Israel
and the
Arab World

THE WORLD STUDIES SERIES

VOLUMES PUBLISHED

Malaysia and its Neighbours, J. M. Gullick.

The European Common Market and Community, Uwe Kitzinger, Fellow
of Nuffield College, Oxford.

The Politics of John F. Kennedy, Edmund Ions, Department of
History, Columbia University, New York.

Apartheid, a Documentary Study of Modern South Africa, Edgar H.
Brookes, M.A., D.Litt., Hon. LL.D.

Israel
and the
Arab World

C. H. Dodd
Department of Government, University of Manchester

and

M. E. Sales
*Centre for Middle Eastern and Islamic Studies,
University of Durham*

NEW YORK
BARNES & NOBLE, Inc.

Published in *The United States of America* 1970
by *Barnes & Noble, Inc., New York, N.Y.* 10003
© *C. H. Dodd and M.E. Sales* 1970
SBN 389 01091 x

956
D 66 i
72581
January, 1971

Printed in Great Britain

Contents

	page
GENERAL EDITOR'S PREFACE	xi
VOLUME EDITORS' PREFACE	xiii
ACKNOWLEDGMENTS	xv
INTRODUCTION	1

SELECT DOCUMENTS

PART I: PLACE AND PEOPLE

(a) Map: North Africa and Arab Asia in *c.* 1900 and in 1968 — 28

(b) Map: Husain–McMahon Correspondence, 1915 — 29

(c) Map: Sykes–Picot Agreement, 1916 — 30

(d) Map: Peace Settlement, 1923 — 31

(e) Map: Royal Commission Partition Plan, 1937 — 32

(f) Map: UN Partition Plan borders, 1947 — 32

(g) Map: 1949 Armistice Agreements' boundaries — 33

(h) Map: Area occupied by Israel after 1967 war — 33

(i) Graph: Arab and Jewish populations of Palestine and Israel, 1914–66 — 34

PART II: THE BASIC ARGUMENT

(a) Excerpts from Chaim Weizmann, *The Jewish People and Palestine*, statement made before the Palestine Royal Commission in Jerusalem, 25 November 1936 — 35

(b) Excerpts from Constantine Zurayk, 'The Conflict between Principle and Force in the Palestine Problem', *Al-'Amal*, December 1947 — 47

CONTENTS

page

PART III: THE WRITTEN UNDERTAKINGS

(*a*) Excerpts from the Husain–McMahon Correspondence, July 1915 to January 1916   55

(*b*) Excerpts from the Sykes–Picot Agreement, May to October 1916   59

(*c*) The Balfour Declaration, 2 November 1917   63

PART IV: THE PEACE SETTLEMENT

(*a*) Article 22 of the Covenant of the League of Nations, April/June 1920   65

(*b*) Excerpts from the Mandatory Instrument for Palestine, 1922   67

PART V: 'PARTITION MEANS THAT NEITHER WILL GET ALL IT WANTS'?

(*a*) Excerpts from the Palestine Royal Commission Report, July 1937   72

(*b*) The Biltmore Programme, 11 May 1942   74

(*c*) Principles submitted to the UN *ad hoc* Committee by the Higher Arab Committee as the Basis for the Future Constitutional Organization of Palestine, 30 September 1947   76

PART VI: THE UN AND THE EMERGENCE OF THE STATE OF ISRAEL

(*a*) Excerpts from the UN General Assembly Resolution on the future government of Palestine, 29 November 1947   78

(*b*) Proclamation of the Independence of Israel, 14 May 1948   82

(*c*) Statement issued by the Governments of the Arab League States on the occasion of the entry of the Arab armies into Palestine, 15 May 1948   84

CONTENTS

page

PART VII: AN EARLY UN ATTEMPT AT PEACE:
THE CONCILIATION COMMISSION FOR PALESTINE

(a) The Lausanne Protocol, signed by Israeli and Arab
delegates to the Lausanne Conference, 12 May 1949   92

(b) Excerpt from the Fourth Progress Report of UN
Conciliation Commission for Palestine, 22 September
1949   94

PART VIII: THE BASIS OF RELATIONS:
THE ARMISTICE REGIME

(a) Excerpts from Egyptian–Israeli Armistice Agreement,
24 February 1949   97

(b) Security Council Resolution, 1 September 1951   102

PART IX: THE RE-ENTRY OF RUSSIA

(a) The Tripartite Declaration by Britain, France and the
United States, 25 May 1950   105

(b) Excerpt from Prime Minister Nasser's speech on the
occasion of the Arms Deal with Czechoslovakia,
27 September 1955   106

(c) Excerpts from W. Z. Laqueur, *The Soviet Union and the
Middle East*, pp. 211–2 and 221–2   111

PART X: FROM CO-EXISTENCE TO WAR

(a) Excerpt from Earl Berger, *The Covenant and the Sword:
Arab–Israeli Relations, 1948–56*, pp. 203–8   115

(b) Excerpt from A. Hourani, 'The Middle East and the
Crisis of 1956', *St Antony's Papers, 4, Middle Eastern
Affairs*, p. 35   121

PART XI: THE SUEZ PEACE

(a) Resolution of the UN General Assembly, 2 February
1957   124

page

(*b*) *Aide-mémoire* from the United States to Israel, 11 February 1957   124

(*c*) Excerpt from broadcast by President Eisenhower, 20 February 1957   127

(*d*) Statement on Israel's decision to withdraw from Sharm-el-Sheik and the Gaza Strip by Israeli Foreign Minister, Mrs Golda Meir, 1 March 1957   129

PART XII: ARAB UNITY AND ISRAEL, 1964–65

(*a*) and (*b*) Excerpts from Georgiana S. Stevens, *Jordan River Partition*, pp. 14–17 and 4–12   132

(*c*) Principle articles of the Palestine National Charter, 2 June 1964   140

(*d*) Excerpts from President Bourguiba's speech to students, 21 April 1965   142

PART XIII: THE OUTBREAK OF WAR, 1967

(*a*) Excerpt from speech by President Nasser, 25 May 1967   147

(*b*) Statement by President Nasser to a press conference, 28 May 1967   150

(*c*) Harold Jackson, 'Egyptian Blockade Would Close Israel's Oil Port', *The Guardian*, 23 May 1967   153

(*d*) Account of President Johnson's meeting with Abba Eban, 26 May 1967, by Theodore Draper, *Israel and World Politics*, pp. 90–1   156

(*e*) Excerpt from private memorandum on UN Emergency Force by Former UN Secretary-General, Dag Hammarskjöld, 5 August 1957   157

(*f*) Excerpts from Report by UN Secretary-General, U. Thant, on the withdrawal of the UN Emergency Force, 18 May 1967   159

PART XIV: THE ARABS IN DEFEAT

(*a*) Resolutions of the Arab summit conference in Khartoum, 29 August—1 September 1967   174 *page*

(*b*) Excerpt from editorial in Syrian newspaper, *Al-Ba'th*, 31 August 1967   175

(*c*) Excerpt from M. Rodinson, 'Israel: the Arab Options', *The Yearbook of World Affairs, 1968*, pp. 89–92   176

PART XV: THE UN ATTEMPT AT A PEACE AND THE
ISRAELI NINE-POINT PEACE PLAN

(*a*) UN Security Council Resolution, 22 November 1967   182

(*b*) Excerpts from speech by President Nasser, 25 November 1967   183

(*c*) Israeli Nine-Point Peace Plan, 10 October 1968: excerpt from Statement to UN General Assembly by the Israeli Foreign Minister   187

PART XVI: CONTINUING PROBLEMS: GUERILLA WARFARE,
THE MILITARY BALANCE, JERUSALEM, REFUGEES

(*a*) Excerpts from Radio Algiers interview of leader of *El Fatah*, Yasir Arafat (Abu Ammar), by Harresh bin Jaddu, 5 June 1968   193

(*b*) Excerpt from H. Haykal, 'Death and Hope', *Al-Ahram*, 16 August 1968   196

(*c*) Excerpt from G. Kemp, *Arms and Security: The Egypt–Israel Case*, pp. 13–4   199

(*d*) (i) Comparative holdings of arms: Israel and the principal Arab states (extracted from *The Military Balance, 1968–69*, (Institute of Strategic Studies)   201

       (ii) Further excerpt from G. Kemp, *Arms and Security: The Egypt–Israel Case*, pp. 22–5   201

(*e*) UN Resolutions on Jerusalem, 1947 and 1948   208

(*f*) White House statements on Jerusalem, 28 June 1967   208

(*g*) UN General Assembly Resolution on Jerusalem, 4 July 1967   209

(*h*) Excerpts from statement by Israeli Foreign Minister, Mr Abba Eban, on Jerusalem, 12 July 1967   209

CONTENTS

page

(*i*) Excerpt from report of Commissioner-General of UNRWA for Palestine, 1 July 1966—30 June 1967, pp. 11–4   213

(*j*) Excerpts from report of Commissioner-General of UNWRA for Palestine, 1 July 1967—30 June 1968, pp. 2 and 4–8   215

(*k*) Excerpt from Don Peretz, 'Israel's New Arab Dilemma', *Middle East Journal*, Vol. 22, No. 1 (1968), pp. 49–53   220

CONCLUSION: FOR FURTHER DISCUSSION   226

APPENDIX   Suggested topics for discussion   235

GUIDE TO FURTHER READING   236

SUBJECT INDEX   238

General Editor's Preface

The World Studies Series is designed to make a new and important contribution to the study of modern history. Each volume in the Series will provide students in colleges and universities with a range of contemporary material drawn from many sources, not only from official and semi-official records, but also from contemporary historical writing and from reliable journals. The material is selected and introduced by a scholar who establishes the context of his subject and suggests possible lines of discussion and enquiry that can accompany a study of the documents.

Through these volumes the student can learn how to read and assess historical documents. He will see how the contemporary historian works and how historical judgements are formed. He will learn to discriminate among a number of sources and to weigh evidence. He is confronted with recent instances of what Professor Butterfield has called 'the human predicament' revealed by history; evidence concerning the national, racial and ideological factors which at present hinder or advance man's progress towards some form of world society.

The authors of this volume have succeeded in making the story of Arab-Israeli relations grow out of the documentation. What they have revealed as underlying the tortuous complexity of religious, economic and political issues is the stark confrontation in the Middle East of two collective wills, each burdened with the accumulated passions of the past. Students of these documents will be impressed by the grave objectivity with which the evidence on both sides is marshalled, but they will also most properly feel themselves under compulsion to make fair historical judgements.

JAMES HENDERSON

Volume
Editors' Preface

Relations between the Arab World and Israel have always been complex. In this book we try to reduce the complexity of the subject, whilst trying to avoid over-simplification, by presenting basic documentation on the course of Arab-Israeli relations. We hope that in a subject where impartiality is so difficult to achieve we do go some way at least towards providing the basic documentation on which impartial assessment must depend. It has not been our intention, however, simply to provide a collection of documents for reference purposes. The book is addressed chiefly to the reader who is new, or fairly new, to the subject of Arab-Israeli relations and who wishes to acquire a well authenticated knowledge of its main features. Consequently, we have sought to make the documents tell the story of Arab-Israeli relations or, rather, to make the story grow out of the documentation. To this end we provide a variety of documentation of fact and opinion not only from official and semi-official documents, but also from the work of contemporary historians and from journals and newspapers. From a study of the documents and supporting explanatory comment and background information the student should be in a position to go some distance in the discussion of the variety of topics suggested in the Appendix.

C. H. DODD AND M. E. SALES

Acknowledgments

Inevitably the documents selected represent only a small proportion of those considered for inclusion and we are aware of many important omissions which considerations of space force upon us. For help in gathering together the documentation from which the selection has been made we should like to express a debt of gratitude to members of the library staffs of the Universities of Manchester and Durham, the Manchester Central Reference Library, the Royal Institute of International Affairs, and the American University of Beirut.

For permission to reproduce material already published elsewhere we are grateful to the following:

The Zionist Federation (Document II (a), from Chaim Weizmann, *The Jewish People and Palestine*); Professor C. K. Zurayk, Professor R. Bayly Winder and the Khayat Book and Publishing Company S. A. L. (Document II (b), from C. K. Zurayk, *The Meaning of the Disaster*, trans. by R. Bayly Winder); Hamish Hamilton Ltd (Document III (a), from George Antonius, *The Arab Awakening*); the Controller of H. M. Stationery Office (Documents III (b), (c), IV (a), (b), V (a)); The Zionist Federation and the Jewish Agency for Israel (Document V (b), from *The Zionist Review*, 22 May 1942); The United Nations (Documents V (c), VI (a), from *The United Nations Yearbook, 1947–48*); Dr Z. Vilnay (Document VI (b), from his book, *Israel Guide*); Dr Muhammad Khalil (Document VI (c), from *The Arab States and the Arab League*, ed. Muhammal Khalil); Professor J. C. Hurewitz (Documents VIII (a), (b), IX (a), (b), from his book *Diplomacy in the Near and Middle East*); Frederick A. Praeger Inc. (Document IX (c), from W. Z. Laqueur, *The Soviet Union and the Middle East*); Mr Earl Berger (Document X (a), from his book, *The Covenant and the Sword*); Chatto & Windus Ltd and A. H. Hourani (Document X (b), from A. H. Hourani, 'The Middle East and the Crisis of 1956', *St. Anthony's Papers No. 4, Middle Eastern Affairs*); Oxford University Press (for the Royal Institute of International Affairs) (Documents XI (b), (c), (d), from *Documents on International Affairs, 1957*, ed. Noble Frankland); The Hoover Institution on War, Revolution, and Peace, Stanford

University (Documents XII (a), (b), from *Jordan River Partition* by Georgiana G. Stevens, © 1965 by the Board of Trustees of the Leland Stanford Junior University); The Palestine Liberation Organisation Center (Document XII (c), from Leila S. Kadi, *Arab Summit Conferences and the Palestine Problem*); The Tunisian Embassy London (Document XII (d)); The BBC Monitoring Service's Summary of World Broadcasts ME/2473/A/1pf (Documents XIII (a), (b), XIV (a), (b), XV (b), XVI (a), (b)); *The Guardian* (Document XIII (c), Harold Jackson, 'Egyptian Blockade Would Close Israel's Oil Port', *The Guardian*, 23 May 1967); Secker & Warburg Ltd and The Viking Press, Inc. (Document XIII (d), from Theodore Draper, *Israel and World Politics*, copyright © 1967, 1968 by Theodore Draper, all rights reserved); The London Institute of World Affairs and Stevens & Sons, the publishers (Document XIV (c), from M. Rodinson, 'Israel: The Arab Options' in *The Year Book of World Affairs 1968*); The Institute for Strategic Studies (Document XVI (d), (i), (ii), from G. Kemp, *Arms and Security* and from *The Military Balance*, ed. Richard Booth); Keesing's Contemporary Archives, 22237 A (Document XVI (f)); and Dr Don Peretz and *The Middle East Journal* (Document XVI (k), from Don Peretz, 'Israel's New Arab Dilemma' in *The Middle East Journal* Winter 1968).

Introduction

The Arab-Israeli conflict does not arise from a mere clash of interests of two states. It is a deep and fundamental disagreement between Arabs and Israelis about the place, even the existence, of Israel in the Middle East.

We therefore treat the problem historically. We seek to discover how the deeply conflicting attitudes of Arab and Israeli have emerged; how they have been modified by time and events; how and why on three occasions the conflict has broken out into war and whether it will lead to war again. In doing this, we hope to arrive at a clear idea of the nature and temper of the conflict and at some assessment of the factors that increase or diminish its potency.

THE SETTING

We begin at the end of the nineteenth century. The geographic area of the present conflict was then part of the Ottoman Empire (Document I(a)). It contained an agglomeration of peoples of different ethnic origins most of whom were, however, overwhelmingly Muslim and mainly Arab in religion and culture. For some three hundred years it had been governed or misgoverned from Istanbul by Ottoman Turkish Sultan-Caliphs who had countenanced over the period an increasing degree of European interference in imperial affairs. The word 'Palestine' had no administrative or constitutional significance until 1923, but was used to refer to the south-western part of the Arab provinces of the Empire (see Document I(b), areas number 3, south of Tyre, and number 8).

The Arab population of Palestine was overwhelmingly peasant, knit together by a complex clan structure. Typically illiterate and poor, the villagers farmed, by primitive methods, holdings which had been reduced to hopelessly uneconomic units by antiquated and quasi-feudal systems of land tenure and taxation. Indebtedness to money-lenders and landlords was endemic. The relatively educated middle and professional classes populated the few towns of size where, however, they largely maintained traditional family and clan loyalties. The heads of these family and clan groups, the aristocrats, were usually substantial landowners, often absentee. They sometimes held Ottoman office and were invariably rich. To the east and in the south, on the edge of the desert, roamed the Bedouin. Acknowledging no authority other than that of their tribal chiefs, they were frequently at war among themselves or raiding against the settled and the sown.

In the later years of the nineteenth century, a tiny minority of Arabs had begun to question the quality of Ottoman rule. Among modernist Arab Islamic thinkers there was a disposition to blame Ottoman misgovernment and decadence for the decline and weakness of Islam in the face of Western technological societies which were threatening the very existence of the Islamic Ottoman Empire. This disposition was deepened by suspicion and hostility when the Ottomans sought to consolidate their hold by reviving the now dormant claims to allegiance which still adhered in the Caliphate. The young Arab urban intelligentsia suspected the centralizing policies, and opposed the despotism, of Ottoman rule. Moreover, among the minority Arab Christian Churches, a quasi-nationalist revolt against the essentially western, non-Arab control of their hierarchy and liturgy had coincided with a new awareness of Arabism in literature and language. These were among the elements which were to coalesce, a little later, into an Arab nationalism which would seek its objectives outside the Ottoman Empire. For the moment, reform and regeneration, whether religious or political, were sought within the existing political framework.

The Jewish minority in Palestine was composed of two distinct groups: the Old Yishuv and the New Yishuv ('Yishuv' = literally 'settlement'). The former was an urban group of students and scholars of the Holy Writings, with their families, and those Jews who had returned from the Diaspora in order to end their days in Zion. It was maintained largely by the charity of Jewish communities overseas and had existed in this way, though fluctuating considerably in size and material fortune, virtually since the final dispersion in AD 70. As a body it evinced neither marked political attitudes nor significant economic activity.

The New Yishuv on the other hand consisted of European immigrants who had begun to come to Palestine in 1882-3. They were rebels against the conservatism and anti-semitism into which they had been born. Contemporary European social and political philosophy had convinced them that Jewish moral, social, economic and political regeneration could be achieved *only* by participation in an autonomous, specifically Jewish national life and by a return to healthy, productive labour on the soil. Some had sought this regeneration in Palestine. Under the auspices of the eastern European Jewish groups to which they belonged, they had acquired land and set up agricultural colonies, some of which soon developed into rural townships. These early settlements had not been notably successful in achieving their ends before 1900, but they provided the seeds from which modern Jewish territorial nationalism was soon to grow. Already their essentially rural economic activity and secular philosophy clearly differentiated the new immigrants from the traditional Yishuv; their European background, literacy, social structure and agricultural methods distinguished them sharply from the mass of the Arab peasantry.

Up to 1900 relations between the tiny Jewish community and the Arab population were largely characterized by the indifference to each other of two totally different cultures, except when new Jewish land settlements violated customary Arab rights of watering or pasturage. Otherwise Jews and Arabs in the countryside shared alike the common difficulties and dangers of water shortage and brigandage. In addition, the Jewish settlers had to cope with the essentially illegal nature of their mere presence in Palestine, whether in town or country: general Ottoman opposition to non-Muslim settlement within the Empire meant that most Jewish colonization took place covertly and by ruse, in spite of Ottoman interdiction rather than because of Ottoman acquiescence.

3

ORIGINS OF CONFLICT: 1900-1919

This period saw the end of the Ottoman Empire, the development of Arab nationalism and Jewish territorial nationalism and the involvement of both nationalisms with outside Powers. A new wave of Jewish immigration into Palestine took place and increasingly secure Jewish settlements were established there. The contradictions which arose between the two nationalisms and between the obligations of the Great Powers to each provide the key to all later antagonisms between the two communities in Palestine.

Increasing Turkish determination to suppress all signs of nascent nationalism within the moribund Ottoman Empire convinced Arab Ottoman discontents that their only course was to remove completely the Arab provinces from Turkish control, even if this could only be achieved by reliance on Western, non-Islamic Powers. This was the beginning of modern Arab *political* nationalism: the desire that Arabs *qua* Arabs should control their own political affairs. It was still a tiny minority movement, even among the intelligentsia, and it encompassed wide differences of opinion on method and precise objective. It did however, receive powerful reinforcement from all classes who suffered Turkish oppression during the First World War.

Among those who aspired to leadership of the early Arab nationalists was Husain, head of the Hashemite family of Hejaz. He seems to have been genuinely disillusioned by Turkish policy *vis-à-vis* the Arabs, though he was also motivated by traditional clan rivalries. Hashemite leadership seems to have been accepted within the movement, if not entirely trusted. At any rate it was Husain who, in 1915, corresponded with Sir Henry McMahon, British High Commissioner in Egypt, and put to Britain the conditions on which the Arabs, under Hashemite leadership, would rebel against the Turks, Germany's war allies. The rising would be concerted with a British drive from Egypt to roll back the Turks from the eastern bank of the Suez Canal. This is the Husain-McMahon Correspondence (Documents I (b) and III (a)), on which are based the arguments about British undertakings to the Arab nationalists. The Correspondence was not published for the time being, though its existence was known in Arab nationalist circles.

4

In 1916, Britain and her European allies secretly reached agreement on the disposition of the Ottoman Empire after the allied victory. They assumed that the Empire would be dismembered and proceeded to stake their claims. This is the Sykes-Picot Agreement (Documents I (c) and III (b)) from which stems the claim that Britain betrayed undertakings to the Arabs in order to promote British and French imperial interests. The agreement remained secret until the Russian copy of it was released by the Bolsheviks after the Russian Revolution and then exploited by German and Turkish propaganda in the Arab Ottoman provinces.

Meanwhile further developments had taken place on the Jewish nationalist front. Theodor Herzl, an Austrian Jewish journalist, had given the original impetus in the middle 1890s. He founded the World Zionist Organization (WZO) in 1897 and this carried on his work after he died in 1904. The varying strands of Jewish nationalist thought and activity now cohered in a movement which always maintained its internal heterogeneity, but had nevertheless produced by 1914 a unified philosophy and programme of action with regard to the essentials of Jewish nationalism—or, as we henceforward call it, 'Zionism'. These essentials were (1) the strengthening of Jewish *national* sentiment by (2) promotion of Jewish colonization and of all aspects of Jewish national life *in Palestine*, and *only* there (*infra* pp. 40–3), through (3) an institution which would organize the material and psychological resources of world Jewry to these ends and which (4) would actively seek the official approval of some Government(s). The Zionist movement in Palestine and the Diaspora was miniscule. Its existence, however, ensured that when further overt persecution provoked a new wave of Russian and Polish Jewish migration in 1904-14, those migrants who went to Palestine faced an essentially new situation. The support of Zionist institutions which were proliferating in Palestine and abroad greatly enhanced their prospects of economic, social and moral success. At the same time Zionist leaders abroad strove to achieve the fourth essential Zionist aim. Several governments were approached with no effective results. It was finally during the war itself, when the collapse of the Ottoman Empire appeared imminent, that the British Government, after some negotiation, announced its support of the Zionist political objective in Palestine. It did so despite the determined opposition of most of the leaders of British Jewry, who feared the dual emotional and political loyalties which Zionism itself and the British approval of it potentially created. This was the Balfour Declaration (Document III (c)) upon which rely the charges that Britain betrayed undertakings to the Arabs in order to promote Zionist interests. The Declaration was released and published immediately.

Much controversy has raged over the precise meanings of these three sets of agreements, over their relation to each other and over the intentions of the various parties to them. We should note that both parties to the Husain-McMahon Correspondence subsequently behaved *as if* an agreement had been reached in the Correspondence, or at any rate *as if* each was satisfied that the other's suspended disagreement would be satisfactorily removed after the war. Each proceeded to play in the war, parts which were supposedly contingent upon agreement in the Correspondence. The immediate release by the British Government of the Balfour Declaration suggests that Britain either saw no incompatibility between the Declaration and previous obligations or felt that the political disadvantages of revealing an acknowledged incompatibility would be outweighed by the immediate political advantages of publication (these advantages have been alleged to include the encouragement of American and Russian Jewish support for joining and for not leaving, respectively, the Allied side in the war against Germany). The *immediate* Arab anxiety occasioned by the publication of 'Balfour' and 'Sykes-Picot' and the repeated British and even Zionist reassurances which this anxiety elicited throughout 1918 and in early 1919 indicate the extent to which the Arab nationalists believed *at the time* that the three sets of agreements did indeed conflict.

Despite, however, the ambiguities and confusions which had characterized the Arab world during the war and early postwar period, the objectives of all parties at the end of 1919 were clear. The Arab nationalists wanted immediate Arab independence and democratic government throughout most of the Arab world; the Zionists wished to obtain conditions in Palestine under which they would build up a Jewish National Home which would eventually manage its own affairs; the British and French sought to acquire, at the expense of Arab independence if necessary, strategic and economic positions in the Middle East from which to maintain their imperialist interests. By the end of 1919, therefore, the basic ingredients of the contemporary conflict between Israel and the Arab world could already be identified: two vigorous and potentially contradictory nationalisms, interacting and conflicting with the interests and obligations of rival external Powers.

THE PEACE SETTLEMENT, 1920-3

That part of the final settlement (1923) which concerned the Asian provinces of the former Ottoman Empire applied the mandatory system which had been enunciated in the Charter of the League of Nations (Document IV (a)) and divided up the area according to French and British interests: the mandated territories of Syria and Lebanon went to France, those of Palestine and Iraq to Britain (Document I (d)). It is beyond the scope of this book to examine the intricacies of policy which led, during the protracted peace negotiations, to this outcome. It is only necessary to point out that the settlement was essentially 'Sykes-Picot' revised in favour of Zionist, French imperialist, and to a greater degree British imperialist, interests. Provisions for the development of a Jewish National Home in Palestine were written into the Palestine Mandate (Document IV (b)), though 'Sykes-Picot' had not mentioned the Home. Through the mandatory system both France and Britain would have much more direct rule in the mandated territories than 'Sykes-Picot' envisaged they would have in their 'zones of influence'. French mandated territories were smaller *in toto*, but the British larger *in toto* than were the respective zones of influence combined with areas of direct rule marked out by 'Sykes-Picot'. 'Palestine' consisted of territory on both sides of the Jordan and was to be mandated and British, whereas in 'Sykes-Picot' it consisted only of the West Bank and was to be 'internationalized'.

The Mandatory Instruments themselves and the attitude of Arab nationalists, Zionists and British to them and to that of Palestine in particular are examined in Part IV.

7

As for the remainder of the Arab world: the Hejaz was recognized as independent; the remainder of the Peninsula was ignored; the British position in Egypt and Sudan, and the French position in Morocco and Tunisia were recognized. The new Turkey renounced all title to these territories, and her own Asian territory was confined to Asia Minor proper. With the exception of the Peninsula, and arguably of Asia Minor, the overall settlement favoured Great Power convenience at the expense of Arab independence.

THE MANDATE: 1923 TO FEBRUARY 1947

We have seen what were the basic positions of the interested groups up to 1923. Virtually without exception, these positions were maintained throughout the Mandate. It is this consistent adherence to bascially simple propositions which clarifies what otherwise appears to be a period of total confusion.

The Arabs consistently opposed the Mandates with argument, strikes and violence. Gradually all the central Arab territories which had emerged from the First World War under foreign tutelage increased their control over their own affairs. By the end of 1946, Iraq, Egypt, Syria, Lebanon and Transjordan were all at least theoretically independent and were members of the UN. Even in the Peninsula change had occurred: the Saudi family had consolidated most of the area into the single unitary state of Saudi Arabia. Only the rump of Palestine remained unchanged. The Palestinian Arabs therefore not only resented the settlement of 1923 itself and the shabby treatment meted out to them then by the Allies, particularly Britain: they also felt a sense of unjustifiable isolation from, and down-grading in relation to, the rest of the Arab world. Their retarded political emancipation seemed to be explicable *only* in terms of the Mandate's provisions for a Jewish National Home. Naturally, therefore, the National Home became the major issue in Palestine and between the Arabs and the outside world. To this political frustration was added a very real fear of the impact on land and society of what was regarded as expansionist and modernist Zionist immigration.

The Palestinian Arabs, therefore, refused to co-operate with any measure which implied recognition of the Mandate or assumed differentiated Palestinian Arab and Zionist political entities rather than a single body politic coincident with the territorial state of Palestine. On these grounds, they rejected the Mandate's proposals for a representative Legislative Council, for a non-official Advisory Council and for an Arab Agency. (In 1928–9 Arab leaders asked for re-consideration of Legislative Council proposals. Discussion was aborted, however, by the violence of 1939. In 1936, Zionists refused to discuss any further Legislative Council proposals until the Arabs recognized the Jewish National Home Clauses of the Mandate. The Peel Report (Document V (a)) recommended that all Legislative Council proposals be dropped as it was clear neither the proportional nor parity principle would work. From 1923 Britain in fact ruled Palestine through a High Commissioner assisted by an official British Advisory Council.) Increasing fear led them to extend their position until, in the 1930s, they demanded that both Zionist immigration and land purchase should cease altogether. Throughout the period the Arabs accused the British, in continuing to operate the Mandate at all, of favouring the Jews at Arab expense. They argued that Britain was enabling the Zionists to build up a Jewish National Home—population, land, institutions, property—in Palestine which would eventually become a Jewish state. This would prevent for ever the achievement of Arab national independence in Palestine.

The Zionists took their stand on the Mandate which, they argued, gave them the right to a National Home in Palestine. They stressed the material benefits which their presence brought to Palestine, and they proceeded to develop within the constitution a vigorous system of local government. They accused Britain, however, of a negative attitude to the Jewish National Home and complained of active hostility in the Palestinian administration. In the later 1930s they claimed that British policy in Palestine directly breached Mandatory obligations. They asserted that Britain constantly gave way to Arab violence and thus positively encouraged extremist Arab non-co-operation; that Britain failed to invest in large-scale economic and social development programmes and thus deliberately exposed the vast differences between the two

9

communities. In these ways, they claimed, Britain failed to provide the psychological and material conditions in which Zionist-Arab relations, which they asserted most Palestinians sought, might flourish. The Zionists co-operated with the early constitutional proposals of the Mandatory, but not with the later ones (*supra* p. 9). They reacted to violence when it occurred and in the 1930s they openly armed in self-defence, particularly in the outlying settlements. At the same time they subscribed to the Jewish Agency's doctrine of self-restraint.

Until the middle 1930s, Britain attempted to maintain the general principle of 'equality of obligation', under the Mandate, to both Arabs and Zionists, and to stress the feasibility of Arab-Zionist harmony in Palestine. To this end they tried to promote constitutional development in which both communities might participate (*supra*, p. 9). They refused repeated Arab demands for the complete abrogation of the Mandate and the establishment of an independent state based, like the other new Arab states, on majority rule expressed through representative institutions. Britain refused equally to accept the implicit object of the Palestinian Zionist community, namely, the ultimate establishment of a Jewish state.

Throughout the 1920s and 1930s the two communities developed along almost completely separate lines—economically, socially and culturally, as well as politically. The maintenance of their basic positions without any essential modification led to increasing enmity between them and each became more hostile to Britain. In this precarious situation, violence erupted periodically. Outbreaks occurred in 1920, 1921, 1928, 1929, 1933 and 1936. Fear escalated. Weapons were stockpiled. Britain set up a series of Enquiries, culminating in the Royal Commission of 1936 which conducted a comprehensive review of the whole period of the Mandate. Its Report concluded that the basic obligations of the Mandate were not only unequal but also irreconcilable, and that the Mandate was therefore unworkable. It recommended partition (Documents I (e) and V (a)).

The Zionists disagreed with the analysis but nevertheless reluctantly agreed to consider partition. The Arabs objected violently to partition for it would not only perpetuate a Zionist political entity in Palestine, but would actually violate the territorial integrity of Palestine itself. They decided to challenge the authority of the Mandate. The result was the Arab Rebellion of 1937. For a time law and order practically broke down in the face of Arab murder, sabotage and obstruction. Among extremist Zionist groups the traditional principle of self-restraint collapsed. Organized guerilla warfare by both sides began in early 1938. British troops were poured in. Order was finally restored only in the summer of 1939. By then the British Government, having abandoned partition and having failed to reach an agreed settlement with Arabs or Zionists had put forward another solution (White Paper, May 1939). This required strict regulation of Zionist land purchase and immigration immediately; and thereafter complete prohibition of immigration save with Arab consent. Britain hoped that this would lead in ten years time to the establishment of an independent unitary state of Palestine in whose government both peoples of the country would co-operate. The plan satisfied none. For the Arabs it clearly fell short of immediate and total abolition of the Mandate, Zionist land purchases and immigration, and from their stand on these objectives they would not move. For the Zionists, the White Paper was a crucial disillusionment; for many it rendered implacable the hostility to Britain which had been growing throughout the Mandate and was to constitute the backbone of Zionist resistance in the 1945–8 period. It now seemed finally clear that Britain had neither the will nor the ability to assist them in achieving in Palestine the Jewish National Home which they envisaged.

Throughout the Second World War, Britain froze the constitutional position in Palestine and held land transfers and immigration at White Paper levels. Jewish refugees from Nazi Europe desperately tried to enter Palestine in defiance of the regulations. If they succeeded and were detected, they were deported to Cyprus, Mauritius, even Europe itself. In an atmosphere of bitterness, Zionist extremist terrorism revived in Palestine from 1943. Previously moderate nationalist attitudes polarized. Nationalist positions were re-stated (e.g. Documents V (b) and (c)).

As the war ended in 1945, and the independent Arab states combined in a loosely organized League for regional co-operation and defence, and the United Nations Organization was born, Britain maintained in Palestine the White Paper policy, despite the enormous build-up of immigrant pressure from Europe. The Zionists employed all means to bring in forbidden refugees. Violence followed, terrorism became a daily occurrence. Zionist settlements were cut off from supplies and markets, the British established a blockade of the sea approaches. This was the bloody, desperate background in Palestine to diplomatic moves elsewhere.

The rising chaos in Palestine and the urgent problem of European Jewish refugees required that a settlement of the Palestine question should not be long delayed. During 1945-6 variants of a partition-type solution were suggested by the British, and also by the American, governments. But throughout these manoeuvres, as always, the Arabs rejected any solution which did not make Palestine a unitary, democratic state; the Zionists rejected any solution which did not at the very least guarantee them eventual control of immigration and land transfers.

In February, 1947 Britain finally gave up attempting to find a solution and referred the whole question to the United Nations. This referral marks a totally new stage of the proceedings on the diplomatic front, although in Palestine itself terrorism and the pressure of frustrated immigration continued to produce desperation.

THE UNITED NATIONS, WAR, ISRAEL, CEASEFIRE: FEBRUARY 1947—DECEMBER 1948

A special session of the General Assembly of the UN opened to debate the Palestine question in April 1947. In May it appointed a Special Committee on Palestine (UNSCOP) which recommended that the Mandate should end and that Palestine should be partitioned. In November 1947 the General Assembly resolved to adopt what were in effect the UNSCOP majority report recommendations (Documents VI (a) and I(f)).

Finally, therefore, a strong stand for partition, which Peel had argued in 1937 to be the only feasible solution, had been taken. The Zionists accepted the resolution and proceeded to make their arrangements for the transitional process to partition and independence for which the resolution provided. Thus, by March 1948 a provisional Jewish government had been announced. The Arabs were profoundly shocked, partly because they opposed partition as a solution in any case, but partly also because they had never seriously expected that it would become the solution. Before the resolution was passed, they tried to prevent the adoption of the UNSCOP report by putting forward alternative proposals, including one for reference to the International Court of Justice of the whole question of the legality of the Mandate and of that of any UN action modifying the Mandate, but their proposals were defeated. After the resolution was passed, they refused to accept it. They announced in December 1947 that they would intervene with military force to prevent its implementation and they abstained from making any of the arrangements for the transitional process.

An overwhelming vote for partition had thus been taken in the Assembly, but no provision had been made there for the enforcement of partition should powerful opposition to it arise in Palestine itself. The British, however, while accepting the partition principle, refused to co-operate with the UN in Palestine in the period transitional to partition for which the resolution provided. On the contrary, having announced in December 1947 that she would relinquish the Mandate on 15 May 1948, Britain declared in February that she would not admit the UN Palestine Commission before 1 May 1948, and in March actually began phased troop withdrawals, while maintaining a relatively effective sea blockade and a much less effective closure of the land borders. Thus, throughout the period from the partition resolution in November 1947 to the completion of British withdrawal on 15 May 1948, a state of non-exercised sovereignty and of undeclared war existed within Palestine. As the Arabs infiltrated men and arms over the land borders to engage in fighting and terrorism, and five neighbouring Arab states massed their armies on the borders, the Zionists organized their fighting and terrorist forces in opposition, smuggled the few arms and men they could through the sea blockade, and prepared for more to come in once the blockade should have ended. In this period, too, began active hostilities within Palestine and a large-scale Arab exodus from Zionist-held areas. The origins of this flight have long been the subject of bitter controversy. There is, however, no evidence that the flight was pre-planned by Arab or Zionist leaders, or by the British. It seems more likely that people decided to go because they were at best inconvenienced and at worst terrified by political anarchy, by the fighting and, above all, by barbaric acts of terrorism. Once the flight had started, there were Zionist terrorists and others who saw its advantages and did not abstain from encouraging it. The Arabs who fled probably thought that they would soon return since, in common with everyone except a very few military and diplomatic observers on the spot, they believed that in the event of wholescale war the Arab states' armies, trained and armed for some years by the west, would in fact, invade and decimate the tiny Zionist population, which was comparatively ill-armed and trained. Thus, with fighting, terrorism, blockade, population upheaval, and the massing of official and unofficial aggressive armies, order within Palestine broke down completely. The UN tried to implement its resolution, held further discussions, called for truces, but was impotent. It finally became clear that the *impasse* would find issue only through war in Palestine.

The British left Palestine and lifted the blockade on 14-15 May 1948. The Zionists simultaneously invoked the UN Partition Resolution and proclaimed a Jewish State, to be called Israel (Document VI (b)). They immediately received a flood of supplies and of immigrants and other man-power as the blockade vanished. The Arab states invaded, proclaiming their justification as they did so (Document VI (c)), and the Arab population continued to flee. The war which followed, interspersed with truces and ceasefires organized by the UN Mediator, finished at the ceasefire of 29 December 1948. Israel had virtually routed the Arab regular and irregular forces and at the ceasefire held the whole of Palestine minus the west bank of the Jordan (which Transjordan was later to incorporate), the Old City of Jerusalem (which was soon integrated with Transjordan in the teeth of the opposition of most other Arab states) and the Gaza Strip (which was to be administered by Egypt after the 1948 war). The armistice agreements (Part VIII) which were negotiated in a series of bilateral meetings during 1949 between Israel and the several Arab states contiguous to her, involved some modifications of the position on the ground at the ceasefire but ended by essentially confirming it (Document I (g)). Thus the Arabs even lost to Israeli arms parts of Palestine allocated to them in the UN Partition Plan.

THE FAILURE TO SECURE A PEACE

The world now looked forward to a negotiated settlement of the Palestine problem. A UN Conciliation Commission was set up to achieve this end, but failed to secure a settlement at what was probably the most propitious time for a solution in the history of the Arab-Israeli conflict. In Part VII we see how close to a solution the two sides were brought. With the failure of the Commission's efforts, the attitudes of both sides hardened.

Evidence of hardening attitudes was provided by the Egyptian maintenance of the war-time denial of Suez to ships carrying goods to Israel. In 1949 Egypt also set up military installations on the islands of Sanafir and Tiran, whence they could control the three-mile-wide straits and deny the Gulf of Aqaba to Israel. The dispute over Suez led to the Arab claim that a 'state of war' existed with Israel, despite the armistice regime. In the discussion of the Suez dispute in the Security Council in 1951, the fundamental incompatibility of Israeli and Arab views on the nature of their conflict emerged. They differed on the nature of the relations established between them by the armistice agreements. Their differing interpretations of that relationship still determine their attitudes to each other today. In Part VIII we have excerpts from the Israeli-Egyptian Armistice Agreement—which is typical of the agreements Israel signed with the other Arab states—and the 1951 Security Council Resolution relating to the Suez Canal and the question of the alleged state of war.

The 1948 war and the subsequent armistice agreements did not, then, solve the Arab-Israeli problem. Rather, a firm foundation was laid for continuing dispute. In essence, the Arab-Israeli conflict has changed in character very little over the years, but it has taken different forms and has been powerfully affected by trends in international politics.

Until 1955 the Western Powers had a free hand to solve the Arab-Israeli dispute, but they were not able to do so. The best they could manage in the early years was a concerted effort by Britain, France and the United States to prevent an arms race or any violation of armistice and frontier lines. The three Powers did this by signing a Tripartite Declaration in May 1950 (Document IX (a)). It was a stop-gap measure that could have been valuable as a means of providing a breathing space for an attempt to find a real solution.

INTERNATIONAL PRE-OCCUPATIONS OF THE POWERS

Unfortunately, however, these problems were difficult to contain. International factors now began to enter. First, there was the complication of French and British withdrawal from empire in North Africa and the Middle East, respectively. The French were not at all disposed to leave Algeria. They therefore naturally enough resented Egyptian support for the Algerian nationalists. In consequence, they began secretly to supply Israel with armaments. This unavoidably began to undermine the Tripartite Declaration and alerted Egypt to the need for arms from some source of supply or other.

The British were meanwhile painfully extricating themselves from their dominant position on the Suez Canal. Their physical weakness after the war was an open invitation to the United States to participate in the defence of the Middle East against possible Russian aggression.

Britain now sought to engage the Arab states in a defensive league, but faced indifference, particularly in Egypt where the temper was still anti-imperialist. The old imperialists were suspected of new designs and Arab leaders could not taint themselves by co-operating with them. Iraq was an exception. She co-operated with Britain, but her leader, Nuri-as-Said, was 'old school' and vied with the new Egyptian revolutionary leader, Nasser, for the leadership of the Arab Middle East. Egypt was irritated by Britain's adherence to Nuri's Turco-Iraqi Pact in April 1955; she was infuriated in December 1955, when Britain tried unsuccessfully to recruit Jordan for what was now the Baghdad Pact. The British initiative was rejected by Jordan and resulted in March 1956 in the ejection from Jordan of Glubb Pasha, the famous British Commander of the Arab Legion. Britain suspected Egyptian plotting and the two countries were at loggerheads. The British were not prepared to admit that their policies for Jordan and for Middle East defence were subject to Egyptian approval. This did not, however, mean that the British were pro-Israeli. As late as October 1956, on the occasion of an Israeli attack on the Jordanian town of Qalqilya, Britain promised aid to Jordan if attacked by Israel. This is alleged by pro-Arab writers to be a ruse to show there was no collusion between Britain and Israel.

Over the Arab-Israeli dispute the British were indeed prepared to go a long way towards seeing the Arab point of view. In the midst of these international manoeuvrings there emerged two sets of proposals for a solution of the Arab-Israeli conflict. One was American and inspired by Dulles; the other was British and inspired by Eden. The Eden proposals were much more favourable to the Arabs than the more detailed Dulles suggestions. Eden was in fact taunted with appeasement by the Leader of the Opposition, the late Hugh Gaitskill!

The western moves to find a solution were certainly prompted by the historic Egyptian decision in September 1955 to buy arms from the Eastern Bloc. If there were no Arab-Israeli problem there would be little justification for outside supplies of arms, and much less opportunity than has occurred for the Russians to establish a foothold in the Arab countries. The Arab-Israeli conflict also provided Egypt with a legitimate reason for building up armaments that could also be used in the new struggle between Arab socialist and Arab traditionalist states. Russia now stepped in. Immediately, the Arab-Israeli conflict became one of vital international importance and it has remained so ever since. For the circumstances of Nasser's arms deal with Czechoslovakia and the effects of the Russian re-entry on the scene, see Documents IX (b) and (c).

REASONS FOR WAR

These international developments created considerable concern in Israel. First, the British withdrawal from Suez meant that Egyptian hostility towards Israel would not henceforth be restrained by a British presence. Secondly, the arms deal with the East raised fears for Israeli military capacity. Moreover, it should be remembered in this connection that many Israelis were emigrants from countries which had a profound awareness of the strength of the Russian bear. He was a creature better known to many Israelis than to many Arabs.

Nor, naturally, were the Americans kindly disposed to Nasser after the arms deal. They had to grin and bear it; and they had to put up with Nasser's recognition of Communist China, a great offence. These factors indeed contributed to the American decision to withdraw their offer to finance in part the building of the Aswan Dam in Upper Egypt. The details cannot be entered into here and are fully catalogued in books on the Suez crisis. This decision led to the Egyptian nationalization of the Suez Canal Company, which infuriated the French and outraged the British. For their various reasons, then, by 1956 the French, the British and the Americans were smarting under Egyptian blows to their often inept policies, whilst the Israelis were becoming seriously alarmed. The reasons for Israeli alarm and their decision to go to war with Egypt are given in Document X (a).

The Israelis complained of a lack of proper supervision of the armistice regime by the UN authorities, whom they came to regard as either biased or ineffective. They consequently took the law into their own hands by adopting a policy of retaliation for which they were repeatedly condemned by the Security Council. The most significant incident occurred on the Egyptian frontier in February 1955 when, after some provocation from Arab infiltrators, Israel, now with Ben Gurion back as Defence Minister, launched a powerful military attack on Gaza. Thirty-eight Egyptian soldiers were killed and thirty-one wounded. Egypt was not intimidated, but seemed to be provoked into more extreme measures. *Fedayeen* (Arab guerrillas) now began to make deep incursions into Israeli territory and to terrorize the Israeli population. Egypt also realized at Gaza the weakness of her arms. It was more than ever imperative to be well armed, and Arab fears of Israeli expansionism redoubled. A brief assessment of Israeli 'expansionism' is given in Document X (b).

By November 1955 Ben Gurion was back in full power as Prime Minister, with a 'backs to the wall' policy. The Israelis entered into secret agreements with the French and then the British—of French and British collusion there is now no doubt.

On 29 October 1956 Israel attacked and, with Anglo-French air support, won a resounding victory in the Suez War.

THE SUEZ PEACE

After the Suez War came to an end, Britain and France were urged out of their gains by the United States and Russia acting in uncharacteristic unison. In November 1956 Egypt agreed to the presence of a UN Emergency Force in Egypt, but under certain conditions, which became subject to some dispute in 1967 when Egypt asked for the withdrawal of the Force (see Documents XIII (e) and (f)).

Israel was not deprived of her gains from the war as easily as were the French and British. Under American pressure she evacuated nearly all Sinai, but persisted for a while in occupying (1) a strip of land running from Eilat to Sharm el-Sheikh and the islands of Tiran and Sanafir and (2) the Gaza Strip.

The process by which Israel was pressed to renounce these gains is dealt with in the documents in Part XI. We see from these documents the nature of the 'guarantee' for freedom of navigation in Aqaba gained by Israel, and for freedom from guerrilla attacks from the Gaza Strip that Israel so greatly desired.

The Americans were alerted by Nasser's diplomatic success at Suez to the dangers of a Nasserite Middle East. In this they probably exaggerated the closeness of connection between leftist regimes like Nasser's and the Soviet Union. It is often said that after Suez the United States muffed an opportunity to get on good terms with the new Arab states through excessive resentment at their socialist trends. Certainly, the United States (with Britain) now aligned herself firmly with anti-revolutionary forces in the Arab world. The Eisenhower Doctrine emerged as the basis of American Middle Eastern policy. It amounted to a promise to provide upon request (1) military and economic aid and (2) US forces to protect territorial integrity and political independence against overt armed oppression from any nation controlled by international communism. The policy did not go far enough to prevent the indigenous Iraqi revolution of 1958 and with it the overthrow of Nuri as-Said's over-confident, pro-western regime. Alarmed by events in Iraq, Lebanon and Jordan now called for aid from the West. The United States and Britain responded by supplying troops, and they did not fuss too much whether the dangers were international communist or local leftist in character.

ARAB POLITICS AND ISRAEL, 1958-67

At this point in the history of the Middle East Nasser's prestige was high. He was the Arab champion in the fight against a western imperialism that still seemed intent on re-asserting itself in a new form through the Eisenhower Doctrine. The high-water-mark of Nasser's prestige was reached in 1958, when, allegedly fearing a communist take-over, but also fearful of the Iraqi monarchy, the Baathist (Arab socialist) leaders in Syria brought that country into unison with Egypt in the United Arab Republic. For the moment all lines led to the successful President Nasser, whose nationalist and now socialist programme would surely harness the energies of the Arab world. Yet before long, with the easing of imperialist pressures, rivalries began to appear. Nasser did not get on well with the rather pretentious Baathists, whom he distrusted and sought to supplant in the new centralized state. He also did not see eye to eye with the new leader of Iraq, Kasim, whose regime was more leftist than Nasser's. He was in fact engaged against Iraq when the latter laid claim to Kuwait, whose defence was at first undertaken, at Kuwaiti request, by the British. Nasser's quarrel with the Baathists and Kasim to some extent re-established his reputation with the West, but could do no good for any claims to the leadership of the Arab world. In 1961 Syria seceded from the union with Egypt.

With the fall of Kasim's regime in 1963, but particularly with the assumption of power in Iraq by President Arif later in the year, Iraqi-Egyptian relations improved. This was a gain for Arab unity, but Egypt, true to her anti-imperialist, and now socialist, convictions—and not without an eye on the oil riches of the Arabian peninsula—had meanwhile become embroiled with Saudi Arabia over the Yemen. Here Nasser intervened on the side of the revolution with some 40,000 troops.

So the Arab world was now rent by two major quarrels. One was between the revolutionaries—Egypt, Syria, Iraq, Algeria and the new regime in the Yemen—on the one hand, and the traditionalist regimes led by Saudi Arabia on the other. The other quarrel was between Nasserites and Baathists for the leadership of the socialist revolution. This latter was essentially a quarrel between Syria and Egypt, but had serious repercussions in the turbulent politics of Iraq.

Against this background of Arab dissension, Israel enjoyed an uneasy security. Egypt showed herself to be as adamant as ever that Israel-bound shipping should not use the Suez Canal. A particularly determined Israeli effort to force the issue in 1959–60 came to nothing. Two foreign ships carrying cargoes to Israel were obliged to unload them at Port Said. In fact, as western imperialism retreated from the Middle East, the tendency among the Arabs was to become even more hostile towards Israel, regarded as one of the last bastions of western imperialism in the Middle East. This anti-imperialism was also bolstered by another and novel factor. The more or less socialist regimes of Egypt, Iraq and Syria thought of Israel not only as an imperialist, but also now as a capitalist, enemy and tied, moreover, to the apron strings of American capitalism. Rendered uneasy by these new emphases in Arab attitudes, Israel did not, however, see any salvation in the arming by the West of traditionalist or moderate Arab regimes. These conservative regimes were almost as prone to hatred of Israel as the more modern. Would the Arab leaders not one day sink their differences and use against Israel the arms they had acquired for their own struggles?

Impelled by their own need for respite from inter-Arab strife and by increased hostility for Israel occasioned by a revival of the River Jordan dispute, the Arab world tried to find a new measure of unity in 1964. Arab Summit conferences were held in January and September 1964 and in September 1965.

The Arab world did not find in these two years quite the harmony it was seeking. Not all Arab states, it turned out, were equally anti-Israeli; and Tunisia rocked the Arab world in 1965 with a call for negotiations with Israel. In Part XII we document the result of the Arab drive for unity and include in Documents XII (a) and (b) material on the dispute over the use of the Jordan waters.

As we can see from the documents, during 1964–5 moderate views, on the whole, prevailed. Nasser successfully reasserted his leadership both against the Arab conservative and the Arab socialist regimes—and to a degree he managed to isolate Bourguiba (see Document XII(d) for Bourguiba's views on Palestine). Yet he was walking on a tightrope. In November 1964 Ibn Saud of Saudi Arabia was succeeded by his brother Feisal. He made more explicit Saudi Arabia's natural interests in a pro-western policy and in security against Arab socialism in the Arabian peninsula. He actively sought out his natural ally, King Hussein of Jordan, and mooted the idea of an Islamic (and conservative) summit conference. This challenge for Arab leadership obliged Nasser to move closer to the Arab socialists. By the middle of 1966 he was engaged in open verbal warfare against Feisal and, in November, signed a Defence Pact with a Syria that was now under a regime more than ever socialist and more than ever unstable. In the circumstances, the policy of guerrilla warfare adopted at the Arab summit meetings in 1964–5 now had ominous implications. Feeling more secure now she was supported by Nasser, Syria openly encouraged the *el Fatah* guerrilla bands operating from her territory. In turn Egypt now encouraged the Palestine Liberation Army. Nasser was riding on the back of a tiger. See Document XII (c) for excerpts from the Palestine National Charter.

THE JUNE WAR, 1967

Israeli determination to stop these guerrilla attacks led to serious Israeli warnings to Syria and, on 7 April 1967, to a major battle between Israeli and Syrian forces. Continued Israeli warnings, it was alleged by Nasser, contained threats to overthrow the Syrian government (see Document XIII (a)). They were taken by Nasser to justify Egyptian troop concentrations on the Israeli border. The Egyptian government then requested the withdrawal of the 3,400-strong UN Emergency Force from the Israeli frontier and from positions on the Straits of Tiran. It was a dramatic gesture which certainly implied a renewal of the blockade of the Gulf of Aqaba; but the UN Force was not strong and was largely composed of contingents whose governments were pro-Egyptian. The UN Secretary-General, U Thant, was much criticized for agreeing to the withdrawal, but as Nasser subsequently made plain, non-compliance would have entailed forcible disarmament of the UN Force. See Documents XIII (e) and (f) for the dispute over U Thant's compliance with the Egyptian request for withdrawal of the UN Force.

At this point the Israeli premier, Eshkol, called for mutual reductions of troops, but the Arabs now seemed to have the bit between their teeth. At this juncture it might have been considered that Syria had been effectively rescued from the alleged danger of Israeli attack. Matters were not, however, to rest there. Nasser now announced that the Straits of Tiran would be closed to Israeli ships and to others carrying strategic goods to Israel. In Arab eyes this was a proper restoration of the pre-1956 position. For Israel closure of the Straits, her leaders had often warned, would be reason for war. See Document XIII (c) for an evaluation of the economic importance of the Straits to Israel. In Document XIII(b) there is an important statement by President Nasser to a press conference held on 28 May.

The Israeli reaction was to call the closing of the Straits an act of pure aggression. Yet the Israeli government hesitated. The Foreign Minister was sent off to Washington for an assurance that the Straits would be kept open (see Document XIII (d)). He was urged to place his trust in the maritime powers and to persuade his government not to attack. Further messages urging restraint were delivered by the United States and the Soviet Union to Israel, but the hawks in the Israeli cabinet were not satisfied with the nature of the Western guarantees. They gained the upper hand. They were influenced, too, by Jordan's decision on 24 May to sign a defence agreement with Egypt, and by the movement of Iraqi troops to Jordan. Israel was being threatened with military concentrations in a way that invited an Israeli attack. As to the Straits, Israel felt that she was her own best support. Would the maritime powers really keep Aqaba open? If there was no vigorous response to the Egyptian aggression would it not encourage further pressure? With Major-General Moshe Dayan now as Defence Minister, Israel attacked on 6 June.

News of war was greeted with joy by the Cairo crowds, but to their intense disillusion the Egyptian army was totally routed in Sinai in a lightning Israeli victory. Very important was the destruction of the Arab air forces before they got off the ground.

This highly efficient air strike was loudly proclaimed by the Arab governments to have been carried out by American and British planes, but these statements, very damaging at the time, were later retracted. Not only the Egyptian, but also the Jordanian army was devastatingly defeated. It was then the turn of the Syrians, who were overwhelmed after fierce battles for the Syrian heights. All three Arab states accepted a cease-fire. The Israelis established themselves on the cease-fire lines, which meant principally that they occupied Sinai and Jerusalem and the West Bank of the Jordan. This latter frontier is regarded by some Israelis as the natural frontier for Israel. The occupation of the West Bank certainly greatly shortens the frontier to be defended. The 1967 cease-fire frontiers are shown in Document I (h).

ATTEMPTS AT PEACE

Any war is a disaster, but wars sometimes solve problems. We must, therefore, ask if the 1967 war in any way helped to make a solution of the Arab-Israeli problem any easier.

First, we must note that Israeli success did not topple the Syrian leaders, whose pronounced hostility towards Israel was such a major factor in the development of the crisis. If toppled, would the Syrian leaders anyway have been replaced by others more stable? Nor did Egypt allow Nasser to go, despite his proffered resignation. There has subsequently been considerable disaffection in Egypt, but no voice has been heard calling for a less tough attitude towards Israel than that of the present leaders. In fact, defeat has hardened Arab attitudes. We can see this from reports on the Khartoum Arab Summit conference held in August 1967. Documents XIV (a) and (b) give the decisions of the Summit conference and provide an example of the Syrian attitude to defeat. In Document XIV(c) we have a view of the Arab world in 1968.

If Arabs and Israelis cannot find a solution, neither are the powers able to impose one in unison. Russia does not want war in the Middle East, but she also does not seem to want peace unless she is one of the guarantors of it. After the cease-fire in 1967 she strove unsuccessfully to obtain the condemnation of Israel as the aggressor before the United Nations. Eventually she moderated her course so far as to permit acceptance by the Security Council of a British resolution that offered some slender hope for the future. In Documents XV (a) and (b) we give the text of the Security Council Resolution of 22 November 1967, and the Egyptian reaction to it. Attempts to find common ground between the two sides by the UN appointed mediator, Professor Gunnar Jarring, have so far been of no avail. Recently, in October 1968, a peace initiative came from Israel in the form of nine very general proposals. This nine-point peace initiative is documented in XV (c).

RENEWED DANGERS OF WAR

There is no peace settlement yet. Before a real peace can be achieved shall we see yet another war? There have been ominous developments since the cease-fire.

First, Arab guerrilla warfare continues. Recently it has included attacks on Israeli civil aircraft outside Israel, a form of attack to which Israel has retaliated in kind. The guerrilla warfare proper is waged not now from mercurial Syria, but from patient Jordan. This has brought on Jordan, who deserves it least, severe Israeli retaliatory action. Unhappy Jordan is the state which may attack and be attacked without creating the direst consequences in the Arab world. Will guerrilla warfare be successful? This problem is considered in Documents XVI (a), (b) and (c). Another important factor in the present situation is the re-arming of Egypt by Russia. The present balance of power and the prospects of arms control are demonstrated in Documents XVI (d) (i) and (ii).

Another problem that has arisen in a new form since the war is that of Jerusalem, now integrated into Israel. It is regarded by the Israelis not as a bargaining counter, but as a permanent acquisition—one that Arabs in particular and Muslims everywhere will permanently resent. The Jerusalem problem is documented in Documents XVI (e) to (h).

The last continuing problem—that which, with boundaries, has been the most important since 1948—is the refugee problem. In its latest aspects it is documented in XVI (i) and (j). A consideration of the effects on Israel of the present enlargement of her territories follows this in Document XVI (k).

PART I

Place and People

In this section, we show graphically how political boundaries in the Arab world and the composition of the population of Palestine/Israel have changed over the period covered by this book. Reference to this section should be made throughout the book since limitation of space prevents us from providing detailed discussion of the geographic and demographic aspects of the problem.

It must suffice to say that from 1918 to 1938 the Jewish population of Palestine grew from some 7 per cent to about 29 per cent of the total population. (The total population increase was from 0.65 million to 1.4 million.) The main areas of Jewish settlement were essentially those parts of Palestine, except the Negev, allocated to Israel under the UN Partition Plan of 1947 (Document I (f)). As we have seen, the UN plan was rejected by the Arab states at the time, but it has subsequently been the only basis for an independent Arab state that the Arabs have been prepared to recognize. The 1948 war left Israel with boundaries more generous than those of the UN plan, which the Jews had accepted (Document I (g)). In addition to occupying all the northern area of Palestine they gained considerably in the central southern area. Not only did they thus escape the inconvenience of the linked, but not continuous, Jewish territory which the UN had ingeniously provided for, they also gained a broad corridor up to and including part of Jerusalem.

As we shall see, after the 1956 war, international pressures forced Israel back to the 1949 lines. After the 1967 war Israel announced the incorporation of Jordanian Jerusalem into Israel; otherwise Israel as yet regards her other gains as militarily occupied territory (Document I (h)). It may have been administrative convenience that required this change from 'enemy territory', but the Arabs are not convinced that the change is not more significant. On the three occasions now that Israel has defeated the Arab states in war she has sought to enlarge her territory, thus lending credence to Arab charges of expansionism. Yet apart from Jerusalem, Israel seems to be interested in further territorial acquisitions only for strategic reasons. Israel needs a shorter frontier, which occupation of the west bank of the Jordan would provide. Israel also needs greater security from Syrian attacks, which occupation of the Golan heights would ensure. (They are now partly occupied by Israeli settlements.) Whether Israel ever withdraws from these areas depends largely on how belligerent the Arab states continue to be.

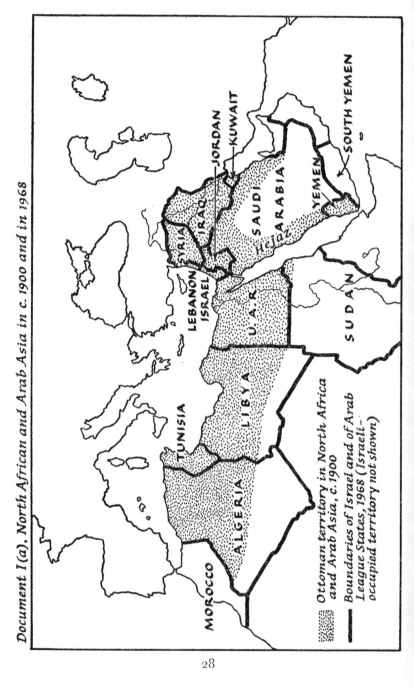

Document I (a), North African and Arab Asia in c. 1900 and in 1968

MOROCCO
ALGERIA
TUNISIA
LIBYA
U.A.R.
SUDAN
SYRIA
IRAQ
LEBANON
ISRAEL
JORDAN
KUWAIT
SAUDI ARABIA
Hejaz
YEMEN
SOUTH YEMEN

Ottoman territory in North Africa and Arab Asia, c. 1900

Boundaries of Israel and of Arab League States, 1968 (Israeli–occupied territory not shown)

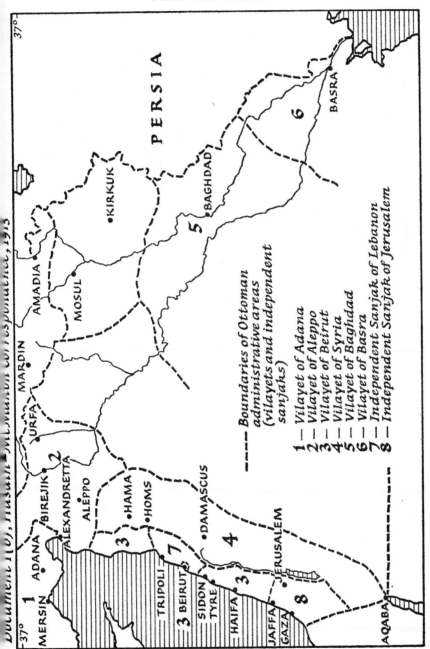

PERSIA

BASRA

KIRKUK

BAGHDAD

6

5

AMADIA

MOSUL

MARDIN

URFA

BIREJIK

ALEXANDRETTA

ALEPPO

HAMA

HOMS

DAMASCUS

2

3

4

7

TRIPOLI

BEIRUT

SIDON

TYRE

HAIFA

JAFFA

GAZA

JERUSALEM

3

3

8

AQABA

MERSIN

ADANA

1

Boundaries of Ottoman
administrative areas
(vilayets and independent
sanjaks)

1 — Vilayet of Adana
2 — Vilayet of Aleppo
3 — Vilayet of Beirut
4 — Vilayet of Syria
5 — Vilayet of Baghdad
6 — Vilayet of Basra
7 — Independent Sanjak of Lebanon
8 — Independent Sanjak of Jerusalem

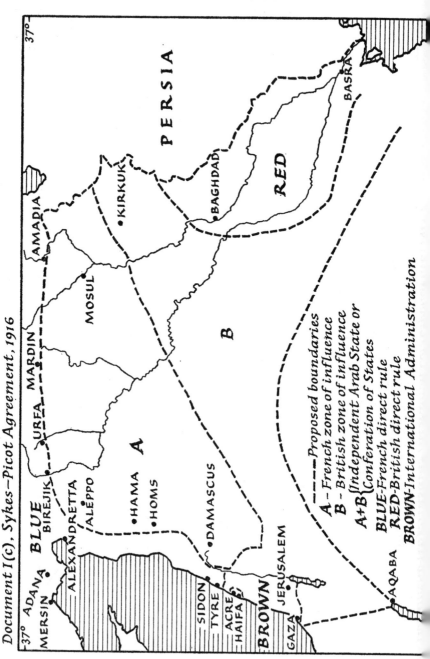

Document I(c). Sykes—Picot Agreement, 1916

- - - - Proposed boundaries
A – French zone of influence
B – British zone of influence
A+B {Independent Arab State or
Conferation of States
BLUE–French direct rule
RED–British direct rule
BROWN–International Administration

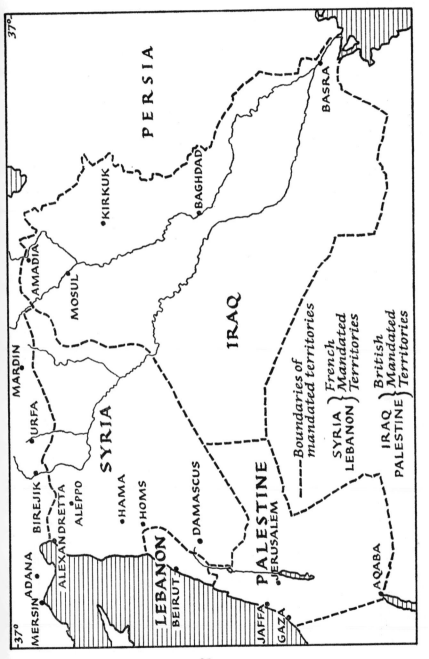

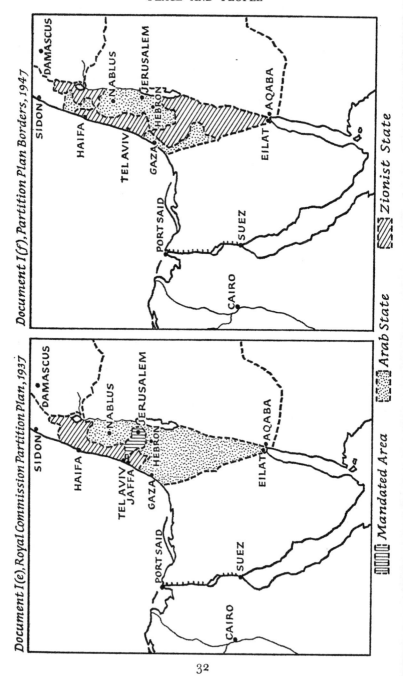

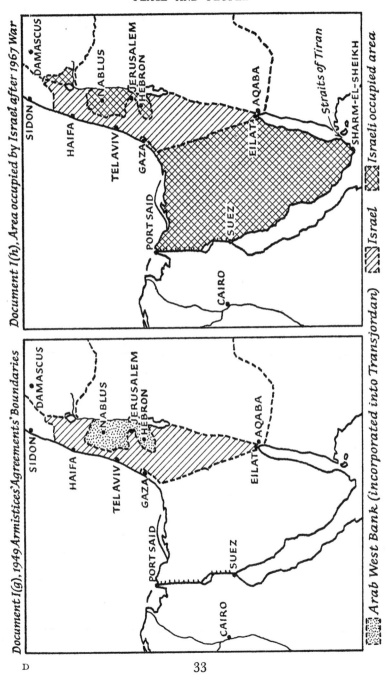

Document I(h), Area occupied by Israel after 1967 War

Document I(g), 1949 Armistices'Agreements'Boundaries

Arab West Bank (incorporated into Transjordan)   Israel   Israeli occupied area

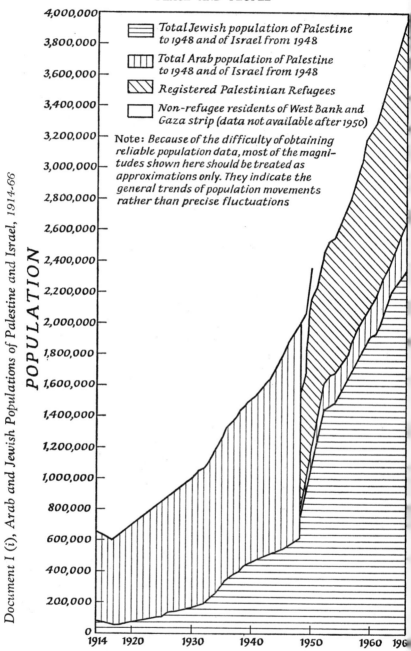

Document I (i), Arab and Jewish Populations of Palestine and Israel, 1914-66

Total Jewish population of Palestine to 1948 and of Israel from 1948

Total Arab population of Palestine to 1948 and of Israel from 1948

Registered Palestinian Refugees

Non-refugee residents of West Bank and Gaza strip (data not available after 1950)

Note: Because of the difficulty of obtaining reliable population data, most of the magnitudes shown here should be treated as approximations only. They indicate the general trends of population movements rather than precise fluctuations

POPULATION

PART II

The Basic Argument

The documents given below illustrate the moderate mainstream of Zionist and Arab nationalist thought on Palestine and show the historical and political arguments which each side has employed through most of the present century.

DOCUMENT II (a). EXCERPTS FROM CHAIM WEIZMANN, *The Jewish People and Palestine*, STATEMENT MADE BEFORE THE PALESTINE ROYAL COMMISSION IN JERUSALEM, 25 NOVEMBER 1936.

I should like to put briefly before you the Jewish problem as it presents itself to us today. It is a twofold problem; but its nature can perhaps be expressed in one word: it is the problem of the homelessness of a people. Speaking of homelessness, I should like at once to state that individual Jews, and individual groups of Jews, may have homes and sometimes very comfortable homes. . . . But if one draws a line and takes the Rhine as the geographical boundary, almost everything to the east of the Rhine is to-day in a position, politically and economically, which may be described—and I am not given, I think to exaggeration—as something that is neither life nor death; and one may add that if Europe to-day were in the same state as it was in 1914 before the war, with the highways and byways of Europe and the world in general open, then we should have witnessed an emigration of Jews that would probably have dwarfed the pre-war emigration—and that pre-war emigration was not by any means small. I think that in the year 1914 alone there emigrated out of Russia, which then included Poland as well, something in the neighbourhood of 120,000 Jews.
They went in the majority of cases to America, where they

could readily be absorbed in a highly developed industrial country. The emigrant found his livelihood almost immediately on arrival. This, as your lordship and the members of the Commission are well aware, cannot happen to-day. The world is closed; and we have recently heard it said in authoritative quarters in Geneva, in Poland, and in England, that there are a million Jews too many in Poland. This is not the place to enter into a discussion as to why exactly a million *Jews*? They are citizens of Poland; their fate and their destinies have been bound up with the fate and destinies of Poland for well-nigh a thousand years. They passed through all the vicissitudes of the Polish nation. They desire to make their contribution, good, bad or indifferent—like everybody else—to Polish develop-ment. Why should they be singled out as being a million too many? No doubt these elementary facts as to the state of the world to-day are known in Poland just as they are known to every intelligent newspaper reader here. What does it mean? Where can they go? Is there any place in the world which can rapidly absorb a million people, whoever they may be, Jews or non-Jews? The poor Polish peasant, perhaps ignorant and not very subtle, when he hears people in authority making a pronouncement like that, may possibly interpret it as meaning: here is a superfluous people standing in my way, which must be got rid of somehow.

I do not want to press the point any further. I shall not waste the time of the Commission by describing in any way what is happening in Germany. It is too well known to need elabora-tion. This accounts for the position of something like 3,600,000 Jews. Poland has slightly over three millions; Germany had in 1932 or 1933 something like 600,000 but that number has since diminished. If one goes further afield, and takes the Jewries of Roumania, Latvia, Austria, one sees practically the same picture, and it is no exaggeration on my part to say that to-day almost six million Jews—I am not speaking of the Jews in Persia and Morocco and such places, who are very inarticulate, and of whom one hears very little—there are in this part of the world six million people pent up in places where they are not wanted, and for whom the world is divided into places where they cannot live, and places into which they may not enter. . . .

36

Now we think this is not merely a problem which concerns the Jewish community. It is in our view a world problem of considerable importance. Naturally it is one which affects primarily the Jewish community, and secondarily the state of affairs in that particular part of the world, a part of the world which since the War has moved towards new forms of political and social life and which is not very strong or very mature either politically or economically. These six million people to whom I have referred are condemned to live from hand to mouth, they do not know to-day what is going to happen tomorrow. I am not speaking now of organized anti-Semitism; even assuming the host-nations were quite friendly, there would still be purely objective reasons in those parts of the world which would tend to grind down the Jewish community and make it into the flotsam and jetsam of the world—grind it into the economic dust, so to speak.

Far be it from me, in saying that, to try to harrow your feelings, but it is too little known. Though it is generally known that the position of the Jewish people is not very happy, I think the depth of its misery is too little appreciated; and that is why I have permitted myself to dwell on it at some length. After all, it affects the fate of six million people. I am thinking of the young people and leaving aside for the moment the old people. I compare the fate of these young men and women—I myself come from the same social stratum—with the fate, the not very enviable fate, of young men and women in, say, the depressed areas of England. There are quite a number of young men and women in England whose state, whose feelings, are not very happy; young men who know that they are superfluous, that they cannot find employment, that the ordinary elementary right of the human being to work, and to live by the work of his hands and his brain, is refused them. It is tragic enough, but at least a man may feel, in Durham or Newcastle, at any rate, that there is a State that takes care of him as far as it can. There is a hope. There may be an opportunity. Unemployment is going down, his turn may come, and a man can put up with a good deal of suffering if he sees a hope in front of him. That is not applicable to the masses, the hundreds, the thousands, and the millions of young men and women in the areas of Central and Eastern Europe. They cannot go out, they cannot find employment, they are not surrounded by a friendly atmosphere, there is nobody who is concerned for them. They are doomed, they are exasperated, they are in despair.

Since my early youth, my lord, I have fought destructive tendencies in Jewry—but it is almost impossible to avoid destructive tendencies amongst a younger generation which lives in the state I have described, unless some hope is given to the young people that one day, some day in some distant future, one in five, one in ten, one in twenty, will find a refuge somewhere where he can work, where he can live, and where he can straighten himself up and look with open eyes at the world and at his fellow-men and women. It is no wonder that a certificate for Palestine is considered the highest boon in this part of the world. One in twenty, one in thirty, may get it, and for them it is redemption; it is tantamount to freedom, the opportunity to live and work, and that is why they watch with such intensity all that is going on here, and whether or not the doors of Palestine will remain open or will remain closed.

I believe I have said enough; it would require special treatment, detailed statistical treatment, to explain why this state of affairs has come about. . . .

Gradually, and I can prove it by statistical data, the Jews are being displaced, and that is the inner meaning of the statement that there are one million Jews too many in Poland. They are too many because their place is gradually being taken by the Poles. The same process, on perhaps a smaller scale, is being repeated in other countries, in the Succession States which sprang up after the War. Such, my lord and gentlemen, is the state of a great part of Jewry in that part of the world.

I could turn to the West and say that, if there is no material problem or economic problem of such acuteness as I have described in the East, there is an uncomfortable feeling in the West, with a few exceptions—it is easy to be a Jew in England—but that uneasy feeling which used to stop at the Vistula has now reached the Rhine and gradually crossed the Rhine. It infiltrates across the Channel and across the Atlantic. It has not become so acute as to make our life unbearable, but it is there, and what has happened in Germany is the writing on the wall even for the Western communities. . . .

Here was a Western community in a civilized state, to all intents and purposes an integral part of the life of Germany, playing a very considerable part economically and intellectually, an old community—the communities on the Rhine are much older than the Prussian communities. I shall not dwell here on the contribution which German Jewry has made to modern Germany—I could quote a galaxy of names of international fame and repute—and in one day, almost overnight, it has been destroyed. First came the destruction of the intellectuals, then the destruction of the merchant class, and so on and so forth, and Hitler and his satellites are saying they will not rest until the German Jewish community is reduced to beggary. It came upon us overnight and naturally it is a warning. . . .

I could go on dwelling on the tense position in Jewry to-day aggravated, as it naturally has been, by the effects of the Great War. This is the moral side of the problem. In all countries we try to do our best, but somehow in many countries we are not entirely accepted as an integral part of the communities to which we belong. This feeling is one of the causes which have prompted Jews throughout the ages, and particularly in the last hundred years, to try to make a contribution towards the solution of the problem and to normalize—to some extent to normalize—the position of the Jews in the world. We are sufficiently strong, my lord, to have preserved our identity, but an identity which is *sui generis* and not like the identity of other nations. When one speaks of the English or the French or the German nation, one refers to a definite State, a definite organization, a language, a literature, a history, a common destiny; but it is clear that when one speaks of the Jewish people, one speaks of a people which is a minority everywhere, a majority nowhere which is to some extent identified with the races among which it lives, but still not quite identical. It is, if I may say so, a disembodied ghost of a race, without a body, and it therefore inspires suspicion, and suspicion breeds hatred. There should be one place in the world, in God's wide world, where we could live and express ourselves in accordance with our character, and make our contribution towards the civilized world, in our own way and through our own channels. Perhaps if we had, we would be better understood in ourselves, and our relation to other races and nations would become more normal. We would not have to be always on the defensive, or on the contrary, become too aggressive, as always happens with a minority forced to be constantly on the defensive. I hope I may be forgiven if I have dwelt too long on this problem, but I feel it is essential that I should make it as clear as I possibly can.

What has produced this particular mentality of the Jews which makes me describe the Jewish race as a sort of dis-embodied ghost—an entity and yet not an entity in accordance with the usual standards which are applied to define an entity? I believe the main cause which has produced the particular state of Jewry in the world is its attachment to Palestine. We are a stiff-necked people and a people of long memory. We never forget. Whether it is our misfortune or whether it is our good fortune, we have never forgotten Palestine, and this steadfastness, which has preserved the Jew throughout the ages and throughout a career that is almost one long chain of inhuman suffering, is primarily due to some physiological or psychological attachment to Palestine. We have never forgotten it nor given it up. We have survived our Babylonian and Roman conquerors. The Jews put up a fairly severe fight and the Roman Empire, which digested half of the civilized world, did not digest small Judea. And whenever they once got a chance, the slightest chance, there the Jews returned, there they created their literature, their villages, towns and communities. And, if the Commission would take the trouble to study the post-Roman period of the Jews and the life of the Jews in Palestine, they would find that during the nineteen centuries which have passed since the destruction of Palestine as a Jewish political entity, there was not a single century in which the Jews did not attempt to come back.

It is, I believe, a fallacy to regard these 1,900 years as, so to say, a desert of time; they were not. When the material props of the Jewish commonwealth were destroyed, the Jews carried Palestine in their hearts and in their heads wherever they went. That idea continued to express itself in their ritual and in their prayers. In the East End of London the Jew still prays for dew in the summer and for rain in the winter, and his seasons and festivals are all Palestinian seasons and Palestinian festivals. When Rome destroyed their country, the intellectual leader of the Jewish community came to the Roman commander and said, 'You have destroyed all our material possessions; give us, I pray, some refuge for our houses of learning'. A refuge was found; the place still exists, it was then a big place, and is now a tiny railway station by the name of Yebna, in Hebrew 'Yavneh'. There were schools there, and there the Jews continued their intellectual output, so that those schools became, so to speak, the spiritual homes, not only of Palestinian Jewry, but of Jewry at large, which was gradually filtering out of Palestine and dispersing all over the world. They replaced the material Palestine, the political Palestine, by a moral Palestine which was indestructible, which remained indestructible; and this yearning found its expression in a mass of literature, sacred and non-sacred, secular and religious.

Later on, whenever the opportunity arose, there were also material movements, movements of masses of Jews into Palestine. When the Jews were driven out of Spain at the end of the fifteenth century they wandered all over the world. Two hundred thousand of them turned their faces towards the East. We are not unmindful of the reception given to us then by the Moslem world. We came to Turkey, and from Turkey we drifted to Palestine. . . . Four great Jewish communities were created: in Hebron, Jerusalem, Safad and Tiberias. They became great centres of Jewish learning, they grew from nothing to communities which sometimes contained as many as 20,000 inhabitants. The darkest period, the period when Jewish Palestine was, so to speak, at its lowest ebb, was after the Crusades and the Tartar invasion. But apart from those hundred or hundred-and-twenty years, there was never a time when Jews did not attempt, not only in prayer, not only in yearning, not only in moral and religious striving, but actually and physically, to go to Palestine.

Messianic movements which were semi-religious and semi-secular—a less rationalistic form of the modern Zionist Movement—sprang up. . . . According to Jewish tradition, the Messiah will come on the day when the Dispersion is complete. [In the 17th century—eds.] there were no Jews in England, and Cromwell invited the return of the Jews to England in order that the Dispersion should be complete, and the advent of the Messiah thus facilitated. I am not quoting these facts merely as a historical curiosity, but in order to point out that the idea of the Return to Zion still survived not only in the consciousness of the Jews, but also in the consciousness of a great part of the non-Jewish world, particularly of the English world, three hundred years before the Balfour Declaration. And throughout the three hundred years which preceded the Balfour Declaration, English people—statesmen, divines— advocated the return of the Jews to Palestine (Lord Shaftesbury, Lord Palmerston, and many more). In the time of Palmerston this idea assumed the form of definite proposals, definite projects, which proved to be impracticable, and finally the British Government proclaimed (and instructed all its Consuls in the East accordingly) that the Jews in Palestine, from whatever country they might have come, were under the protection of Great Britain. If you have an opportunity of travelling through the southern Jewish villages, you will see one of the oldest of the settlements, Rishon-le-Zion, which is, if I may say so, one of the most interesting. When the settlers first tried to acquire that land—and the acquisition of land in the time of the Turks was even more of a science than it is now—they did it through the influence and the help of the British Vice-Consul at Jaffa.

. . . I think the Balfour Declaration is nothing but the final link in the chain of attempts made by the British people to help us to come back to Palestine.

Before I close, I should like to mention two or three things which preceded the Balfour Declaration. When we first started our work in 1897, at the first Zionist Congress, and Dr Herzl, who was then the leader of the Movement, tried to negotiate with the Sultan for our return to Palestine, the Sultan, in the usual Turkish way, never said 'Yes' and never said 'No', and things were uncertain. But the Jewish position grew worse from day to day and finally, in 1903, there was a massacre in Kishinev which started a wave of pogroms that swept over the whole of Russia. The position of the Jews became desperate.

The hope of ever obtaining anything definite from the Turkish Government dwindled, and the leader of the Zionist movement, who always hoped that some day England might help us with the Return, met Joseph Chamberlain. Joseph

Chamberlain had then just returned from a tour to Africa, and he made an offer of a country which then was called Uganda (and is now part of Kenya) to the Jews. And so we found ourselves—a movement far from any practical realization of its aspirations—treated very seriously by the mightiest government in the world who made us a generous offer, an offer of a territory almost as big as the mandated territory of Palestine. I think the territory which was then discussed was something like 8,000 square miles, a plateau in Uganda—I have never been there, but as far as I know, good land. We had the rope round our necks; and yet, when this offer was brought to the Zionist Congress, a great discussion ensued and finally the offer was accepted in this form: that a Commission should be sent to the country in question to see what it was. But that was carried by a small majority; the minority, a very important minority, consisted primarily of Jews from Eastern Europe (I myself was amongst them), and they refused the offer for one reason only: 'It is not Palestine, and it never will be Palestine'. I remember we proposed that our leader should write a letter to the British Government and say something like this to the British Government: 'We are extremely grateful for your generous offer, but we cannot accept it, just as we could not agree to cease to be Jews. Some day it may be given to you to make us another offer'. We said, 'We have waited two thousand years, and we shall wait a few more years; and in the fullness of time God will keep His promise to His people'. Our Leader died, and the offer was refused. Twelve or thirteen years later Mr Balfour, who was Prime Minister in the Cabinet which had made the Uganda offer, gave us the Balfour Declaration.

Mr Balfour, when I had the pleasure of making his acquaintance, tried to understand why we felt like this, and the only reason which appealed to him was when I told him: 'It is not Jerusalem, and it never will be'. This tenacity, this steadfastness, is, my lord and gentlemen, perhaps our misfortune. If it had disappeared, there would be no Jewish problem. But here we are; it is our destiny. . . .

What did the Balfour Declaration mean? It meant something quite simple at that time, and I am saying so advisedly. It meant that Judea was restored to the Jews or the Jews were restored to Judea. I could submit to the Commission a series of utterances of responsible statesmen and men in every walk of life in England to show that this Declaration was at the time regarded as the *Magna Carta* of the Jewish people; it was in a sense comparable with another Declaration made thousands of years before, when Cyrus allowed a remnant of the Jews to return from Babylon and to rebuild the Temple. To the ordinary man at that time reading the Declaration, what it meant is broadly indicated by the various speeches at a solemn meeting at the Opera House in London, where (among others) Lord Cecil spoke and said: 'Arabia for the Arabs, Judea for the Jews, Armenia for the Armenians'. Much water and much blood have flowed under the various bridges of the world since that time, and not all of his predictions have been realized; but we read into the Declaration what the statesmen of Great Britain told us it meant. It meant a National Home, 'national' meaning that we should be able to live like a nation in Palestine, and 'Home' a place where we might live as free men in contradistinction to living on sufferance everywhere else. To English people I need not explain what the word 'home' means, or what it does *not* mean, to us everywhere else.

The meaning was clear, and the Jewry of the world, in the trenches of Europe, in the pogrom-swept area of Russia, saw it like that. . . .

It meant, as I say, at that time, and speaking in political parlance, a Jewish State; and when I was asked at the Peace Conference, quite impromptu, by Mr Lansing, 'What do you mean by a Jewish National Home?' I gave this answer: 'To build up something in Palestine which will be as Jewish as England is English'. Of course, we have always borne in mind, and our teachers and mentors at that time, British statesmen, repeatedly told us: 'There is a second half to the Balfour Declaration. That second part provides that nothing should be done which might injure the interests of the non-Jewish communities in Palestine'. Well, I must leave it to the Commission to test this and to ascertain whether, throughout the work of these last sixteen years, we have done anything which has in any way injured the position of the non-Jewish population. I go further than that. The Balfour Declaration says that the civil and religious rights of the non-Jewish communities should not be interfered with. I would humbly ask the Commission to give the broadest possible interpretation to that, not merely a narrow interpretation of civil and religious rights; put it as broadly as the Commission may wish, and test it, and I think I can say before the Commission, before God, and before the world, that in intention, consciously, nothing has been done to injure their position. On the contrary, indirectly we have conferred benefits on the population of this country. I should like to be perfectly frank: We have not come for that purpose. We have come for the purpose of building up a National Home for the Jewish people; but we are happy and proud that this upbuilding has been accompanied by considerable benefits to the country at large. . . .

Another difficulty with which we had to contend, was that the very causes which might have hastened the issue of the Balfour Declaration also produced resisting forces. One of these forces is the growth of Arab nationalism. The Arab race emerged out of the war more conscious of itself, and rightly so; and they look upon Palestine as an Arab country and upon us as intruders. This is not the time to discuss it, but by implication, I think, I have answered this particular charge. It may perhaps be interesting to read to you a quotation from a speech by the late Lord Milner in a debate in the House of Lords in 1923:

If the Arabs go to the length of claiming Palestine as one of their countries in the same sense as Mesopotamia [the name of Mesopotamia was then current] or Arabia proper is an Arab country, then I think they are flying in the face of facts, of all history, of all tradition and all associations of the most important character, I had almost said, the most sacred character. The future of Palestine cannot possibly be left to be determined by the temporary impressions and feelings of the Arab majority in the country at the present day.

I should like to add that as soon as the Balfour Declaration was issued, and even before that, British statesmen and those who had negotiated with British statesmen, were well aware both of Arab susceptibilities and of the necessity for making our position clear to the Arabs. The difficulty with which we were faced, and are unfortunately still faced to-day, is that there were and are very few Arabs who can really speak authoritatively on behalf of the Arab people. In 1918 there was one distinguished Arab who was the Commander-in-Chief of the Arab armies which were supporting the right flank of Allenby's army, the then Emir Feisal—subsequently King Feisal. At the suggestion of General Allenby I went to the camp of the Emir. I frankly put to him our aspirations, our hopes, our desires, our intentions, and I can only say—if any oath of mine could convince my Arab opponents—I can only say that we found ourselves in full agreement; and that first meeting was the beginning of a lifelong friendship. Our relationship was expressed subsequently in a treaty—perhaps treaty is too ambitious a word—I was not a contracting party—but in a document whose moral value cannot be contested. It lays down the lines of relationship between the Jews in Palestine and the Arabs in Palestine and their general relationship with the Arabs at large. I may submit to the Commission that, as far as we are concerned, that has not changed.

One feature of this treaty to which I refer is that the intermediary who negotiated it and actually contributed to its drafting was the late Colonel Lawrence. He also acted as interpreter. Of this treaty I gave cognisance to the Foreign Office and to the various authorities who dealt with us at that time.

It may be that we have come to this country as a people which was looked upon primarily as a western people with western training. We have been engaged too much and too deeply with our own work, which has taxed all our energies, and it may be that we have not done all that we could have done in normal circumstances, to find our way to our Arab friends. History will have to judge of that; but many attempts were made by us, here, in Cairo, in Damascus, in Beirut, to make the Arabs understand our point of view, to ask them to co-operate with us, to help to find a *modus vivendi*. The hand which we repeatedly stretched out was always repelled, and to-day we stand in this position which the Royal Commission faces. Anything which my Organization or myself or our friends can contribute towards helping the Royal Commission, if they need our help, in finding a solution of this thorny problem, you will find us only too ready to offer.

THE BASIC ARGUMENT

NOTE

CHAIM WEIZMANN, born in Russian Poland in 1874, studied chemistry in Germany and Switzerland and became one of the leaders of the WZO in the years after Herzl died and Weizmann himself went to live in Britain (1904). There he continued his career as a chemist, achieving distinction in both university and government employment. At the same time he played a leading role in the negotiations which issued in the Balfour Declaration and thereafter remained in the forefront of WZO politics, though he was not always the Organization's titular head. In 1948 he went to live in Israel as first President of the new State, an office which he retained until his death in 1952.

DOCUMENT II (b). EXCERPTS FROM CONSTANTINE ZURAYK, 'THE CONFLICT BETWEEN PRINCIPLE AND FORCE IN THE PALESTINE PROBLEM', *Al-'Amal*, DECEMBER 1947.

. . . Let us strip this problem of its external appearances and penetrate to the inner essence. What do we find?

We find that we have a problem in which principle on the one hand is confronted by force and interest on the other. Thus, the effect of this problem is not limited to Arabs and Zionists. In fact it involves the whole world, for it is a touchstone of the conscience of the world and of the strength of international organization. Furthermore, it is an indication of the direction in which human society will move: towards justice and peace, or toward oppression and continuous war.

In this question the principle is the right of every people to the land on which they live and on which their forefathers have lived for long centuries—to the land which has been dyed red with their blood, and with whose soil the sweat of their brow has been mixed. It is the right to exploit the land's resources and to establish therein any political, social, or cultural system which they choose, provided that they do not infringe on the liberty and rights of other peoples.

Mankind has struggled for centuries to have this right acknowledged and in its name has spilled blood and made other sacrifices. In the First World War, when the leaders of the Allied nations proclaimed it, the world imagined that it would be the basis of international organization after the war, but it was not long before this vision cracked on the rock of self-interest, and once more force and balance of power began to steer the world. The recent war was similar: the proclamation

47

of lofty principles in the Atlantic Charter and elsewhere and a new international organization, the United Nations, but, unfortunately, force, interest, and balance of power are still the effective factors in international politics.

If we review all the decisions and measures which have been taken in connection with Palestine, we find that they are contrary to the natural right of the Arabs and to the fundamental principle of the right of self-determination for which the nations proclaimed they were fighting and in the name of which they sacrificed themselves to an extraordinary degree.

The Balfour Declaration which Britain gave to the Jews and which the Zionists take as the foundation stone of their legal claims, was completely contrary to the aforementioned principle. The British had no right from any point of view to dispose of a land which was not their own or to determine the future of any people other than their own. I do not here refer to the contradiction between the Balfour Declaration and the pledges which the British made to the Arabs, despite its importance, for I am limiting my inquiry to the principle involved, regardless of political or other points of view, which also favour the Arabs.

Some may say that the British acquired the right to dispose of Palestine because they conquered it and obtained it as spoils of war from the Ottoman Turks. One refutation of this argument is that the British did not conquer it alone but in partnership with the Arabs, who allied themselves with them and who rose up in their well-known revolt in order to liberate their country. However, the more important refutation from the point of view of principle is that the right of conquest can no longer be considered a basis for world organization. If it can be, we have turned civilization back to the Dark Ages and have trampled under foot the fundamental principle of nationalism, namely, the right of every people to its land and to the determination of its own destiny.

Others may say that the Balfour Declaration acquired an international legal character when the League of Nations endorsed it and made it one of the bases of the British mandate for Palestine. The answer to this claim is that what is built on a false foundation will continue to be false even if the whole world endorses it. Furthermore, the mandate over Palestine is itself contrary to the general principle of mandates enunciated

in Article twenty-two of the Covenant of the League of Nations
. . . paragraph four. . . .

In the light of this . . . the inclusion of the Balfour Declaration
in the text of the mandate for Palestine was not only a trans-
gression of the natural rights of the Arabs, but also contrary to
the fundamental principle relevant to all mandates for territories which had been under Ottoman control and whose
independence was provisionally recognized. For beyond any
doubt the policy of immigration and of acting to build a
national Jewish home impaired this previously recognized
independence, not to mention the fact that the wishes of the
people of Palestine were never considered either as to the mandate itself or as to the choice of the mandatory power.

Palestine was thus ruled for a period of twenty-five years by
a regime based neither on natural nor legal principles, but
instead on force and self-interest. Through this force the
sovereignty of the Arabs was violated instead of being preserved,
and their existence in their own land was encompassed by
danger and threatened with extinction.

Now the United Nations has committed the same crime and
sacrificed principle on the altar of interest. Its decision on
partition transgresses the right of the people of Palestine to
determine their future in accordance with well-established
democratic processes and is also contrary to both the letter and
the spirit of the United Nations Charter itself. Even if we assume
that the mandate for Palestine was based on a legal foundation
—and we have demonstrated that it was not—we find no article
in the twelfth chapter of the Charter (which deals with mandated territories) that gives the United Nations the right to
partition the country or to dispose of it as it wants. There is one
single inescapable principle: to aid this country to attain its
independence and to determine its own fate.

Thus the decision of the United Nations—like the mandate—
rests on neither a moral nor a legal foundation. The Arab
delegations came forward with the proposal of submitting this
question to the International Court of Justice so that it might
give its opinion on the competence of the United Nations to
decide on partition. Even this proposal was turned down—a
fact showing that the United Nations, under the pressure of

various forces and interests, was not in this case prepared to listen to the voice of the highest legal authority in the world.

We deduce from all that has preceded that the struggle against Zionism and against the establishment of a Jewish state in Palestine is not, from the Arab point of view, merely a national struggle, but a struggle for the sake of a lofty human ideal—a struggle between right and might, between principle and interest.

Some may ask: 'do the Zionists not have principles on which they build their movement and in which they clothe their propaganda and through which they acquire sympathy and support?'

They do indeed flaunt many 'principles', but none of them will stand before fact and evidence.

The Zionists claim that Palestine is the national home of the Jews because they inhabited it for many generations in the past, that they were then driven from it, and that they now have the right to return to it. The fact is that the Jews infiltrated Palestine in ancient time as other Semitic tribes infiltrated the countries of the Fertile Crescent, but they established a unified kingdom in it only during the period of David and Soloman (1017–937 BC), and this kingdom lasted only for a limited period. Even during that short period their rule did not include all of Palestine, for the Philistines and others continued to have power and influence in the country. Then the Jewish kingdom was divided into two states—north and south. The first fell in 722 BC and the second in 586 BC. During the following centuries they were scattered, and although they tried to rebuild their political life, they failed time after time until finally, during the first two Christian centuries, they were completely dispersed. One thing which shows that their relationship with Palestine was transitory is that the name by which the country has been known throughout history is not derived from them but from their bitterest enemies, the Philistines. Further it is important to note that even at the peak of their power they did not inhabit the regions which they now occupy and which were given them by the partition—that is, the plains and the coast. These were the home of the Philistines and the centre of their power.

In addition, the Zionist Jews who are now immigrating to Palestine bear absolutely no relation to the Semitic Jews. In fact they are from another stock which is completely different from the Semitic stock. Historians affirm that the great majority of the eastern European Jews—and they are the ones who are now pouring into Palestine—trace their origins back to the Khazar tribes who embraced Judaism in the eighth Christian century and who later spread throughout eastern and central Europe. Thus their only bond with the Jews who settled in Palestine in ancient times is religion, which is not a valid basis on which to build nationalism or to found a state.

On the other hand, the Arabs in Palestine represent not only the tribes which migrated from the [Arabian] Peninsula in the seventh century—those tribes were in fact small in number—but all the inhabitants, Semites and others (Philistines, Canaanites, Amorites, Aramaeans, etc.) who have come to Palestine one after another since the dawn of history and who were Arabicized in the seventh century and thereafter. Thus they are the original inhabitants of the country, and the sojourn of the Jews in their country was only transitory and temporary when compared with the long history of the country.

Even if we grant the Jews an historical right in the past, what right does that confer on them in the present? If historical relationship is a valid basis for claiming title to a country, the Arabs would today have the right to claim Spain, the Italians would have the right to claim England, and all the population of the United States would have to leave it and return it to the American Indians.

From whatever point of view we examine the historical principle to which the Zionists appeal, we find that their case has no foundation and cannot be proved.

The Zionist Jews claim that Palestine is their land, that God promised it to them, and that the prophets prophesied their certain return to it. Some Christians have been taken in by these claims in view of certain prophecies which appear in some books of the Bible. But these Christians forget that the Jews refused the Christian message in its entirety and that they, by surrendering to this Jewish claim, surrender the cradle of their religion to a group which has refused it and has fought it throughout the centuries. Further, how can we accept the view that any one people is the special people of God, that there is a covenant between God and them, or that God has singled them out for a particular relationship or distinction. The idea of a 'chosen people' is closer to that of Nazism than to any other idea, and [in the end] it will fall and collapse just as Nazism did.

Let us note that the Zionist state which is now being built in Palestine is as far as possible from religion, for it is a secular state in every sense of the word. It uses the principle of religion, among other things, merely as a vehicle for propaganda, for in fact the state centres on such basic concepts of the secular state as land, industry and culture. In fact its fundamental bases are conquest and seizure by force—and how remote are they from true religion!

The Zionists attempt to support their case for the establishment of a state in Palestine on the persecution and agonies which the Jews have suffered throughout the ages, especially under Nazi rule and during the recent war. They point to the tens of thousands who still live in refugee camps in Germany and elsewhere.

If we assume for the sake of argument that the Jews had no hand in bringing about the persecution which has befallen them, that they in no way contributed to it, and that it was all the fault of other peoples, who then is responsible for it and at whose expense should it be rectified? Is it proper that the Arabs be asked to pay the price of the persecution and suffering which the peoples of Europe preserved, and on the basis of it the political structure should be established by recognized democratic means.

These are some of the 'principles' on which Zionists base their propaganda. These 'principles', and others like them which we cannot treat in this article, do not, as we have seen, rest on a valid or strong foundation. All of them collapse and fall apart before one clear truth which cannot be refuted, namely, the right of the Arabs to determine their own future and to preserve the natural legacy which they inherited from their forefathers.

What then forbids them this right?

Power and self-interest.

The power is the world-wide power of the Jews—politically, financially, and culturally.

This power became clear during the First World War. It extracted the Balfour Declaration from the British government, then imposed on the members of the League of Nations the inclusion of this declaration in the text of the mandate, and continued under the mandate to act in England and America so as to secure continued support for its aggressive policy, despite the awakening of British politicians to its dangers and despite successive Arab revolts. In recent years this power has been centred in the United States. No one who has not stayed in that country and studied its conditions can truly estimate the extent of this power or visualize the awful danger of it. Many American industries and financial institutions are in the hands of Jews, not to mention the press, radio, cinema, and other media of propaganda, or Jewish voters in the states of New York, Illinois, Ohio, and others which are important in presidential elections, especially in these days when the conflict between Democrats and Republicans is at a peak and both parties are trying to acquire votes from any quarter possible.

To estimate the danger of Jewish power in the United States, and consequently in all the world, it suffices to know that the Jews of the United States collected one hundred and five million dollars in 1946 and one hundred and seventy million this year, and that they are now making provisions to collect three hundred and fifty million—all for the support of the new Jewish state.

This is the power: the power of the Jews. Let us turn to the self-interest. There are, in the first place, the domestic interests of American parties, which, as well-informed Americans know, are contrary to the higher interests of America as a state with important stakes in the Arab world. Then there is Russia's interest in finding for itself an opening in the Near East behind the strong points with which the Anglo-Saxon states are building in her face in Greece, Turkey and Iran. Thus if the situation in Palestine is disturbed and the Security Council intervenes, either as a body or by means of some of its members, the Soviets will have an opportunity to penetrate into this vital region of the world behind the Anglo-Saxons' first line of defence.

These two interests, the American internal and the Soviet external, coincided with other imperialistic interests and with the world-wide power of the Jews and led to the partition decision and to the sacrifice of right and principle.

53

NOTE

CONSTANTINE ZURAYK, born in Damascus in 1909, has pursued a brilliant academic career in Oriental Languages, Literature and History mainly in Lebanon and the USA. In 1952 and 1957 respectively he became Vice-President and Distinguished Professor of History at the American University of Beirut. The latter appointment he still holds, and his scholarship has received international recognition with appointments to UNESCO and the International Association of Universities. He held Syrian diplomatic posts in the US and at the UN during 1945-7, and has been among the foremost intellectual Arab nationalists. Immediately after the Arab defeats in 1947-8, he published notable and deeply searching critical analyses of the Arab predicament.

PART III

The Written Undertakings

We reproduce in this section the crucial documents upon which charges of conflicting promises, betrayal and bad faith rely. When studying the texts constant reference should be made to Documents I (b) and (c).

The crucial question raised by the Husain-McMahon Correspondence is a semantic one. Both writers used the Arabic word *wilaya*, akin to the Turkish *vilayet* (*infra* Document III (a), words marked *), the largest unit of Ottoman local administration. Was the word intended to refer strictly to Ottoman administrative areas, or to refer loosely to areas defined in a vague geographical sense only? Or were *both* meanings employed, but inconsistently? Britain has always officially claimed that McMahon's phraseology, as well as the intentions behind it, were such as to except Palestine from the area in which Britain had undertaken to support Arab independence. The Arabs claim that the phraseology is either nonsensical or does *not* except Palestine. We should compare Document III (a) with Document I (b) and ask which explanation seems inherently more likely.

Further, in studying all three documents, we should ask what promises were actually made, whether they conflicted and, if so, how. We shall also want to know whether there is evidence of bad faith or whether apparent bad faith can be explained by postulating mere misunderstandings. A very brief consideration of certain circumstantial evidence which bears upon the interpretation of these three sets of agreements is given in the Introduction (*supra* p. 6).

DOCUMENT III (a). EXCERPTS FROM THE HUSAIN-MCMAHON CORRESPONDENCE, JULY 1915 TO JANUARY 1916 (We reproduce

only the first and fourth letters of the sequence, translated by
G. Antonius.)

The Sharif Husain's first note to Sir Henry McMahon

Mecca, 2 Ramadan 1333
(14 July 1915)

[complimentary titles]

Whereas the entire Arab nation without exception is determined to assert its right to live, gain its freedom and administer its own affairs in name and in fact;

And whereas the Arabs believe it to be in Great Britain's interest to lend them assistance and support in the fulfilment of their steadfast and legitimate aims to the exclusion of all other aims;

And whereas it is similarly to the advantage of the Arabs, in view of their geographical position and their economic interests and in view of the well-known attitude of the Government of Great Britain, to prefer British assistance to any other;

For these reasons the Arab nation has decided to approach the Government of Great Britain with a request for the approval through one of their representatives if they think fit, of the following basic provisions which, as time presses, have not been made to include matters of relatively smaller importance, since such matters can wait until the time comes for their consideration.

1. Great Britain recognizes the independence of the Arab countries which are bounded: on the north, by the line Mersin-Adana to parallel 37° N. and thence along the line Birejik-Urfa - Mardin - Midiat - Jazirat (ibn 'Umar) - Amadia to the Persian frontier; on the east, by the Persian frontier down to the Persian Gulf; on the south, by the Indian Ocean (with the exclusion of Aden whose status will remain as at present); on the west, by the Red Sea and the Mediterranean Sea back to Mersin.

2. Great Britain will agree to the proclamation of an Arab Caliphate for Islam.

3. The Sharifian Arab Government undertakes, other things being equal, to grant Great Britain preference in all economic enterprises in the Arab countries.

4. With a view to ensuring the stability of Arab independence and the efficacy of the promised preference in economic enterprises, the two contracting parties undertake, in the event of any foreign state attacking either of them, to come to each other's assistance with all the resources of their military and naval forces; it being understood that peace will be concluded only when both parties concur.

In the event of one of the two parties embarking upon a war of offence, the other party will adopt an attitude of neutrality, but, if invited to join, will agree to confer with the other party as to the conditions of joint action.

5. Great Britain agrees to the abolition of Capitulations [i.e. the 'chapters' of the concessions which Ottoman Sultans had granted to certain foreign powers to exempt the latters' subjects from Ottoman administrative and legal jurisdiction within certain areas of the Empire. Capitulations had become a symbol of Muslim humiliation at the hands of western powers. *Eds.*] in the Arab countries, and undertakes to assist the Sharifian Government in summoning an international congress to decree their abolition.

6. Clauses 3 and 4 of the present Agreement are to remain in force for a period of fifteen years. Should either party desire an extension, due notice of one year before the expiry of that period will have to be given.

Therefore since the entire Arab nation is (God be praised!) united in its resolve to pursue its noble aim to the end, at whatever cost, it requests the Government of Great Britain to return an answer, whether negatively or in the affirmative, within thirty days of the receipt of this message, in default of which it reserves its right to complete freedom of action, just as we will consider ourselves absolved from the letter and the spirit of the declaration which we made earlier through 'Ali Efendi.

[compliments]

Sir Henry McMahon's second note to the Sharif Husain

Cairo, 24 October 1915

[complimentary titles]
I have, with gratification and pleasure, received your note of

29 Shawwal 1333, and its tokens of sincere friendship have filled me with satisfaction and contentment.

I regret to find that you inferred from my last note that my attitude towards the question of frontiers and boundaries was one of hesitancy and lukewarmth. Such was in no wise the intention of my note. All I meant was that I considered that the time had not yet come in which that question could be discussed in a conclusive manner.

But, having realized from your last note that you considered the question important, vital and urgent, I hastened to communicate to the Government of Great Britain the purport of your note. It gives me the greatest pleasure to convey to you, on their behalf, the following declarations which, I have no doubt, you will receive with satisfaction and acceptance.

The districts* of Mersin and Alexandretta, and portions of Syria lying to the west of the districts* of Damascus, Homs, Hama and Aleppo, cannot be said to be purely Arab, and must on that account be excepted from the proposed delimitation. Subject to that modification, and without prejudice to the treaties concluded between us and certain Arab Chiefs, we accept that delimitation.

As for the regions lying within the proposed frontiers, in which Great Britain is free to act without determent to the interests of her ally France, I am authorized to give you the following pledges on behalf of the Government of Great Britain, and to reply as follows to your note:

1. That, subject to the modifications stated above, Great Britain is prepared to recognize and uphold the independence of the Arabs in all the regions lying within the frontiers proposed by the Sharif of Mecca;

2. That Great Britain will guarantee the Holy Places against all external aggression, and will recognize the obligation of preserving them from aggression;

3. That, when circumstances permit, Great Britain will help the Arabs with her advice and assist them in the establishment of governments to suit those diverse regions;

4. That it is understood that the Arabs have already decided to seek the counsels and advice of Great Britain exclusively; and that such European advisers and officials as may be needed to establish a sound system of administration shall be British;

5. That, as regards the two vilayets* of Baghdad and of Basra, the Arabs recognize that the fact of Great Britain's established position and interests there will call for the setting up of special administrative arrangements to protect those regions from foreign aggression, to promote the welfare of their inhabitants, and to safeguard our mutual economic interests.

I am confident that this declaration will convince you, beyond all doubt, of Great Britain's sympathy with the aspirations of her friends the Arabs; and that it will result in a lasting and solid alliance with them, of which one of the immediate consequences will be the expulsion of the Turks from the Arab countries and the liberation of the Arab peoples from the Turkish yoke which has weighed on them all these long years.

I have confined myself in this note to vital questions of primary importance. If there are any other matters in your notes, which have been overlooked, we can revert to them at some suitable time in the future.

I have heard with great satisfaction and pleasure that the Sacred Kiswa and the charitable gifts which had gone with it had arrived safely and that, thanks to your wise directions and arrangements, they were landed without trouble or damage in spite of the risks and difficulties created by the present deplorable war. We pray Almighty God that He may bring a lasting peace and freedom to mankind.

I am sending this note with your faithful messenger, Shaikh Muhammad ibn 'Aref ibn 'Uraifan, who will lay before you certain interesting matters, which, as they are of secondary importance, I have abstained from mentioning in this note.

[compliments]

DOCUMENT III (b). EXCERPTS FROM THE SYKES-PICOT AGREEMENT, MAY TO OCTOBER 1916. (So called after Sir Mark Sykes and M. Georges-Picot who carried out the negotiations at the end of 1915 and beginning of 1916 which led to the Agreement. The latter was contained in correspondence between Grey, British Foreign Minister, and Cambon, French Ambassador in London. We reproduce only the fourth letter of the sequence. Tsarist Russia was third party to the Agreement.)

Sir Edward Grey to M. Paul Cambon, 16 May 1916.

I have the honour to acknowledge the receipt of your Excellency's note of the 9th instant, stating that the French Government accept the limits of a future Arab State, or Confederation of States, and of those parts of Syria where French interests predominate, together with certain conditions attached thereto, such as they result from recent discussions in London and Petrograd on the subject.

I have the honour to inform your Excellency in reply that the acceptance of the whole project, as it now stands, will involve the abdication of considerable British interests, but, since His Majesty's Government recognize the advantage to the general cause of the Allies entailed in producing a more favourable internal political situation in Turkey, they are ready to accept the arrangement now arrived at, provided that the co-operation of the Arabs is secured, and that the Arabs fulfil the conditions and obtain the towns of Homs, Hama, Damascus, and Aleppo.

It is accordingly understood between the French and British Governments—

1. That France and Great Britain are prepared to recognize and protect an independent Arab State or a Confederation of Arab States in the areas (A) and (B) marked on the annexed map, under the suzerainty of an Arab chief. That in area (A) France, and in area (B) Great Britain, shall have priority of right of enterprise and local loans. That in area (A) France and in area (B) Great Britain, shall alone supply advisers or foreign functionaries at the request of the Arab State or Confederation of Arab States.

2. That in the blue area France, and in the red area Great Britain, shall be allowed to establish such direct or indirect administration or control as they desire and as they may think fit to arrange with the Arab State or Confederation of Arab States.

3. That in the brown area there shall be established an international administration, the form of which is to be decided upon after consultation with Russia, and subsequently in consultation with the other Allies, and the representatives of the Shereef of Mecca.

4. That Great Britain be accorded (1) the ports of Haifa and Acre, (2) guarantee of a given supply of water from the Tigris and Euphrates in area (A) for area (B). His Majesty's Government, on their part, undertake, that they will at no time enter into negotiations for the cession of Cyprus to any third Power without the previous consent of the French Government.

5. That Alexandretta shall be a free port as regards the trade of the British Empire, and that there shall be no discrimination in port charges or facilities as regards British shipping and British goods; that there shall be freedom of transit for British goods through Alexandretta and by railway through the blue area, whether those goods are intended for or originate in the red area, or (B) area, or area (A); and there shall be no discrimination, direct or indirect, against British goods on any railway or against British goods or ships at any port serving the areas mentioned.

That Haifa shall be a free port as regards the trade of France, her dominions and protectorates, and there shall be no discrimination in port charges or facilities as regards French shipping and French goods. There shall be freedom of transit for French goods through Haifa and by the British railway through the brown area, whether those goods are intended for or originate in the blue area, area (A), or area (B), and there shall be no discrimination, direct or indirect, against French goods on any railway, or against French goods or ships at any port serving the areas mentioned.

6. That in area (A) the Baghdad Railway shall not be extended southwards beyond Mosul, and in area (B) northwards beyond Samarra, until a railway connecting Baghdad with Aleppo via the Euphrates Valley has been completed, and then only with the concurrence of the two Governments.

7. That Great Britain has the right to build, administer, and be sole owner of a railway connecting Haifa with area (B), and shall have a perpetual right to transport troops along such a line at all times.

It is to be understood by both Governments that this railway is to facilitate the connection of Baghdad with Haifa by rail, and it is further understood that, if the engineering difficulties and expense entailed by keeping this connecting line in the brown area only make the project unfeasible, that the French

Government shall be prepared to consider that the line in question may also traverse the polygon Banias-Keis Marib - Salkhab Tell Otsda - Mesmie before reaching area (B).

8. For a period of twenty years the existing Turkish customs tariff shall remain in force throughout the whole of the blue and red areas, as well as in areas (A) and (B), and no increase in the rates of duty or conversion from *ad valorem* to specific rates shall be made except by agreement between the two powers.

There shall be no interior customs barriers between any of the above-mentioned areas. The customs duties leviable on goods destined for the interior shall be collected at the port of entry and handed over to the administration of the area of destination.

9. It shall be agreed that the French Government will at no time enter into any negotiations for the cession of their rights and will not cede such rights in the blue area to any third Power, except the Arab State or Confederation of Arab States without the previous agreement of His Majesty's Government, who, on their part, will give a similar undertaking to the French Government regarding the red area.

10. The British and French Governments, as the protectors of the Arab State, shall agree that they will not themselves acquire and will not consent to a third Power acquiring territorial possessions in the Arabian peninsula, nor consent to a third Power installing a naval base either on the east coast, or on the islands, of the Red Sea. This, however, shall not prevent such adjustment of the Aden frontier as may be necessary in consequence of recent Turkish aggression.

11. The negotiations with the Arabs as to the boundaries of the Arab State or Confederation of Arab States shall be continued through the same channel as heretofore on behalf of the two Powers.

12. It is agreed that measures to control the importation of arms into the Arab territories will be considered by the two Governments.

I have further the honour to state that, in order to make the agreement complete, His Majesty's Government are proposing to the Russian Government to exchange notes analogous to those exchanged by the latter and your Excellency's Government on 26 April last. Copies of these notes will be communicated to your Excellency as soon as exchanged.

I would also venture to remind your Excellency that the conclusion of the present agreement raises, for practical consideration, the question of the claims of Italy to a share in any partition or rearrangement of Turkey in Asia, as formulated in article 9 of the agreement of 26 April 1915, between Italy and the Allies.

His Majesty's Government further consider that the Japanese Government should be informed of the arrangements now concluded.

DOCUMENT III (c). THE BALFOUR DECLARATION, 2 NOVEMBER 1917.

Foreign Office
2 November 1917

Dear Lord Rothschild,[1]

I have much pleasure in conveying to you, on behalf of His Majesty's Government, the following declaration of sympathy with Jewish Zionist aspirations which has been submitted to, and approved by, the Cabinet.

'His Majesty's Government view with favour the establishment in Palestine of a National Home for the Jewish people, and will use their best endeavours to facilitate the achievement of this object, it being clearly understood that nothing shall be done which may prejudice the civil and religious rights of existing non-Jewish communities in Palestine, or the rights and political status enjoyed by Jews in any other country.'

I should be grateful if you would bring this declaration to the knowledge of the Zionist Federation.[2]

signed

Arthur James Balfour[3]

[1] The 2nd Baron, Walter Rothschild, was one of the few prominent British Jews who were Zionist. Chiefly known for his learned work as a zoologist, the origins of his interest in Zionism are not known, but he took part in the political negotiations throughout 1917 which led to the Declaration.

[2] The British Zionist Federation, of which Weizmann was at this time President, represented all the constituent Zionist societies of Great Britain.

[3] Secretary of State for Foreign Affairs.

PART IV

The Peace Settlement

The Mandatory Instruments for Lebanon, Syria and Iraq were roughly identical. They provided, *inter alia*, for the introduction of an organic law by the Mandatory within three years of the coming into force of the Mandate and for the promotion by the Mandatory of the progressive development of the mandated territories as independent states. The Mandatory Instrument for Palestine, however, (Document IV (b)), was quite different: it provided specifically for a Jewish National Home (preamble and Articles 2, 4, 6, 11, 22) and failed to provide either for a constitution or for independence at all, let alone within some defined period of time. Instead it restricted itself to provisions for 'self-governing institutions' and 'local autonomy' (Articles 2 and 3). Moreover, since it excluded parts of Palestine from certain of its provisions, it appeared to envisage a division of the territory (Article 25).

All the Instruments fell short of Arab hopes and, more important, of Arab expectations: those for Lebanon, Syria and Iraq because they revealed unequivocally that the principles of immediate independence and democratic government had been scrapped in return for an arrangement, albeit transitional, which the people concerned had specifically said[1] they did not want; the Palestine Instrument because it went even further and actually suspended those principles indefinitely in order, it seemed, to allow an alien majority to establish itself in Palestine. In Arab eyes, the Mandatory regimes not only contravened Article 22 of the Charter of the League (Document IV (a)), but also betrayed the principle of self-determination

[1] In evidence before a US Commission of Enquiry; through Faisal, son of Husain and unofficial representative of Syria and Iraq at Paris Peace Conference; in resolutions of Arab Congresses held in Syria and Palestine, etc.

which the allies had boasted during the First World War and on which they had caused the Arabs to rely when they had sought Arab military assistance. For the Arabs the Palestine Mandate was merely allied manipulation of allied 'principles' in defiance of British promises. Arab feelings about Palestine thus reflected their disillusionment and resentment about the Arab mandatory regimes as a whole. For the Zionists, the Palestine Mandate was an internationally recognized instrument which invalidated any previous conflicting undertakings. Moreover the instrument safeguarded Arab civil and religious rights. The Zionists asserted that they wished to live in peace and friendship with the Arabs. How, they asked could the Arabs, now 'given' enormous pieces of ex-Ottoman territory in which they would eventually enjoy independence and self-government, begrudge the Jews a tiny corner of that territory which had been conquered by the allies in the War. Britain argued that the Palestine Mandate was not a breach of the McMahon Correspondence for, it was claimed, Palestine had been excepted from the territory within which Britain had undertaken to support Arab independence (*supra* p. 55). In any case, Britain stated, Arab rights in Palestine were safeguarded by the terms of the Balfour Declaration which had been written into the Palestine Mandatory Instrument.

DOCUMENT IV (a). ARTICLE 22 OF THE COVENANT OF THE LEAGUE OF NATIONS, APRIL/JUNE 1920.

1. To those colonies and territories which as a consequence of the late war have ceased to be under the sovereignty of the States which formerly governed them and which are inhabited by peoples not yet able to stand by themselves under the strenuous conditions of the modern world, there should be applied the principle that the well-being and development of such peoples form a sacred trust of civilization and that securities for the performance of this trust should be embodied in this Covenant.

2. The best method of giving practical effect to this principle is that the tutelage of such peoples should be entrusted to advanced nations who by reason of their resources, their experience or their geographical position can best undertake

this responsibility, and who are willing to accept it, and that this tutelage should be exercised by them as Mandatories on behalf of the League.

3. The character of the mandate must differ according to the stage of the development of the people, the geographical situation of the territory, its economic conditions and other similar circumstances.

4. Certain communities formerly belonging to the Turkish Empire have reached a stage of development where their existence as independent nations can be provisionally recognized subject to the rendering of administrative advice and assistance by a Mandatory until such time as they are able to stand alone. The wishes of these communities must be a principal consideration in the selection of the Mandatory.

5. Other peoples, especially those of Central Africa, are at such a stage that the Mandatory must be responsible for the administration of the territory under conditions which will guarantee freedom of conscience or religion, subject only to the maintenance of public order and morals, the prohibition of abuses such as the slave trade, the arms traffic and the liquor traffic and the prevention of the establishment of fortifications, or military and naval bases and of military training of the natives for other than police purposes and the defence of territory, and will also secure equal opportunities for the trade and commerce of other Members of the League.

6. There are territories, such as Southwest Africa and certain of the South Pacific Islands, which, owing to the sparseness of their population, or their small size, or their remoteness from the centres of civilization, or their geographical contiguity to the territory of the Mandatory, and other circumstances, can be best administered under the laws of the Mandatory as integral portions of its territory, subject to the safeguards above-mentioned in the interests of the indigenous population.

7. In every case of mandate, the Mandatory shall render to the Council an annual report in reference to the territory committed to its charge.

8. The degree of authority, control or administration to be exercised by the Mandatory shall, if not previously agreed upon by the Members of the League, be explicitly defined in each case by the Council.

9. A permanent Commission shall be constituted to receive and examine the annual reports of the Mandatories and to advise the Council on all matters relating to the observance of the mandates.

DOCUMENT IV (b). EXCERPTS FROM THE MANDATORY INSTRUMENT FOR PALESTINE, 1922.

The Council of the League of Nations:

Whereas the principal Allied Powers have agreed, for the purpose of giving effect to the provisions of Article 22 of the Covenant of the League of Nations, to entrust to a Mandatory selected by the said Powers the administration of the territory of Palestine, which formerly belonged to the Turkish Empire within such boundaries as may be fixed by them; and

Whereas the Principal Allied Powers have also agreed that the Mandatory should be responsible for putting into effect the declaration originally made on 2 November 1917, by the Government of His Britannic Majesty, and adopted by the said Powers, in favour of the establishment in Palestine of a National Home for the Jewish people, it being clearly understood that nothing should be done which might prejudice the civil and religious rights of existing non-Jewish communities in Palestine, or the rights and political status enjoyed by Jews in any other country; and

Whereas recognition has thereby been given to the historical connection of the Jewish people with Palestine and to the grounds for reconstituting their national home in that country; and

Whereas the Principal Allied Powers have selected His Britannic Majesty as the Mandatory for Palestine; and

Whereas the mandate in respect of Palestine has been formulated in the following terms and submitted to the Council of the League for approval; and

Whereas His Britannic Majesty has accepted the mandate in respect of Palestine and undertaken to exercise it on behalf of the League of Nations in conformity with the following provisions; and

Whereas by the afore-mentioned Article 22 (paragraph 8) it is provided that the degree of authority, control or administration to be exercised by the Mandatory, not having been previously agreed upon by the Members of the League, shall be explicitly defined by the Council of the League of Nations; Confirming the said mandate, defines its terms as follows:

Article 1. The Mandatory shall have full powers of legislation and of administration, save as they may be limited by the terms of this mandate.

Article 2. The Mandatory shall be responsible for placing the country under such political, administrative and economic conditions as will secure the establishment of the Jewish national home, as laid down in the preamble, and the development of self-governing institutions, and also for safeguarding the civil and religious rights of all the inhabitants of Palestine, irrespective of race and religion.

Article 3. The Mandatory shall, so far as circumstances permit, encourage local autonomy.

Article 4. An appropriate Jewish agency shall be recognized as a public body for the purpose of advising and co-operating with the Administration of Palestine in such economic, social and other matters as may affect the establishment of the Jewish national home and the interests of the Jewish population in Palestine, and, subject always to the control of the Administration, to assist and take part in the development of the country.

The Zionist organization, so long as its organization and constitution are in the opinion of the Mandatory appropriate, shall be recognized as such agency. It shall take steps in consultation with His Britannic Majesty's Government to secure the co-operation of all Jews who are willing to assist in the establishment of the Jewish national home.[1]

Article 5. The Mandatory shall be responsible for seeing that no Palestine territory shall be ceded or leased to, or in any way placed under the control of, the Government of any foreign Power.

---

[1] WZO represented only that minority of world Jewry which was Zionist. In order, therefore, to fulfil the requirements of this sentence, the Jewish Agency was established in 1929. It was constitutionally linked to WZO through a shared President, 50 per cent Zionist membership (theoretically) of its governing organs, and its function in effect as the Palestine Executive of WZO. Britain recognized it for the purposes of Article 4 in 1929–30.

Article 6. The Administration of Palestine, while ensuring that the rights and position of other sections of the population are not prejudiced, shall facilitate Jewish immigration under suitable conditions and shall encourage, in co-operation with the Jewish agency referred to in Article 4, close settlement by Jews on the land, including State lands and waste lands not required for public purposes.

Article 7. The Administration of Palestine shall be responsible for enacting a nationality law. There shall be included in this law provisions framed so as to facilitate the acquisition of Palestinian citizenship by Jews who take up their permanent residence in Palestine.

Article 8. The privileges and immunities of foreigners, including the benefits of consular jurisdiction and protection as formerly enjoyed by capitulation or usage in the Ottoman Empire, shall not be applicable in Palestine.

Unless the Powers whose nationals enjoyed the afore-mentioned privileges and immunities on 1 August 1914 shall have previously renounced the right to their re-establishment, or shall have agreed to their non-application for a specified period, these privileges and immunities shall, at the expiration of the mandate, be immediately re-established in their entirety or with such modifications as may have been agreed upon between the Powers concerned.

Article 9. The Mandatory shall be responsible for seeing that the judicial system established in Palestine shall assure to foreigners, as well as to natives, a complete guarantee of their rights.

Respect for the personal status of the various peoples and communities and for their religious interests shall be fully guaranteed. In particular, the control and administration of Wakfs shall be exercised in accordance with religious law and the dispositions of the founders.

Article 10. Pending the making of special extradition agreements relating to Palestine, the extradition treaties in force between the Mandatory and other foreign Powers shall apply to Palestine.

Article 11. The Administration of Palestine shall take all necessary measures to safeguard the interests of the community in connection with the development of the country, and, subject to any international obligations accepted by the Mandatory, shall have full power to provide for public ownership or control of any of the natural resources of the country or of the public works, services and utilities established or to be established therein. It shall introduce a land system appropriate to the needs of the country, having regard, among other things, to the desirability of promoting the close settlement and intensive cultivation of the land.

The Administration may arrange with the Jewish agency mentioned in Article 4 to construct or operate, upon fair and equitable terms, any public works, services and utilities, and to develop any of the natural resources of the country, in so far as these matters are not directly undertaken by the Administration. Any such arrangements shall provide that no profits distributed by such agency, directly or indirectly, shall exceed a reasonable rate of interest on the capital, and any further profits shall be utilized by it for the benefit of the country in a manner approved by the Administration. . . .

Article 24. The Mandatory shall make to the Council of the League of Nations an annual report to the satisfaction of the Council as to the measures taken during the year to carry out the provisions of the mandate. Copies of all laws and regulations promulgated or issued during the year shall be communicated with the report.

Article 25. In the territories lying between the Jordan and the eastern boundary of Palestine as ultimately determined, the Mandatory shall be entitled, with the consent of the Council of the League of Nations, to postpone or withold application of such provisions of this mandate as he may consider inapplicable to the existing local conditions, and to make such provision for the administration of the territories as he may consider suitable to those conditions, provided that no action shall be taken which is inconsistent with the provisions of Articles 15, 16 and 18.

Article 26. The Mandatory agrees that, if any dispute whatever should arise between the Mandatory and another Member of the League of Nations relating to the interpretation or the application of the provisions of the mandate, such dispute, if it cannot be settled by negotiation, shall be submitted to the Permanent Court of International Justice provided for by Article 14 of the Covenant of the League of Nations.

Article 27. The consent of the Council of the League of Nations is required for any modification of the terms of this mandate.

Article 28. In the event of the termination of the mandate hereby conferred upon the Mandatory, the Council of the League of Nations shall make such arrangements as may be deemed necessary for safeguarding in perpetuity, under guarantee of the League, the rights secured by Articles 13 and 14, and shall use its influence for securing, under the guarantee of the League, that the Government of Palestine will fully honour the financial obligations legitimately incurred by the Administration of Palestine during the period of the mandate, including the rights of public servants to pensions or gratuities.

PART V

'Partition means that neither will get all it wants'?

Throughout the Mandate both Arab Nationalists and Zionists maintained essentially unaltered their basic positions with regard to Palestine. Thus, the novel Partition proposal of the Palestine Royal Commission in 1937 (Document V (a) and Document I (e) were greeted with rebellion by the Arabs and misgiving by the Zionists. By the end of the Mandate nationalist objectives had been forcefully restated on both sides (e.g. Documents V (b) and (c)).

DOCUMENT V (a). EXCERPTS FROM THE PALESTINE ROYAL COMMISSION REPORT (THE 'PEEL REPORT'), JULY 1937.

. . . Manifestly the problem cannot be solved by giving either the Arabs or the Jews all they want. The answer to the question 'Which of them in the end will govern Palestine?' must surely be 'Neither'. We do not think that any fair-minded statesman would suppose, now that the hope of harmony between the races has proved untenable, that Britain ought either to hand over to Arab rule 400,000 Jews, whose entry into Palestine has been for the most part facilitated by the British Government and approved by the League of Nations; or that, if the Jews should become a majority, a million or so of Arabs should be handed over to their rule. But, while neither race can justly rule all Palestine, we see no reason why, if it were practicable, each race should not rule part of it. . . .

'Half a loaf is better than no bread' is a peculiarly English proverb; and, considering the attitude which both the Arab and the Jewish representatives adopted in giving evidence before us, we think it improbable that either party will be satisfied at first sight with the proposals we have submitted for the adjustment of their rival claims. For Partition means that neither will get all it wants. It means that the Arabs must acquiesce in the exclusion from their sovereignty of a piece of territory, long occupied and once ruled by them. It means that the Jews must be content with less than the Land of Israel they once ruled and have hoped to rule again. But it seems to us possible that on reflection both parties will come to realize that the drawbacks of Partition are outweighed by its advantages. For, if it offers neither party all it wants, it offers each what it wants most, namely freedom and security.

The advantages to the Arabs of Partition on the lines we have proposed may be summarized as follows:

1. They obtain their national independence and can co-operate on an equal footing with the Arabs of the neighbouring countries in the cause of Arab unity and progress.

2. They are finally delivered from the fear of being 'swamped' by the Jews and from the possibility of ultimate subjection to Jewish rule.

3. In particular, the final limitation of the Jewish National Home within a fixed frontier and the enactment of a new Mandate for the protection of the Holy Places, solemnly guaranteed by the League of Nations, removes all anxiety lest the Holy Places should ever come under Jewish control.

4. As a set-off to the loss of territory the Arabs regard as theirs the Arab State will receive a subvention from the Jewish State. It will also, in view of the backwardness of Trans-Jordan, obtain a grant of £2,000,000 from the British Treasury; and, if an arrangement can be made for the exchange of land and population, a further grant will be made for the conversion, as far as may prove possible, of uncultivable land in the Arab State into productive land from which the cultivators and the State alike will profit.

The advantages of Partition to the Jews may be summarized as follows:

1. Partition secures the establishment of the Jewish National Home and relieves it from the possibility of its being subjected in the future to Arab rule.

2. Partition enables the Jews in the fullest sense to call their National Home their own: for it converts it into a Jewish State.

Its citizens will be able to admit as many Jews into it as they themselves believe can be absorbed. They will attain the primary objective of Zionism—a Jewish nation, planted in Palestine, giving its nationals the same status in the world as other nations give theirs. They will cease at last to live a 'minority life'.

To both Arabs and Jews Partition offers a prospect—and we see no such prospect in any other policy—of obtaining the inestimable boon of peace. It is surely worth some sacrifice on both sides if the quarrel which the Mandate started could be ended with its termination. It is not a natural or old-standing feud. An able Arab exponent of the Arab case told us that the Arabs throughout their history have not only been free from anti-Jewish sentiment but have also shown that the spirit of compromise is deeply rooted in their life. And he went on to express his sympathy with the fate of the Jews in Europe. 'There is no decent-minded person,' he said, 'who would not want to do everything humanly possible to relieve the distress of those persons,' provided that it was 'not at the cost of inflicting a corresponding distress on another people.' Considering what the possibility of finding a refuge in Palestine means to many thousands of suffering Jews, we cannot believe that the 'distress' occasioned by Partition, great as it would be, is more than Arab generosity can bear. And in this, as in so much else connected with Palestine, it is not only the peoples of that country that have to be considered. The Jewish Problem is not the least of the many problems which are disturbing international relations at this critical time and obstructing the path to peace and prosperity. If the Arabs at some sacrifice could help to solve that problem, they would earn the gratitude not of the Jews alone but of all the Western world.

DOCUMENT V (b). THE BILTMORE PROGRAMME, 11 MAY 1942.

1. American Zionists assembled in this Extraordinary Conference reaffirm their unequivocal devotion to the cause of democratic freedom and international justice to which the people of the United States, allied with the other United Nations, have dedicated themselves, and give expression to their faith in the ultimate victory of humanity and justice over lawlessness and brute force.

2. This Conference offers a message of hope and encouragement to their fellow Jews in the Ghettos and concentration camps of Hitler-dominated Europe and prays that their hour of liberation, may not be far distant.

3. The Conference sends it warmest greetings to the Jewish Agency [*supra* p. 68] Executive in Jerusalem, to the Va'ad Leumi [lit. = National Council, i.e. the elected supreme organ of the Jewish community in Palestine during the Mandate. *Eds.*] and to the whole Yishuv [*supra* p. 2] in Palestine, and expresses its profound admiration for their steadfastness and achievements in the face of peril and great difficulties. The Jewish men and women in field and factory, and the thousands of Jewish soldiers of Palestine in the Near East who have acquitted themselves with honour and distinction in Greece, Ethiopia, Syria, Libya and on other battlefields, have shown themselves worthy of their people and ready to assume the rights and responsibilities of nationhood.

4. In our generation, and in particular in the course of the past twenty years, the Jewish people have awakened and transformed their ancient homeland; from 50,000 at the end of the last war their numbers have increased to more than 500,000. They have made the waste places to bear fruit and the desert to blossom. Their pioneering achievements in agriculture and in industry, embodying new patterns of co-operative endeavour, have written a notable page in the history of colonization.

5. In the new values thus created, their Arab neighbours in Palestine have shared. The Jewish people in its own work of national redemption welcomes the economic, agricultural and national development of the Arab peoples and states. The Conference reaffirms the stand previously adopted at Congresses of the World Zionist Organization, expressing the readiness and the desire of the Jewish people for full co-operation with their Arab neighbours.

6. The Conference calls for the fulfilment of the original purpose of the Balfour Declaration and the Mandate which 'recognizing the historical connection of the Jewish people with Palestine' was to afford them the opportunity, as stated by President Wilson, to found there a Jewish Commonwealth.

The Conference affirms its unalterable rejection of the White Paper of May 1939 and denies its moral or legal validity. The

White Paper seeks to limit, and in fact to nullify Jewish rights to immigration and settlement in Palestine, and, as stated by Mr Winston Churchill in the House of Commons in May 1939, constitutes 'a breach and repudiation of the Balfour Declaration'. The policy of the White Paper is cruel and indefensible in its denial of sanctuary to Jews fleeing from Nazi persecution; and at a time when Palestine has become a focal point in the war front of the United Nations, and Palestine Jewry must provide all available manpower for farm and factory and camp, it is in direct conflict with the interests of the allied war effort.

7. In the struggle against the forces of aggression and tyranny, of which Jews were the earliest victims, and which now menace the Jewish National Home, recognition must be given to the right of the Jews of Palestine to play their full part in the war effort and in the defence of their country, through a Jewish military force fighting under its own flag and under the high command of the United Nations.

8. The Conference declares that the new world order that will follow victory cannot be established on foundations of peace, justice and equality, unless the problem of Jewish homelessness is finally solved.

The Conference urges that the gates of Palestine be opened; that the Jewish Agency be vested with control of immigration into Palestine and with the necessary authority for upbuilding the country, including the development of its unoccupied and uncultivated lands; and that Palestine be established as a Jewish Commonwealth integrated in the structure of the new democratic world.

Then and only then will the age-old wrong to the Jewish people be righted.

DOCUMENT V (c). PRINCIPLES SUBMITTED TO THE UN *ad hoc* COMMITTEE[1] BY THE HIGHER ARAB COMMITTEE[2] AS THE BASIS FOR THE FUTURE CONSTITUTIONAL ORGANIZATION OF PALESTINE, 30 SEPTEMBER 1947.

[1] In September, 1947, the UN General Assembly created an *ad hoc* Committee of all member nations to deal with the UNSCOP Report (*supra* p. 12 and *infra* p. 78). It approved partition by 25 votes to 13, 17 abstentions and 2 absentees.
[2] Formed in 1936, the Committee consisted of representatives of most of the Arab political groups in Palestine, and is thought to have organized, directly or indirectly, all subsequent Palestinian Arab opposition to the Mandate until 1948.

1. That an Arab State in the whole of Palestine be established on democratic lines.

2. That the Arab State of Palestine would respect human rights, fundamental freedoms and equality of all persons before the law.

3. That the Arab State of Palestine would protect the legitimate rights and interests of all minorities.

4. That freedom of worship and access to the Holy Places would be guaranteed to all.

[In addition], the following steps would have to be taken to give effect to the above-mentioned four principles:

(1) A Constituent Assembly should be elected at the earliest possible time. All genuine and law-abiding nationals of Palestine would be entitled to participate in the elections of the Constituent Assembly.

(2) The Constituent Assembly should, within a fixed time, formulate and enact a Constitution for the Arab State of Palestine, which should be of a democratic nature and should embody the above-mentioned four principles.

(3) A government should be formed within a fixed time, in accordance with the terms of the Constitution, to take over the administration of Palestine from the Mandatory Power.

Such a programme was the only one which the Arabs of Palestine were prepared to adopt, and the only item on the Committee's agenda with which the Arab Higher Committee would associate itself was Item 3. . . .[1]

The representative of the Arab Higher Committee said he had not commented upon the UNSCOP Report because the Arab Higher Committee considered that it could not be used as a basis for discussion. Both the majority and the minority plans contained in the Report were inconsistent with the United Nations Charter and the Covenant of the League of Nations. The Arabs of Palestine were solidly determined to oppose with all the means at their disposal any scheme which provided for the dissection, segregation or partition of their country or which gave to a minority special and preferential rights and status.

[1] The Saudi and Iraqi proposal that the termination of the Mandate over Palestine and the recognition of its independence as one state be placed on the agenda of the General Assembly.

PART VI

The UN and the Emergence of the State of Israel

The UN General Assembly Resolution of 29 November 1947 (Document VI (a)) is the document to which above all others Israel has referred as the basis of her constitutional legitimacy; her spiritual (or cultural) legitimacy has rested on other grounds. Both are set out succinctly in Document VI (b) and refuted in Document VI (c). The Arabs have explicitly or implicitly maintained this refutation ever since, as we shall see.

DOCUMENT VI (a). EXCERPTS FROM UN GENERAL ASSEMBLY RESOLUTION ON THE FUTURE GOVERNMENT OF PALESTINE, 29 NOVEMBER 1947. (The voting was 33 to 13, 10 abstentions and 1 absentee).

The General Assembly,
    Having met in special session at the request of the mandatory Power to constitute and instruct a special committee to prepare for the consideration of the question of the future government of Palestine at the second regular session;
    Having constituted a Special Committee and instructed it to investigate all questions and issues relevant to the problem of Palestine, and to prepare proposals for the solution of the problem, and
    Having received and examined the report of the Special Committee [In August 1947 the eleven-man UNSCOP unanimously recommended the termination of the Mandate; seven members recommended partition; three recommended a Federal State; one abstained. *Eds.*] including a number of unanimous recommendations and a plan of partition with economic union approved by the majority of the Special Committee,

Considers that the present situation in Palestine is one which is likely to impair the general welfare and friendly relations among nations;

Takes note of the declaration by the mandatory Power that it plans to complete its evacuation of Palestine by 1 August 1948;

Recommends to the United Kingdom, as the mandatory Power for Palestine, and to all other Members of the United Nations the adoption and implementation, with regard to the future government of Palestine, of the Plan of Partition with Economic Union set out below;

Requests that

1. The Security Council take the necessary measures as provided for in the plan for its implementation;

2. The Security Council consider, if circumstances during the transitional period require such consideration, whether the situation in Palestine constitutes a threat to the peace. If it decides that such a threat exists, and in order to maintain international peace and security, the Security Council should supplement the authorization of the General Assembly by taking measures, under Articles 39 and 41 of the Charter to empower the United Nations Commission, as provided in this resolution, to exercise in Palestine the functions which are assigned to it by this resolution;

3. The Security Council determine as a threat to the peace, breach of the peace or act of aggression, in accordance with Article 39 of the Charter, any attempt to alter by force the settlement envisaged by this resolution;

4. The Trusteeship Council be informed of the responsibilities envisaged for it in this plan;

Calls upon the inhabitants of Palestine to take such steps as may be necessary on their part to put this plan into effect;

Appeals to all Governments and all peoples to refrain from taking any action which might hamper or delay the carrying out of these recommendations, . . .

Plan of Partition with Economic Union
Part I.—Future Constitution and Government of Palestine

A. Termination of Mandate, Partition and Independence

1. The Mandate for Palestine shall terminate as soon

79

as possible but in any case not later than 1 August 1948.

2. The armed forces of the mandatory Power shall be progressively withdrawn from Palestine, the withdrawal to be completed as soon as possible but in any case not later than 1 August 1948.

The mandatory Power shall advise the Commission, as far in advance as possible, of its intention to terminate the Mandate and to evacuate each area.

The mandatory Power shall use its best endeavours to ensure that an area situated in the territory of the Jewish State, including a seaport and hinterland adequate to provide facilities for a substantial immigration, shall be evacuated at the earliest possible date and in any event not later than 1 February 1948.

3. Independent Arab and Jewish States and the Special International Regime for the City of Jerusalem, set forth in part III of this plan, shall come into existence in Palestine two months after the evacuation of the armed forces of the mandatory Power has been completed but in any case not later than 1 October 1948. The boundaries of the Arab State, the Jewish State, and the City of Jerusalem shall be described in parts II and III below.

4. The period between the adoption by the General Assembly of its recommendation on the question of Palestine and the establishment of the independence of the Arab and Jewish States shall be a transitional period.

B. Steps preparatory to independence

1. A Commission shall be set up consisting of one representative of each of five Member States. The Members represented on the Commission shall be elected by the General Assembly on as broad a basis, geographically and otherwise, as possible.

2. The administration of Palestine shall, as the mandatory Power withdraws its armed forces, be progressively turned over to the Commission, which shall act in conformity with the recommendations of the General Assembly, under the guidance of the Security Council. The mandatory Power shall to the fullest possible extent co-ordinate its plans for withdrawal

with the plans of the Commission to take over and administer areas which have been evacuated.

In the discharge of this administrative responsibility the Commission shall have authority to issue necessary regulations and take other measures as required.

The mandatory Power shall not take any action to prevent, obstruct or delay the implementation by the Commission of the measures recommended by the General Assembly.

3. On its arrival in Palestine the Commission shall proceed to carry out measures for the establishment of the frontiers of the Arab and Jewish States and the City of Jerusalem in accordance with the general lines of the recommendations of the General Assembly on the partition of Palestine. Nevertheless, the boundaries as described in part II of this plan are to be modified in such a way that village areas as a rule will not be divided by state boundaries unless pressing reasons make that necessary.

4. The Commission, after consultation with the democratic parties and other public organizations of the Arab and Jewish States, shall select and establish in each State as rapidly as possible a Provisional Council of Government. The activities of both the Arab and Jewish Provisional Councils of Government shall be carried out under the general direction of the Commission.

If by 1 April, 1948 a Provisional Council of Government cannot be selected for either of the States, or, if selected, cannot carry out its functions, the Commission shall communicate that fact to the Security Council for such action with respect to that State as the Security Council may deem proper, and to the Secretary-General for communication to the Members of the United Nations.

5. Subject to the provisions of these recommendations, during the transitional period the Provisional Councils of Government, acting under the Commission, shall have full authority in the areas under their control, including authority over matters of immigration and land regulation.

6. The Provisional Council of Government of each State, acting under the Commission, shall progressively receive from the Commission full responsibility for the administration of that State in the period between the termination of the Mandate and the establishment of the State's independence.

7. The Commission shall instruct the Provisional Councils of Government of both the Arab and Jewish States, after their formation, to proceed to the establishment of administrative organs of government, central and local.

DOCUMENT VI (b). PROCLAMATION OF THE INDEPENDENCE OF ISRAEL, 14 MAY 1948.

The Land of Israel was the birthplace of the Jewish people. Here their spiritual, religious and national identity was formed. Here they achieved independence and created a culture of national and universal significance. Here they wrote and gave the Bible to the world.

Exiled from the Land of Israel, the Jewish people remained faithful to it in all the countries of their dispersion, never ceasing to pray and hope for their return and the restoration of their national freedom.

Impelled by this historic association, Jews strove throughout the centuries to go back to the land of their fathers and regain their statehood. In recent decades they returned in their masses. They reclaimed the wilderness, revived their language, built cities and villages, and established a vigorous and ever-growing community, with its own economic and cultural life. They sought peace yet were prepared to defend themselves. They brought the blessings of progress to all inhabitants of the country and looked forward to sovereign independence.

In the year 1897 the First Zionist Congress, inspired by Theodor Herzl's vision of the Jewish State, proclaimed the right of the Jewish people to national revival in their own country.

This right was acknowledged by the Balfour Declaration of 2 November 1917, and re-affirmed by the Mandate of the League of Nations which gave explicit international recognition to the historic connection of the Jewish people with Palestine and their right to reconstitute their National Home.

The recent holocaust, which engulfed millions of Jews in Europe, proved anew the need to solve the problem of the homelessness and lack of independence of the Jewish people by means of the re-establishment of the Jewish State, which would open the gates to all Jews and endow the Jewish people with equality of status among the family of nations.

The survivors of the disastrous slaughter in Europe, and also

Jews from other lands, have not desisted from their efforts to reach Erets-Israel, in face of difficulties, obstacles and perils; and have not ceased to urge their right to a life of dignity, freedom and honest toil in their ancestral land.

In the Second World War the Jewish people in Palestine made their full contribution to the struggle of the freedom-loving nations against the Nazi evil. The sacrifices of their soldiers and their war efforts gained them the right to rank with the nations which founded the United Nations.

On 29 November 1947 the General Assembly of the United Nations adopted a Resolution requiring the establishment of a Jewish State in Palestine. The General Assembly called upon the inhabitants of the country to take all the necessary steps on their part to put the plan into effect. This recognition by the United Nations of the right of the Jewish people to establish their independent State is unassailable.

It is the natural right of the Jewish people to lead, as do all other nations, an independent existence in its sovereign State.

ACCORDINGLY WE, the members of the National Council, representing the Jewish people in Palestine, and the World Zionist Movement, are met together in solemn assembly today, the day of termination of the British Mandate for Palestine; and by virtue of the natural and historic right of the Jewish people and of the Resolution of the General Assembly of the United Nations.

WE HEREBY PROCLAIM the establishment of the Jewish State in Palestine, to be called 'Medinat Israel' (State of Israel).

WE HEREBY DECLARE that, as from the termination of the Mandate at midnight, 14—15 May 1948, and pending the setting up of the duly elected bodies of the State in accordance with a Constitution, to be drawn up by the Constituent Assembly not later than 1 October 1948, the National Council shall act as the Provisional State Council, and that the National Administration shall constitute the Provisional Government of the Jewish State, which shall be known as Israel.

THE STATE OF ISRAEL will be open to the immigration of Jews from all countries of their dispersion; will promote the development of the country for the benefit of all its inhabitants; will be based on the principles of liberty, justice and peace as conceived by the Prophets of Israel; will uphold the full social and political equality of all its citizens, without distinction of religion, conscience, education and culture; will safeguard the Holy Places of all religions; and will loyally uphold the principles of the United Nations Charter.

THE STATE OF ISRAEL will be ready to co-operate with the organs and representatives of the United Nations in the implementation of the Resolution of the Assembly of 29 November 1947, and will take steps to bring about the Economic Union over the whole of Palestine.

We appeal to the United Nations to assist the Jewish people in the building of its State and to admit Israel into the family of nations.

In the midst of wanton aggression, we yet call upon the Arab inhabitants of the State of Israel to preserve the ways of peace and play their part in the development of the State, on the basis of full and equal citizenship and due representation in all its bodies and institutions—provisional and permanent.

We extend our hand in peace and neighbourliness to all the neighbouring states and their peoples, and invite them to co-operate with the independent Jewish nation for the common good of all. The State of Israel is prepared to make its contribution to the progress of the Middle East as a whole.

Our call goes out to the Jewish people all over the world to rally to our side in the task of immigration and development and to stand by us in the great struggle for the fulfilment of the dream of generations for the redemption of Israel.

With trust in Almighty God, we set our hand to this Declaration, at this Session of the Provisional State Council, on the soil of the Homeland, in the city of Tel-Aviv, on this Sabbath eve, the fifth of Iyar 5708, the fourteenth day of May 1948.

DOCUMENT VI (c). STATEMENT ISSUED BY THE GOVERNMENTS OF THE ARAB LEAGUE STATES ON THE OCCASION OF THE ENTRY OF THE ARAB ARMIES INTO PALESTINE, 15 MAY 1948.

1. Palestine was part of the former Ottoman Empire subject to its law and represented in its parliament. The overwhelming majority of the population of Palestine were Arabs. There was in it a small minority of Jews that enjoyed the same rights and bore the same responsibilities as the [other] inhabitants, and

did not suffer any ill-treatment on account of its religious beliefs. The holy places were inviolable and the freedom of access to them was guaranteed.

2. The Arabs have always asked for their freedom and independence. On the outbreak of the First World War, and when the Allies declared that they were fighting for the liberation of peoples, the Arabs joined them and fought on their side with a view to realizing their national aspirations and obtaining their independence. England pledged herself to recognize the independence of the Arab countries in Asia, including Palestine. The Arabs played a remarkable part in the achievement of final victory and the Allies have admitted this.

3. In 1917 England issued a declaration in which she expressed her sympathy with the establishment of a National Home for the Jews in Palestine. When the Arabs knew of this they protested against it, but England reassured them by affirming to them that this would not prejudice the right of their countries to freedom and independence or affect the political status of the Arabs in Palestine. Notwithstanding the legally void character of this declaration, it was interpreted by England to aim at no more than the establishment of a spiritual centre for the Jews in Palestine, and to conceal no ulterior political aims, such as the establishment of a Jewish State. The same thing was declared by the Jewish leaders.

4. When the war came to an end England did not keep her promise. Indeed, the Allies placed Palestine under the Mandate system and entrusted England with [the task of carrying it out], in accordance with a document providing for the administration of the country, in the interests of its inhabitants and its preparation for the independence which the Covenant of the League of Nations recognized that Palestine was qualified to have.

5. England administered Palestine in a manner which enabled the Jews to flood it with immigrants and helped them to settle in the country. [This was so] notwithstanding the fact that it was proved that the density of the population in Palestine had exceeded the economic capacity of the country to absorb additional immigrants. England did not pay regard to the interests or rights of the Arab inhabitants, the lawful owners of the country. Although they used to express, by

various means, their concern and indignation on account of this state of affairs which was harmful to their being and their future, they [invariably] were met by indifference, imprisonment and oppression.

6. As Palestine is an Arab country, situated in the heart of the Arab countries and attached to the Arab world by various ties—spiritual, historical, and strategic—the Arab countries, and even the Eastern ones, governments as well as peoples, have concerned themselves with the problem of Palestine and have raised it to the international level; [they have also raised the problem] with England, asking for its solution in accordance with the pledges made and with democratic principles. The Round Table Conference was held in London in 1939 in order to discuss the Palestine question and to arrive at the just solution thereof. The Governments of the Arab States participated in [this conference] and asked for the preservation of the Arab character of Palestine and the proclamation of its independence. This conference ended with the issue of a White Paper in which England defined her policy towards Palestine, recognized its independence, and undertook to set up the institutions that would lead to its exercise of the characteristics of [this independence]. She [also] declared that her obligations concerning the establishment of a Jewish national home had been fulfilled, since that home had actually been established. But the policy defined in that [White] Paper was noᵗ carried out. This, therefore, led to the deterioration of the situation and the aggravation of matters contrary to the interests of the Arabs.

7. While the Second World War was still in progress, the Governments of the Arab States began to hold consultations regarding the reinforcement of their co-operation and the increasing of the means of their collaboration and their solidarity, with a view to safeguarding their present and their future and to participating in the erection of the edifice of the new world on firm foundations. Palestine had its [worthy] share of consideration and attention in these conversations. These conversations led to the establishment of the League of Arab States as an instrument for the co-operation for the Arab States for their security, peace and well-being.

The Pact of the League of Arab States declared that Palestine has been an independent country since its separation from the

Ottoman Empire, but the manifestations of this independence have been suppressed due to reasons which were out of the control of its inhabitants. The establishment of the United Nations shortly afterwards was an event about which the Arabs had the greatest hopes. Their belief in the ideals on which that organization was based made them participate in its establishment and membership.

8 Since then the Arab League and its [member] Governments have not spared any effort to pursue any course, whether with the Mandatory Power or with the United Nations, in order to bring about a just solution of the Palestine problem; [a solution] based upon true democratic principles and compatible with the provisions of the Covenant of the League of Nations and the [Charter] of the United Nations, and which would [at the same time] be lasting, guarantee peace and security in the country and prepare it for progress and prosperity. But Zionist claims were always an obstacle to finding such a solution, [as the Zionists], having prepared themselves with armed forces, strongholds and fortifications to face by force anyone standing in their way, publicly declared [their intention] to establish a Jewish state.

9. When the General Assembly of the United Nations issued, on 29 November 1947, its recommendation concerning the solution of the Palestine problem, on the basis of the establishment of an Arab state and of another Jewish [state] in [Palestine] together with placing the City of Jerusalem under the trusteeship of the United Nations, the Arab States drew attention to the injustice implied in this solution [affecting] the right of the people of Palestine to immediate independence, as well as democratic principles and the provisions of the Covenant of the League of Nations and [the Charter] of the United Nations. [These States also] declared the Arabs' rejection of [that solution] and that it would not be possible to carry it out by peaceful means, and that its forcible imposition would constitute a threat to peace and security in this area.

The warnings and expectations of the Arab States have, indeed, proved to be true, as disturbances were soon widespread throughout Palestine. The Arabs clashed with the Jews, and the two [parties] proceeded to fight each other and shed each other's blood. Whereupon the United Nations began to realize the danger of recommending the partition [of Palestine] and is still looking for a way out of this state of affairs.

10. Now that the British mandate over Palestine has come to an end, without there being a legitimate constitutional authority in the country, which would safeguard the maintenance of security and respect for Law and which would protect the lives and properties of the inhabitants, the Governments of the Arab States declare the following:

First: That the rule of Palestine should revert to its inhabitants, in accordance with the provisions of the Covenant of the League of Nations and [the Charter] of the United Nations and that [the Palestinians] should alone have the right to determine their future.

Second: Security and order in Palestine have become disrupted. The Zionist aggression resulted in the exodus of more than a quarter of a million of its Arab inhabitants from their homes and in their taking refuge in the neighbouring Arab countries.

The events which have taken place in Palestine have unmasked the aggressive intentions and the imperialistic designs of the Zionists, including the atrocities committed by them against the peace-loving Arab inhabitants, especially in Dayr Yasin, Tiberias and others. Nor have they respected the inviolability of consuls, as they have attacked the consulates of the Arab States in Jerusalem. After the termination of the British mandate over Palestine the British authorities are no longer responsible for security in the country, except to the degree affecting their withdrawing forces, and [only] in the areas in which these forces happen to be at the time of withdrawal as announced by [these authorities]. This state of affairs would render Palestine without any governmental machinery capable of restoring order and the rule of law to the country, and of protecting the lives and properties of the inhabitants.

Third: This state of affairs is threatening to spread to the neighbouring Arab countries, where feeling is running high because of the events in Palestine. The Governments of the Member States of the Arab League and of the United Nations are exceedingly worried and deeply concerned about this state of affairs.

Fourth: These Governments had hoped that the United Nations would have succeeded in finding a peaceful and just solution of the problem of Palestine, in accordance with democratic principles and the provisions of the Covenant of the League of Nations and [the Charter] of the United Nations, so that peace, security and prosperity would prevail in this part of the world.

Fifth: The Governments of the Arab States, as members of the Arab League, a regional organization within the meaning of the provisions of Chapter VIII of the Charter of the United Nations, are responsible for maintaining peace and security in their area. These Governments view the events taking place in Palestine as a threat to peace and security in the area as a whole and [also] in each of them taken separately.

Sixth: Therefore, as security in Palestine is a sacred trust in the hands of the Arab States, and in order to put an end to this state of affairs and to prevent it from becoming aggravated or from turning into [a state of] chaos, the extent of which no one can foretell; in order to stop the spreading of disturbances and disorder in Palestine to the neighbouring Arab countries; in order to fill the gap brought about in the governmental machinery in Palestine as a result of the termination of the mandate and the non-establishment of a lawful successor authority, the Governments of the Arab States have found themselves compelled to intervene in Palestine solely in order to help its inhabitants restore peace and security and the rule of justice and law to their country, and in order to prevent bloodshed.

Seventh: The Governments of the Arab States recognize that the independence of Palestine, which has so far been suppressed by the British Mandate, has become an accomplished fact for the lawful inhabitants of Palestine. They alone, by virtue of their absolute sovereignty, have the right to provide their country with laws and governmental institutions. They alone should exercise the attributes of their independence, through their own means and without any kind of foreign interference, immediately after peace, security, and the rule of law have been restored to the country.

At that time the intervention of the Arab states will cease, and the independent State of Palestine will co-operate with the [other member] States of the Arab League in order to bring peace, security and prosperity to this part of the world.

The Governments of the Arab States emphasize, on this occasion, what they have already declared before the London Conference and the United Nations, that the only just solution of the Palestine problem is the establishment of a unitary Palestinian State, in accordance with democratic principles, whereby its inhabitants will enjoy complete equality before the law, [and whereby] minorities will be assured of all the guarantees recognized in democratic constitutional countries, and [whereby] the holy places will be preserved and the right of access thereto guaranteed.

Eighth: The Arab States most emphatically declare that [their] intervention in Palestine was due only to these considerations and objectives, and that they aim at nothing more than to put an end to the prevailing conditions in [Palestine]. For this reason, they have great confidence that their action will have the support of the United Nations; [that it will be] considered as an action aiming at the realization of its aims and at promoting its principles, as provided for in its Charter.

PART VII

An Early UN Attempt at Peace:
The Conciliation Commission for Palestine

The period immediately following the Arab-Israeli Armistice Agreements in 1949 was undoubtedly the most propitious time that has ever existed for a settlement of the Arab-Israeli dispute.

On 11 December 1948 the UN General Assembly set up a Conciliation Commission for Palestine. Its principal functions were to assist the governments and authorities to achieve a final settlement of all outstanding questions; to ensure the protection of the Holy Places with guarantees of full access thereto; to secure the demilitarization and the internationalization of Jerusalem; to seek arrangements for free access to Haifa Port and to Lydda Airport; and to facilitate the rehabilitation and repatriation of refugees. Whilst realizing that peace would not be easily or quickly achieved, the Commission 'found the Governments of the Arab States and the Government of Israel to be in an attitude of mind definitely favourable to peace'. Why then was a peaceful settlement not achieved?

The principal issues at stake were two, though they were closely interconnected. First, there was the problem of what to do about the large numbers of Arab refugees (some 750,000) from Israeli-held territory. Second, there was the boundary question. What were to be the proper boundaries between Israel and her Arab neighbours? The Arabs generally stressed the importance of settling the refugee problem first; the Israelis would settle it only within the framework of a general peace settlement—after twenty years still the main aim of Israeli policy. The Arab States based their approach on the UN General Assembly's Resolution of 11 December 1948, which stated 'that refugees wishing to return to their homes and live in peace with their neighbours should be permitted to do so at the earliest practicable moment and that compensation should be paid for the property of those choosing not to return and for loss of, or damage to, property'. Israel stressed another section of the General Assembly's December Resolution which stated that refugees who returned 'should live in peace with their neighbours'. In the Israeli view this made return of refugees contingent on the establishment of peace between Israel and the Arab States.

Rightly, the Commission stressed the inter-connection of the refugee and the territorial question. A victory for this approach was won early in the Commission's work when, in May 1949, both sides signed a protocol that gave reason for some hope. The text is given below in Document VII (a). The document referred to in the text was a map on which were indicated the boundaries defined in the 1947 UN Partition Plan. The Arabs have maintained that by signing the Protocol Israel gave some sort of recognition to the 1947 Partition Plan boundaries. The Israeli view is that the annexed map was to be taken, as the text says, as *a*, not *the* basis for discussion.

DOCUMENT VII (a). THE LAUSANNE PROTOCOL, SIGNED BY ISRAELI AND ARAB DELEGATES TO LAUSANNE CONFERENCE, 12 MAY 1949.

The United Nations Conciliation Commission for Palestine, anxious to achieve as quickly as possible the objectives of the General Assembly resolution of 11 December 1948 regarding refugees, the respect for their rights and the preservation of their property as well as territorial and other questions, has proposed to the delegations of the Arab states and to the delegation of Israel that the working document attached hereto be taken as a basis for discussions with the Commission.

The interested delegations have accepted this proposal with the understanding that the exchanges of views which will be carried on by the Commission with the two parties will bear upon the territorial adjustments necessary to the above-indicated objectives.

*

The first attempt at a solution of the refugee problem was an Israeli proposal to take over from Egypt the Gaza Strip with its 250,000 Arab residents and refugees. With the Arabs already in Israel this would have raised the Arab population of Israel to one-third of the total. The Arab States rejected this solution. They wanted the immediate return of refugees to Israeli-held territory that was allotted to Arabs under the UN Partition Plan. The intention was that these areas would be Arab territory.

This intention was obviously not one to be recognized by Israel, despite her signing of the Lausanne Protocol. Israel's territorial claims were for boundaries much wider than those of the Partition Plan and incorporated territories won during the 1948 war. The proposals were denounced by the Arabs as 'a flagrant violation of the terms of the Protocol of 12 May 1949'.

With the United States now exerting considerable pressure on Israel a final attempt at a settlement was made. Both sides now agreed *mirabile dictu* to discuss the refugee question first as part of a settlement, though the Arab States still refused direct negotiation with Israel. The story is told in Document VII (b) below, an excerpt from the Conciliation Commission's Report. In this document the crux of the Arab-Israeli problem, as it was in 1949, can be seen. The Arab states could consider the Israeli offer to repatriate 100,000 refugees if they were to go to Israeli territory as allocated in the UN Partition Plan. The Israeli gains of territory by war they did not in effect regard as at the disposition of Israel. If Israel had been prepared substantially to accept the Partition Plan boundaries after the 1948 war, there would no doubt have been a settlement. Naturally enough, after a successful defensive war Israel was not prepared to do so. She needed security and she needed land to develop. Israeli accounts largely blame the Conciliation Commission and the American Government for denouncing the Israeli offer before the Arab states had a real opportunity to consider it. According to Berger, who has studied the press of the period, 'the Arabs were inclined with some misgivings to accept it, the Israeli proposal, as a basis for discussion'. If this is correct—and some more research might usefully be done on this point—then the prospect for peace was greater than the documentary evidence suggests. Yet the fact remains that the Arab States did reject the Israeli proposals, taking a stand that has hardened with time into one of the basic elements of the Arab-Israeli conflict.

DOCUMENT VII (b). EXCERPT FROM THE FOURTH PROGRESS REPORT OF THE UN CONCILIATION COMMISSION FOR PALESTINE, 22 SEPTEMBER 1949.

The Refugee Question

1. Repatriation, resettlement and rehabilitation

7. The delegation of Israel stated on 28 July that, in response to the views of the Commission and in order to facilitate the task of conciliation, the Government of Israel agreed on the following points: the problem of refugees should be placed as the first item on the agenda of joint discussions of a general peace settlement; on the initiation of such discussions, the Israel delegation would be prepared to convey to the Commission and to the Arab delegations the total figure of refugees which the Government of Israel would be ready to repatriate; in the view of the Government of Israel, such repatriation must form part of a comprehensive plan for the settlement of the entire refugee problem; and this repatriation would be put into effect only as an integral part of a general and final peace settlement. The Israel delegation also expressed the wish that these negotiations should be carried out directly with the Arab delegations.

8. On 2 August, the Arab delegations stated to the Commission that, understanding that the Israel delegation would advance concrete proposals within the framework of a final solution of the refugee problem and that these proposals would be considered as a first step towards stabilization of the situation in Palestine, and considering such a course to be in the spirit of General Assembly resolution 194 (III) and the Protocol of 12 May 1949, they agreed to discuss the Israel proposals. They stated that this acceptance in no way prejudged acceptance of any particular plan.

9. Following the reply by the Arab delegations, the delegation of Israel submitted its proposals to the Commission at a meeting on 3 August. After a few general remarks, the Israel representative stated that his Government was prepared to

make its contribution to the solution of the refugee problem. This contribution would be limited by considerations affecting the security and the economy of the State. Thus, the refugees would be settled in areas where they would not come in contact with possible enemies of Israel; moreover, the Government of Israel reserved the right to resettle the repatriated refugees in specific places, in order to ensure that their reinstallation would fit into the general plan of the economic development of Israel. Subject to these conditions, the Government of Israel would be prepared to accept the return to Israel in its present limits of 100,000 refugees, in addition to the total Arab population existing at the end of hostilities (including those who have already returned since then), thus increasing the total number of that population to a maximum of 250,000. This repatriation would form part of a general plan for resettlement of refugees which would be established by a special organ to be created for the purpose by the United Nations.

10. The Commission, considering the Israel delegation's proposal as unsatisfactory, limited itself to communicating that proposal unofficially to the Arab delegations for their information. On 15 August, the Arab delegations transmitted to the Commission, also unofficially, a memorandum containing their observations on the proposals submitted to the Commission by the Israel delegation on 3 August. In the opinion of the Arab delegations, the Israel proposal was contrary to resolution 194 (III), as well as to the Protocol of 12 May 1949. They considered that under the terms of the Protocol the Israel proposal could bear only upon the territories allocated to Israel according to the map attached to that document. The Arab delegations protested the contention of the Israel delegation that the settlement of Arabs in Israel territory must be subordinated to economic and strategic considerations. They recalled, moreover, the memorandum addressed by them to the Commission on 23 May, requesting the repatriation of all refugees originating in territory allocated to the Arabs or to be internationalized, according to the map attached to the Protocol of 12 May 1949. If the Israel proposal were to be interpreted as applying exclusively to refugees originating in areas allocated to Israel on the above-mentioned map, the Arab delegations would not object to its adoption as a basis for discussion of the

disposition of those particular refugees. Finally, the Arab delegations favoured compensation in kind for the refugees who might not return to their homes; this indemnification might take the form of territorial compensation within the terms of the Protocol of 12 May. The text of the Protocol was attached as an annex to the third progress report of the Commission (A/927).

PART VIII

The Basis of Relations:
The Armistice Regime

With the failure of the Conciliation Commission's work the Arab States and Israel had to regulate their relations in accord with the 1949 Armistice Agreements. No other basis existed, or has existed ever since.

Excerpts are given below from the Israeli-Egyptian Armistice Agreement that deal with the relations between the two states. Israeli armistice agreements with the other Arab States were similar. Of the Arab States at war with Israel only Iraq did not sign an armistice agreement.

DOCUMENT VIII (a). EXCERPTS FROM EGYPTIAN-ISRAELI ARMISTICE AGREEMENT, 24 FEBRUARY 1949.

Preamble

The Parties to the present Agreement, responding to the Security Council resolution of 16 November 1948 calling upon them, as a further provisional measure under Article 40 of the Charter of the United Nations and in order to facilitate the transition from the present truce to permanent peace in Palestine, to negotiate an Armistice; having decided to enter into negotiations under United Nations Chairmanship concerning the implementation of the Security Council resolutions of 4 and 16 November 1948; and having appointed representatives empowered to negotiate and conclude an Armistice Agreement;

The undersigned representatives, in the full authority

entrusted to them by their respective Governments, have agreed upon the following provisions:

ARTICLE I. With a view to promoting the return to permanent peace in Palestine and in recognition of the importance in this regard of mutual assurances concerning the future military operations of the Parties, the following principles, which shall be fully observed by both Parties during the Armistice, are hereby affirmed:

1. The injunction of the Security Council against resort to military force in the settlement of the Palestine question shall henceforth be scrupulously respected by both Parties.

2. No aggressive action by the armed forces—land, sea, or air—of either Party shall be undertaken, planned, or threatened against the people or the armed forces of the other; it being understood that the use of the term 'planned' in this context has no bearing on normal staff planning as generally practiced in military organizations.

3. The right of each Party to its security and freedom from fear of attack by the armed forces of the other shall be fully respected.

4. The establishment of an armistice between the armed forces of the two Parties is accepted as an indispensable step toward the liquidation of armed conflict and the restoration of peace in Palestine.

ARTICLE II. 1. In pursuance of the foregoing principles and of the resolutions of the Security Council of 4 and 16 November 1948, a general armistice between the armed forces of the two Parties—land sea and air—is hereby established.

2. No element of the land, sea or air, military or para-military forces of either Party, including non-regular forces, shall commit any warlike or hostile act against the military or para-military forces of the other Party, or against civilians in territory under the control of that Party; or shall advance beyond or pass over for any purpose whatsoever the Armistice Demarcation Line set forth in Article VI of this Agreement except as provided in Article III of this Agreement; and elsewhere shall not violate the international frontier; or enter into or pass through the air space of the other Party or through the waters within three miles of the coastline of the other Party. . . .

ARTICLE IV. With specific reference to the implementation of the resolutions of the Security Council of 4 and 16 November 1948, the following principles and purposes are affirmed:

1. The principle that no military or political advantage should be gained under the truce ordered by the Security Council is recognized.

2. It is also recognized that the basic purposes and spirit of the Armistice would not be served by the restoration of previously held military positions, changes from those now held other than as specifically provided for in this Agreement, or by the advance of the military forces of either side beyond positions held at the time this Armistice Agreement is signed.

3. It is further recognized that rights, claims or interests of a non-military character in the area of Palestine covered by this Agreement may be asserted by either Party, and that these, by mutual agreement being excluded from the Armistice negotiations, shall be, at the discretion of the Parties, the subject of later settlement. It is emphasized that it is not the purpose of this Agreement to establish, to recognize, to strengthen, or to weaken or nullify, in any way, any territorial, custodial or other rights, claims or interests which may be asserted by either Party in the area of Palestine or any part or locality thereof covered by this Agreement, whether such asserted rights, claims or interests, derive from Security Council resolutions, including the resolution of 4 November 1948 and the Memorandum of 13 November 1948 for its implementation, or from any other source. The provisions of this Agreement are dictated exclusively by military considerations, and are valid only for the period of the Armistice.

ARTICLE V. 1. The line described in Article VI of this Agreement shall be designated as the Armistice Demarcation Line and is delineated in pursuance of the purpose and intent of the resolutions of the Security Council of 4 and 16 November 1948.

2. The Armistice Demarcation Line is not to be construed in any sense as a political or territorial boundary, and is delineated without prejudice to rights, claims and positions of either Party to the Armistice as regards ultimate settlement of the Palestine question.

3. The basic purpose of the Armistice Demarcation Line is to delineate the line beyond which the armed forces of the

respective Parties shall not move except as provided in Article III of this Agreement.

4. Rules and regulations of the armed forces of the Parties, which prohibit civilians from crossing the fighting lines or entering the area between the lines, shall remain in effect after the signing of this Agreement with application to the Armistice Demarcation Line defined in Article VI. . . .

ARTICLE XI. No provision of this Agreement shall in any way prejudice the rights, claims and positions of either Party hereto in the ultimate Peaceful settlement of the Palestine question.

ARTICLE XII. The present Agreement is not subject to ratification and shall come into force immediately upon being signed.

2. This Agreement, having been negotiated and concluded in pursuance of the resolution of the Security Council of 16 November 1948 calling for the establishment of an armistice in order to eliminate the threat to the peace in Palestine and to facilitate the transition from the present truce to permanent peace in Palestine, shall remain in force until a peaceful settlement between the Parties is achieved, except as provided in paragraph 3 of this Article.

3. The Parties to this Agreement may, by mutual consent, revise this Agreement or any of its provisions, or may suspend its application, other than Articles I and II, at any time. In the absence of mutual agreement and after this Agreement has been in effect for one year from the date of its signing, either of the Parties may call upon the Secretary-General of the United Nations to convoke a conference of representatives of the two Parties for the purpose of reviewing, revising or suspending any of the provisions of this Agreement other than Articles I and II. Participation in such conference shall be obligatory upon the Parties.

4. If the conference provided for in paragraph 3 of this Article does not result in an agreed solution of a point in dispute, either Party may bring the matter before the Security Council of the United Nations for the relief sought on the grounds that this Agreement has been concluded in pursuance of Security Council action toward the end of achieving peace in Palestine.

5. This Agreement supersedes the Egyptian-Israeli General

Cease-Fire Agreement entered into by the Parties on 24 January 1949.

6. This Agreement is signed in quintuplicate, of which one copy shall be retained by each Party, two copies communicated to the Secretary-General of the United Nations for transmission to the Security Council and to the United Nations Conciliation Commission on Palestine, and one copy to the Acting Mediator on Palestine.

*

The denial of Suez to Israel by Egypt on the grounds of a threat to her security brought the armistice relationship into dispute very soon after it was established. In order to justify the denial of Suez Egypt maintained—and still maintains—that a state of war existed with Israel despite the Armistice Agreement. In defending her views before the Security Council Egypt stressed the traditional meaning of an armistice as no more than a cessation of hostilities. Egypt had also derived strength from a decision of the Mixed Armistice Commission set up under Article X of the Agreement to supervise its implementation. The Commission held that as no Egyptian *military* forces were involved, the closure of Suez to Israeli shipping did not contravene the letter of the Armistice Agreement, much as it denied its spirit.

For her part, Israel has always denied the existence of the 'state of war' claimed by the Arab States. In her arguments in the Security Council Israel based her view not on traditional ideas about the meaning of an armistice, but on the conditions of this particular Agreement. Israel stressed the importance of the phrase in the preamble that described the Agreement as concluded in order to facilitate transition from present truce to permanent peace (note also Articles I and IV). Israel also pointed out that the Agreement provided for security and freedom from attack, which the Arab assertion of the existence of a state of war directly undermined. The Security Council sidestepped the legal complexities of the problem, but directed Egypt to lift the ban on shipping to Israel. Egypt declined to oblige. The Security Council did not force Egypt to comply, nor did they have the whole matter thrashed out in the International Court of Justice. However, the Security Council adopted a resolution in September 1951 which included the view that neither side 'could reasonably assert that it is a belligerent'. The text of the Resolution is given below in Document VIII (b).

DOCUMENT VIII (b). SECURITY COUNCIL RESOLUTION, 1 SEPTEMBER 1951.

The Security Council

1. *Recalling* that in its resolution of 11 August 1949 (S/1376) relating to the conclusion of Armistice Agreements between Israel and the neighbouring Arab States it drew attention to the pledges in these Agreements 'against any further acts of hostility between the Parties'.

2. *Recalling* further that in its resolution of 17 November 1950 (S/1907 and Corr.1), it reminded the states concerned that the Armistice Agreements to which they are parties contemplate 'the return of permanent peace in Palestine', and therefore urged them and other states in the area to take all such steps as will lead to the settlement of the issues between them.

3. *Noting* the report of the Chief of Staff of the Truce Supervision Organization to the Security Council of 12 June 1951 (S/2194).

4. *Further noting* that the Chief of Staff of the Truce Supervision Organization recalled the statement of the senior Egyptian delegate in Rhodes on 13 January 1949, to the effect that his delegation was 'inspired with every spirit of co-operation, conciliation and a sincere desire to restore peace in Palestine', and that the Egyptian Government has not complied with the earnest plea of the Chief of Staff made to the Egyptian delegate on 12 June 1951, that it desist from the present practice of interfering with the passage through the Suez Canal of goods destined for Israel.

5. *Considering* that since the armistice regime, which has been in existence for nearly two-and-a-half years, is of a permanent character, neither party can reasonably assert that it is actively a belligerent or requires to exercise the right of visit, search, and seizure for any legitimate purpose of self-defence.

6. *Finds* that the maintenance of the practice mentioned in

paragraph 4 above is inconsistent with the objectives of a peaceful settlement between the parties and the establishment of a permanent peace in Palestine set forth in the Armistice Agreement.

7. *Finds further* that such practice is an abuse of the exercise of the right of visit, search and seizure.

8. *Further finds* that that practice cannot in the prevailing circumstances be justified on the ground that it is necessary for self-defence.

9. *And further noting* that the restrictions on the passage of goods through the Suez Canal to Israel ports are denying to nations at no time connected with the conflict in Palestine valuable supplies required for their economic reconstruction, and that these restrictions together with sanctions applied by Egypt to certain ships which have visited Israel ports represent unjustified interference with the rights of nations to navigate the seas and to trade freely with one another, including the Arab States and Israel.

10. *Calls upon* Egypt to terminate the restrictions on the passage of international commercial shipping and goods through the Suez Canal wherever bound and to cease all interference with such shipping beyond that essential to the safety of shipping in the Canal itself and to the observance of the international conventions in force.

PART IX

The Re-entry of Russia

With the failure of efforts for peace the Western Powers felt impelled to try at least to contain the Arab-Israeli dispute. Britain, France and the United States therefore issued a Tripartite Declaration, which served to limit an arms race for a short while, but which broke down largely because it was incompatible with Western schemes for Middle Eastern defence. These meant arming certain states, notably Iraq and Jordan. Western arms supplies to Israel's most dangerous adversary, Egypt, were strictly limited, but France began secretly to supply arms to Israel in 1952 as a *quid pro quo* for Egyptian aid to Algerian rebels (see *Suez Ten Years After* (London, BBC, 1967), pp. 60–67). The policy inspiring the Tripartite Declaration finally broke down with the Egyptian-Czechoslovak arms deal of February 1955.

The guarantee of the Armistice lines in the Declaration was partly intended to prevent any Arab attack on Jordan, which had annexed Arab-held central and west Palestine. However, it chiefly sought to stifle any aggressive designs by either side. It did not explicitly impose the Armistice lines on the Arab States; but it came near enough to doing so for the Arab League Council to obtain assurances that the Declaration was not to be regarded as the final settlement of the Arab-Israeli problem. Although broadly satisfied with the Armistice terms, Israel also did not consider the Declaration as a satisfactory settlement of the conflict. Simply to prevent the outbreak of hostilities was not the same as obtaining the peace settlement she demanded. The text of the Tripartite Declaration is given below, Document IX (a).

DOCUMENT IX (a). THE TRIPARTITE DECLARATION BY BRITAIN, FRANCE AND THE UNITED STATES, 25 MAY 1950.

The Governments of the United Kingdom, France and the United States, having had occasion during the recent Foreign Ministers meeting in London to review certain questions affecting the peace and stability of the Arab States and of Israel, and particularly that of the supply of arms and war material to these States, have resolved to make the following statements:

1. The three Governments recognize that the Arab States and Israel all need to maintain a certain level of armed forces for the purposes of assuring their internal security and their legitimate self-defence and to permit them to play their part in the defence of the area as a whole. All applications for arms or war material for these countries will be considered in the light of these principles. In this connection the three Governments wish to recall and reaffirm the terms of the statements made by their representatives on the Security Council on 4 August 1949, in which they declared their opposition to the development of an arms race between the Arab States and Israel.

2. The three Governments declare that assurances have been received from all the States in question, to which they permit arms to be supplied from their countries, that the purchasing State does not intend to undertake any act of aggression against any other State. Similar assurances will be requested from any other State in the area to which they permit arms to be supplied in the future.

3. The three Governments take this opportunity of declaring their deep interest in and their desire to promote the establishment and maintenance of peace and stability in the area and their unalterable opposition to the use of force or threat of force between any of the States in that area. The three Governments, should they find that any of these States was preparing to violate frontiers or armistice lines, would, consistently with their obligations as members of the United Nations, immediately take action, both within and outside the United Nations, to prevent such violation.

*

In the wake of the Tripartite Declaration initiatives by Dulles and Eden to find some formula for the solution of the Arab-Israeli problem completely failed. These new Western attempts at a solution were made the more urgent by the new factor in the situation which we now document—the re-entry of Russia into the Middle East in 1955.

The Arab world was stunned by the Gaza raid carried out by Israel in February 1955. It was a retaliatory raid for Arab frontier attacks of much less weight and it followed the announcement by Egypt of the formation of guerrilla bands. It was certainly inspired by the idea of teaching the Arabs a lesson they would not forget and possibly such retaliation was intended to force Egypt to the conference table. The main result was to provide Egypt with further justification for strengthening her armed forces. Egypt did so in a dramatic way, as we see in Document IX (b). Yet, as we may perceive, Nasser was concerned with other problems besides that of Israel. Arms were needed for the sake of independence of action generally and not only with regard to Israel.

DOCUMENT IX (b). EXCERPT FROM PRIME MINISTER NASSER'S SPEECH ON THE OCCASION OF THE ARMS DEAL WITH CZECHO-SLOVAKIA, 27 SEPTEMBER 1955.

The fifth goal of your Revolution was to set up a strong national army. From the beginning of the Revolution you have all exerted every effort to achieve this goal and we have worked with you with all our might and with every means at our disposal. We have worked with you to achieve this goal because to achieve it means liberty; to achieve it means glory; to achieve it means dignity.

My brothers, we met the greatest obstacles—we met many difficulties in achieving our aim. We did everything we could to set up military factories; we did everything we could to provide the army with the heavy armaments it needed; and we did everything we could so that Egypt's army might be a strong national army.

Yes, my brothers, we did a lot.

But there were the greatest difficulties in our way. We believed that if we wanted to create such an army for Egypt we had to preserve our freedom. We believed that if we wanted to achieve this strong national army for Egypt, we had to become free in our internal and our foreign policies.

My brothers, we will never agree that this army be formed at the expense of this country's freedom, or at the expense of this country's glory, or at the expense of this country's dignity. We have always been determined that the formation of this strong national army should go hand in hand with true liberty and with real glory.

We have proclaimed Egypt's policy on many occasions. We declared that Egypt after the Revolution of 23 July would go forward with its independent policy; it would go forward having rid itself of imperialism; it would go forward having rid itself of domination; and it would go forward having rid itself of foreign influence. These were our hopes and these were your hopes. We did everything we could to preserve these hopes. We did everything we could, my brothers, to preserve these goals— and we were confronted by many obstacles.

You know that heavy weapons are controlled by the big powers. You know that the big powers have never agreed to supply our army with heavy weapons except with conditions and except with stipulations. You know that we refused these conditions and these stipulations because we are jealous of our true freedom and we are jealous of our independent policy. We are anxious that Egypt have a strong independent policy so that we may make of Egypt a new independent personality which will really rid itself of imperialism, will really rid itself of occupation, will really rid itself of foreign domination in all its aspects. We have been making progress along this path.

Today, my brothers, we hear an outcry from London, we hear an outcry from Washington about the arming of Egypt's troops. But I would like to tell you that throughout the last three years we have tried to get heavy weapons for the army by every means, not for aggressive purposes, not to attack, not to make war, but for defence, for security, for peace.

We wanted to strengthen our army so as to provide security for ourselves, to provide security for our nation, to provide security for our 'Arabism'. We wanted to get weapons for the army so that we could always feel secure, safe, and tranquil. We never intended to strengthen our army for aggressive purposes. We never intended to strengthen the army for wars. But the army which is the defender and protector of our homeland must always stand prepared to defend the borders and the country's honour. Such is our purpose and this is our goal. We have always declared this throughout the last three years. We do not want arms for aggression. We want arms so that we can be tranquil, so that we feel at peace and not threatened.

Today, my brothers, I sense an outcry here and I sense an outcry there. I sense these outcries now that we have been able to obtain for the army the weapons of which it is in need, without conditions and without restrictions, so as to achieve the goal which this Revolution undertook—that Egypt should have a strong national army to defend its true independence and protect its true freedom.

On this occasion I would like to tell you, my brothers, the story of the arming of our troops. When the Revolution took place we went to each of the States, we went to every quarter to get weapons for the army. We went to Britain; we went to France; we went to America; we went to the rest of the States to get weapons for the army in the interest of peace and defence. What did we get? We got only demands. They wanted to arm the troops after we had signed a document or after we had signed a pact. We declared that even though we had wanted and had decided to arm our troops, we would never sign a document. We were arming our troops in the interest of our freedom, of our independent personality, of our Revolution of the glory of our country, of Egypt's dignity. We declared that we would not arm our troops at the expense of our freedom.

We requested arms but what was the result? The result, my brothers, is a long and bitter story. I remember now, I remember as I talk to you that we sometimes humiliated ourselves but we never abandoned our principles. We humiliated ourselves when we requested arms—we begged for arms—but at the same time we were determined to hold to our principles and we were determined to preserve our high ideals. And what was the result? Never, my brothers, could we achieve our goal, the greatest goal for which this Revolution was undertaken, the creation of a strong national army.

France always bargained with us. She bargained with us over North Africa. She says to us, 'We will give you arms on the condition that you should not criticize our position in North Africa, and on condition that you relinquish your "Arabism", that you relinquish your humanitarianism and on condition that you should keep silent and close your eyes when you see the massacres in North Africa'.

We said to her, 'How can we relinquish our "Arabism"? How can we give up our humanitarianism? We never can'.

France's arms offer to us was always like a sword above our necks. We were always being threatened, my brothers, with the cutting off of arms. We were always being threatened, my brothers, with the supply of arms to Israel and the cutting off of arms for Egypt. This is the story of France and now I'll tell you the story of America.

From the time of the Revolution we asked for arms and we were promised arms. And what was the result?

The promise was a promise circumscribed with conditions. We would get arms if we signed a mutual security pact. We would get arms if we would sign some form of alliance. We refused to sign a mutual security pact. We refused to sign any form of alliance. And, my brothers, we could never get a single weapon from America.

What was the story of England. England told us that she was ready to supply us arms. We accepted gratefully. What was the result? England provided us with a quantity of arms which was not sufficient to achieve the goals of this Revolution.

What was the result of all this, my brothers? The army opposing us is obtaining arms from various parts of the world. Israel's army has been able to obtain arms from England, France, Belgium, Canada, Italy and from various other states. It can always find someone to supply it arms, while we read in the foreign press—in the British, American or French newspapers—that Israel's army can defeat all the Arab armies combined. It was only last month, my brothers, that I read many articles in that sense, that the Israeli army could defeat Egypt, that the Israeli army could beat the Arabs, that the Israeli army was superior in armament, that the Israeli army was superior in equipment.

This is what they have said in their press and I said to them, since you feel like this why do you prevent us from obtaining arms? I asked them this, and what was the result? France complained about our feelings towards North Africa and prevented us from obtaining arms.

When we saw this, when we saw this domination, when we saw this influence which was being used against us, we decided to ask all the states of the world to supply us arms without conditions. I told them these arms would not be used for aggression, that they would be used for defence, that we had no aggressive intent, that our intentions were peaceful, that we wanted to have a strong independent army to defend our country and help it to achieve its free and independent goals, that we want to have a strong army not for aggression but for defence.

I said this, my brothers, in the name of Egypt to America, to England, to France, to Russia, to Czechoslovakia and to the rest of the states and I waited for their answers. I waited, and what was the result? I got answers from some of them that I could get arms with conditions. I refused, for I have already told you that although we are ready to humiliate ourselves by asking for arms, we will never abandon our principles.

We received a reply from Czechoslovakia saying that she was prepared to supply arms in accordance with our needs and those of Egypt's army on a commercial basis, the transaction to be considered like any other commercial transaction. We agreed and last week Egypt signed a commercial agreement with Czechoslovakia to supply us with arms. This agreement permits Egypt to pay in Egyptian products such as cotton and rice. This offer we gratefully accepted. In this way, my brothers, we achieve one of the goals of the Revolution, the formation of a strong national army.

Today, my brothers, as I talk to you I sense the outcry raised here and there—an outcry in London, an outcry in Washington. These outcries seek to continue to control us, to continue to influence us.

We will fight to destroy this control, We will fight to destroy this influence. We will fight to achieve the goals of the Revolution and we will fight to create a strong national army able to achieve the greatest goals of the Revolution, able to obtain peace. Yes, my brothers, peace—that peace which we proclaimed at Bandung, the peace which we have proclaimed on many occasions.

This army which we create is for the sake of peace. We create is so that we can be secure in our lot, we create it so that Egypt will not be a State of refugees. We create it against aggression, we create it against any territorial designs against our nation's soil.

When I hear someone say that this opens the way for Russian influence or foreign influence in Egypt or the Middle East, I think of the remote past and I say that this commercial agreement without conditions does not open the way for Russian or foreign influence, but, my brothers, it means the eradication of the foreign influence which so long oppressed and dominated us.

*

The reaction of the Israeli Prime Minister was to describe the arms deal as 'a departure liable to bring about a revolutionary and ominous change in Israel's security situation'. The immediate significance of the Czech arms deal was its immense contribution to the arms race. In the longer run it contained broader implications both for the Arab-Israeli conflict and for the Middle East generally. An assessment of the impact of this Russian re-awakening to the potentialities of the Middle East is given in Document IX (c).

DOCUMENT IX (c). EXCERPTS FROM W. Z. LAQUEUR, *The Soviet Union and the Middle East*, PP. 211–12 AND 221–2.

(i)

The Soviet-Egyptian arms deal in September 1955 was regarded at the time as the great turning point in the Middle East, the end of one era and the beginning of another. There is no need to revise that view in retrospect; the arms deal was, indeed, the great divide. That is how it appeared to both the Western and Eastern blocs, with only the Egyptian leaders taking exception. The latter argued that Egypt was an independent country and thus entitled to get weapons wherever it wished. Had not the Turks accepted Soviet arms in the early twenties? And had not the Western Powers themselves been partners in a military alliance with Russia in World War Two? Anyway, the arms agreement was a purely commercial transaction; Egypt was only to import weapons and ammunition from the Soviet bloc, not political ideas.

These were the arguments of the Egyptian leaders, and they were no doubt sincere. The fears of the West (and the hopes of the East) were less concerned with the good intentions than with the objective results of Colonel Nasser's actions. There was nothing morally reprehensible about a policy of playing the two great world blocs against each other, especially since it might have appeared to be in the best interests of the Egyptian people. However, to make neutralism a paying proposition, some prerequisites were required; it had been comparatively easy to take the first and second steps, but then a political chain reaction followed. When Naguib and Nasser took over in July 1952 they solemnly (and sincerely) declared that they merely wanted to purge the country of traitors, and then step down again in three weeks or as many months. But the political situation made this intention illusory and having accepted responsibility, they had to go on ruling the country. It could also be shown that Nasser's road to the eminently respectable Bandung Conference in 1955 eventually led to the 1957 meeting in Cairo (the 'solidarity conference' of the Afro-Asian peoples) which was anything but neutralist. The danger. from the Western point of view, was not in the Soviet arms deal itself (which was relatively unimportant), but in Egypt's dependence on the Soviet Union. Egypt's neutrality, it was feared, would give way to positive neutralism (positive towards the Soviet Union) and this, in turn, would gradually lead toward open hostility to the West and a close alliance with the Soviet bloc.

From the Soviet point of view there were no scruples or hesitations about the arms deal once it had been discovered how attractive such offers were in Arab eyes, and how much sympathy could be gained in the Middle East by such relatively inexpensive outlays. Moral or ideological scruples did not come into the picture; many years had passed since the Soviets had decried the fiendish activities of the 'merchants of death'. The only risks were practical. Would Nasser take the arms but try to preserve his independence? What if he used his new military equipment in a local Middle Eastern war? What if he were defeated and the Soviet arms fell into other hands? And if he were victorious—would he become too strong to be manipulated?

These questions were apparently given careful study in Moscow, but the conclusion reached was that the risks involved were small. It was undoubtedly anticipated that Nasser would try to preserve his independence, but then Egypt's internal and external situation would make the continuation and strengthening of the Soviet alliance imperative for him.

If he used the arms in a Middle Eastern war and was defeated—*tant pis*; it would mean that he needed new arms and these again would come from the Soviet Union. If he won a war, he would have Soviet military assistance to thank, and Russian prestige would increase enormously. Either way Moscow could not lose.

(ii)

The exact details of the arms deal have never been made public; subsequently it became known that there were provisions for the delivery of guns, heavy tanks, submarines, modern jet planes, etc. And it proved to be quite incorrect (as some Western observers had predicted) that Russia would merely use the pact to dump antiquated war material on Egypt. Was it true that Egypt could not receive the arms it wanted from the Western powers? By and large, Nasser's description of Egypt's applications and requests was in accordance with the facts: Washington, London, and Paris had wanted to prevent a Middle Eastern arms race that could only have led to a new war. Nasser was not quite correct in charging the West with giving Israel preferential treatment. If America had not given Egypt the war material it had required, neither had any been given to Israel. Britain supplied Egypt with Vampire and Meteor jets and with heavy Centurion tanks, of which Israel had none. As far as can be established, France had given Israel only small quantities prior to September 1955. Substantial French arms shipments to Israel only came considerably later —after the Egyptian-Soviet arms deal.

But what did Nasser want the heavy equipment for? The official explanation was that he needed it for the defence of Egypt against Israel. If this version had been believed in Western capitals, he would presumably have received the arms he needed. But at the time the general view, rightly or wrongly, was that Nasser needed these weapons not only, and perhaps not mainly, against Israel, but to establish an Egyptian 'co-prosperity sphere' throughout the Middle East and North Africa. He would have clashed with Turkey, with Iraq, with the West over Aden and North Africa, and possibly with Sudan, Jordan, and other neighbouring countries. Such a development was clearly not in the Western interest. The Soviet Union, on the other hand, had no qualms in this respect. No direct Soviet interests were involved in the Middle East, and in whatever direction Colonel Nasser tried to make headway he would clash with the West.

Would Western arms supplied in spring or summer of 1955 have forestalled Nasser's *rapprochement* with the Soviet Union? This is a hypothetical question that could be debated endlessly. In the opinion of the present writer, the West could have prevented the Soviet-Egyptian alliance at the time only if it had (in addition to shipping arms) given up the Baghdad Pact and its remaining positions in the Middle East and North Africa, reached an understanding about the future of Arab oil, and delivered Israel to its fate. Whether such a course of action on the part of the West would have prevented a more gradual and less dramatic *rapprochement* between Egypt and the Soviet Union is doubtful; this long-term process was motivated by inner social and political tensions that could not possibly have been affected by the supply of Western arms. The decision to ask for arms from the Soviet bloc was dictated by political necessities. The main thing for Colonel Nasser was not to obtain more and better arms, important as this was. Above all, he wanted to be free to use the arms as he wished. This aim could not be achieved so long as the 'Western arms monopoly' still existed.

PART X

From Co-existence to War

We have seen how the French supply of arms to Israel was followed by the Czech supply of arms to Egypt and the Russian reappearance in the Middle East. Were these factors alone sufficient to turn the intermittent incidents of the Arab-Israeli conflict into a real war? In order to understand why war broke out in 1956 we should have to examine in the field of international politics the complex reasons for the emergence of the Suez Crisis. This would go beyond our scope, but what we must do is to take into account those factors in the Arab-Israeli conflict that played a powerful part in the move to war. We give in Document X (a) an account of the origins of the war, in so far as they stemmed from Arab-Israeli hostility, by a serious student of the Arab-Israeli conflict.

DOCUMENT X (a). EXCERPT FROM EARL BERGER, *The Covenant and the Sword, Arab-Israeli Relations 1948–56*, PP. 203–8.

The nationalization of the Suez Canal Company, like the Czech arms deal, stands as one of the great advances in Egypt's struggle to free herself from the coils of psychological bondage. It also stands as a convenient mark of the rising tide of war. On this day, we are accustomed to say, Egypt made Britain and France into her enemies and brought them into alliance with Israel. The claim is exaggerated. The forces of war had been afoot for many months. The nationalization of the Suez Canal Company does not mark the beginning of the story but the final chapter. The story is a long and complicated one. To understand how it began we must go back to 1954. Since the subject of this study is Israel we shall begin with her. At the same time we should remember that she did not play a decisive role in creating the conditions which led to the invasion. She had her own game to play, but the only circumstances in which it could be played were set up for her by France, Britain—and Egypt.

In the summer of 1954 the Israelis were undecided about Egypt and her intentions. The *rapprochement* was obviously a failure, propaganda attacks had increased, and the blockade was slowly being tightened again. But it was still not certain which way the Egyptians would jump once their treaty with Britain had been safely negotiated. As soon as the Anglo-Egyptian treaty was initialled, guerrillas were sent into Israel, pipelines dynamited, roads mined, and coincident with this were statements by high Egyptian officials in clear, unmistakeable terms to the effect that Egypt's next task was to liberate Palestine. The Israelis had their answer: the Egyptians were moving towards war. The Israelis reacted by asking for arms to balance those being sent to Egypt, and to Iraq, and for a security pact with the United States. To ensure that there was no mistake about Egypt's intentions Israel sent numerous messages to her through the medium of Britain, France and the U.S. requesting her to stop guerrilla activities or risk retaliation. By February 1955 the Israelis were satisfied that President Nasser could have no doubt of what they would do if his border policy did not change. The Gaza Raid, large and fierce as it was, was similar to those launched against Jordan (except that the Israelis had learned to take care to avoid injuring civilians) and indicated that the Israelis, whatever their public demands for arms, felt capable of handling the Egyptian border in the same way as they had handled the Jordanian. Egypt, unlike Jordan, had the potential to defeat the Israelis, but this could not affect the Israelis' capacity to handle the situation as it existed then and as it was likely to develop over the next years.

One cannot be precise of course, but if one were to point to a time when the Israelis began to consider seriously the prospect of war with Egypt it was during these months between the summer of 1954 and February 1955. It was during this time that the Israelis began to believe that Egypt would go to war as soon as she believed that she could win. However disheartened the Israelis may have been by this knowledge they were still in control of the situation and they knew it. There was no immediate need to prepare for war. It is true that requests for arms were sent out to the Powers but this was part of the normal merry-go-round of 'arms balance'. What the Israelis did was raise their price for not considering war with Egypt. In 1953 or early 1954 they would have accepted a relatively quiet border, a modicum of co-operation between local commanders and some relaxation of the blockade as a satisfactory indication that Egypt did not intend to pursue an aggressive policy. By January 1955 they required more than this. As the months passed and the blockade was tightened, the Gulf of Akaba closed, the boycott extended, the *fedayeen* attacks increased, the propaganda intensified, it took more, for example, than a lull in the border attacks to persuade the Israelis that Egypt had ended her hostile policy. In June, news of Egypt's negotiations with Russia began to come through and the Israeli 'price' rose accordingly. It was then, in early September, that Ben Gurion warned Egypt that if she persisted in keeping the Straits closed Israel would use force to open them within the next twelve months.

It is interesting that Ben Gurion should still have considered the economic situation more pressing than the military. Evidently he felt that Israel could deal with the *fedayeen* on their own terms, and that Russian aid to Egypt did not present any immediate threat to the arms balance. The economic situation was much more serious; apparently so serious that it justified risking war to gain direct access to Asian and African markets. That he did not mention arms, although he knew of the arms negotiations with Russia, indicates that he underestimated the amounts involved. Had he known surely his price for peace would have been higher.

The Czech arms deal completely altered Israel's relations with Egypt and the rest of the Arab world. 'No man in his senses', Ben Gurion said, 'will believe that Nasser and his colleagues might use the Soviet arms for a war against the West, or the British arms for a war against the East.' Israel was the obvious target. All the major Egyptian leaders said so, the radio said so, the Press said so, the border situation implied as much Who were the Israelis to disregard this mass of circumstantial evidence?

It is hard to say how set the Israeli activists were on war. Possibly, if Egypt had met their price by opening up the Gulf of Akaba they might have been persuaded to hold off, possibly not. Israeli strategy always had to start from several unpalatable bases. Israel had no hinterland into which she could withdraw and recover her strength. She had no manpower resources upon which to draw once the main armies were engaged. She had no natural resources by which to sustain and feed herself once she was at war, or once the sea-coast was blockaded. Her land area was attenuated, her lines of communication exposed, invading armies could split her asunder at any one of a dozen places. She always had to be prepared to fight on four fronts at once. Potentially she was far inferior to Egypt alone. She could not afford to cut her corners too finely. She had to strike while the calibre of her individual soldiers was still sufficient to outweigh the quantitative disadvantages. The decisive month seems to have been April 1956; it being then decided, barring unexpected changes in Egypt's attitude or in the international climate, to go to war as soon as all necessary preparations had been made.

April 1956 was a very bad month for the Israelis. The armistice regime was in ruins; the Security Council was useless; the Tripartite Declaration was virtually disowned; the Great Power conferences had achieved nothing. All the safeguards laboriously built up around the cease-fire in 1948 had disappeared. President Nasser was steadily extending his influence over the other Arab countries. No one seemed able to stand before him. *Fedayeen*, controlled by Egyptian military attachés, operated across all four of Israel's borders. General Glubb was expelled from Jordan along with most of the British officers in the Arab Legion (Nasser claimed that he had no hand in this—but the effect, which was what concerned the Israelis, was the same as if he had). It seemed that soon Nasser would be able to do as he wished in the Middle East. Along the border the Egyptians refused to co-operate. The bulk of their army was in the eastern Sinai near the Israeli border and April was the worst month to date for *fedayeen*.

Strategic considerations aside, the effect of all this upon public opinion in Israel was profound. The first and most important function of any government is to provide for the protection of its citizens. A government which cannot do that soon loses its position. By early 1956 the Israeli population was severely exercised by its lack of security and its grim future prospects. Public opinion is seldom rational, particularly in times of stress, and the Israeli population was not likely to heed comments that they had brought many of their troubles down on themselves, or that President Nasser was not the evil genius they made him out to be, or that the Arabs had strong justification for what they were doing. The people had fixed on the one central issue. Their security, present and future, was in serious danger, and they demanded that their government do something about it. No government dare ignore such a summons. The Czech arms deal had darkened Israel's future prospects as nothing else had done. But it was the *fedayeen* who brought that insecurity home to every Israeli, who created that great, swelling tide of public demands for action, which drowned the voice of the moderates, and gave the government no alternative but action sooner rather than later. It is true that the Israelis had suffered less from border marauders than the Arabs. In 1956 (before the Sinai Campaign), about fifty-eight Israelis were killed and one hundred and sixty wounded: the Arabs had about two hundred killed and two hundred wounded. But while the moral implications of killing a man are the same whatever his nation, the political implications are not necessarily so.

In Egypt, only the Palestinians living in Gaza or soldiers and police stationed there or in the area were affected. In Syria, the only people affected were that small number living or stationed in the immediate vicinity of Lake Tiberias. In Lebanon, only those living right next to the border had anything to fear and that from accidental shots. Even in Jordan there were few instances of Israelis penetrating more than four or five miles, and that was mainly in the sparsely populated Hebron hills south of Jerusalem. In Cairo, Damascus, Amman and Beirut—everywhere in the Arab countries except the areas mentioned—the citizens moved about freely and without fear. One could walk in the fields on a lonely afternoon, or travel to see friends in the evening. When one drove from Homs to Aleppo at night, or from Cairo to Alexandria, one did not think of Israeli raiders. In the Arab countries the 'belt of fear' could be drawn by a red pencil running alongside the border. The destruction of Qibya was a terrible thing, but the citizen of Nablus a few miles away was safe. In Israel the 'belt of fear' ran from border to border, north to south, east to west. At night travel anywhere in the country was dangerous—during the day anywhere that was relatively isolated, a highway in the south, an orchard outside Tel Aviv, a suburb of Jerusalem. The *fedayeen* roamed everywhere. A small group of three or four men in one busy night could throw a whole district into panic for months. Parts of the country, even in the fertile north, saw only the occasional military or police patrol; no civilian would go there because of the *fedayeen*. No one felt secure, no place was considered safe.

In such circumstances a comparative analysis of casualty statistics is meaningless. To kill an Israeli is no greater crime than to kill an Arab, but the effect upon public opinion is something else again. Fifty-eight dead is perhaps not very many in one year—more people than that might die in road accidents. But it was the manner of death that was important. The Israelis were not more easily frightened than other people, but when each felt the peril to be so close he was bound to turn to his government and demand his primary, fundamental right: protection. Furthermore, economic development in the whole of the south was seriously hindered and development of the south was one of the keystones of Israeli economic planning. Here was another challenge no government could ignore. Taking the *fedayeen* operation as a whole, the number of casualties, the amount of machinery and goods stolen, the number of mining incidents, the dynamited pipelines: all were less important than their psychological impact. If the Egyptians' intentions were to strike fear into the hearts of Israelis they succeeded. It is odd that they did not consider that such acts would also arouse anger, and that an angry population would demand an end to its fears.

In April it was finally decided by Ben Gurion and those around him that Egypt meant war. Nothing that transpired in the following months indicated that they might be wrong. Israel had to attack first. But the Israelis were not strong enough to attack Egypt and at the same time maintain an adequate defensive posture along the other borders. Arms had to be obtained. There had to be a favourable line-up of Great Powers; but over this the Israelis had little control. They could only wait and seize their opportunity when it arose. They did not have long to wait.

*

Berger stresses the hostile policies adopted by Egypt as one of the chief factors that led to the Israeli attack. Arab writers stress

Israeli expansionism. For what other reason, they ask, did Israel conclude the important arms deal with France in 1952? Was not this the first blow at the Tripartite Declaration? Israel would claim her moves were justified by the Arab States' refusal to conclude a peace treaty, and by Arab bellicosity in closing Suez, by attacking Israel viciously in the press and on radio and in asserting the existence of a state of war. It is the all-too-familiar story. Each side claims fear of the aggressive intentions of the other to justify its own aggressiveness. The pronouncements of the more extreme elements on each side are those that receive publicity; and this rhetoric is important for it creates an atmosphere in which moderation can easily come to be regarded as treachery and cowardice.

On the theme of Israeli expansionism, which occupies so much of popular, and therefore politically important, Arab accounts of the outbreak of war in 1956, we include a brief and moderate assessment by a distinguished student of the Arab world (Document X (b)).

DOCUMENT X (b). EXCERPT FROM A. H. HOURANI, 'THE MIDDLE EAST AND THE CRISIS OF 1956', *St Antony's Papers No. 4, Middle Eastern Affairs*, p. 35.

There is of course another urgent 'problem of Palestine'. It is the problem posed by Arab fears of Jewish expansion, and Jewish fears of Arab attack; fears which, as so often, may themselves bring about what is feared. Both are unjustified in one sense, but not in another. It may be doubted whether any Arab Government seriously considers running the risks of an attack on Israel, and whether the Israeli Government has a plan of expansion lying in one of its pigeon holes. But each side would have something to gain by expansion: the Israelis would gain a better strategic frontier and more water-resources, and the Arabs would gain land for the refugees and the land route between Egypt and Arab Asia. Moreover, neither side objects in principle to expansion: the Zionists have always regarded themselves as possessing rights to a larger area than is included in the present state of Israel, and the Arabs cannot but regard the whole of Palestine as being Arab land. Thus, if either side has or seems to have an opportunity for expansion, the pressure in favour of taking it would be too strong to resist. Such an opportunity would occur if three conditions were fulfilled simultaneously: support by a Great Power, absence of opposition from the other Great Powers, and local superiority. These conditions did indeed seem to be fulfilled in 1956, and the result was a Jewish attack on Egypt. It is true, that attack was generally regarded as being essentially 'defensive', and possibly defence was the first motive in the mind of the Israeli Government; but self-defence is one of the classical motives of expansion, and no doubt if the Israeli attack had succeeded—if that is to say, they had not made a miscalculation about the second of the three conditions—it would have ended in an enlargement of the territories of Israel.

PART XI

The Suez Peace

The 1956 war left Israel in occupation of the Sinai peninsula. Had she remained there the whole character of the Arab-Israeli conflict would have been changed. It would have resembled the situation after the 1967 war.

However, in 1956 Israel was not allowed to retain her gains from war. With extreme reluctance she abandoned them in response to very firm American pressure. Israel was above all, loath to leave the Straits of Tiran and the Gaza Strip. As we may see from the selection of documents below, Israel wanted an assurance that the Gaza Strip would not continue to constitute a base for guerrilla attacks; and that navigation through the Straits would not be at the mercy of the Arab States. In fact, Egypt occupied Gaza as soon as Israeli troops withdrew; but the UN Emergency Force occupied the Straits, which were kept open until closed by Egypt in 1967.

The documents below (1) illustrate the importance of American pressure in restoring the situation to that existing before 1956, (2) provide information on the nature of the important American 'commitment' to keep the Straits open to Israeli shipping, and (3) present the Israeli understanding of the nature of the American 'committment'.

It is clear that Israel obtained an assurance on Gaza and the Straits that was much less firm than she desired. Nevertheless, Israel deemed it wise to bow to American pressure. In 1967 she relied on her own strength more.

Paragraph 8 of the Statement (Document XI (d)) by the Israeli Foreign Minister is of particular interest for the dispute in 1967 over the withdrawal of the UN Emergency Force (see Part XIII).

DOCUMENT XI (a). RESOLUTION OF THE UN GENERAL ASSEMBLY, 2 FEBRUARY 1957.

The General Assembly,

Having received the report of the Secretary-General of 24 January 1957,

Recognizing that withdrawal by Israel must be followed by action which would assure progress towards the creation of peaceful conditions,

1. *Notes with appreciation* the Secretary-General's report and the measures therein to be carried out upon Israel's complete withdrawal;

2. *Calls upon* the Governments of Egypt and Israel scrupulously to observe the provisions of the General Armistice Agreement between Egypt and Israel of 24 February 1949;

3. *Considers* that, after full withdrawal of Israel from the Sharm el–Sheikh and Gaza areas, the scrupulous maintenance of the Armistice Agreement requires the placing of the United Nations Emergency Force on the Egyptian-Israel armistice demarcation line and the implementation of other measures as proposed in the Secretary-General's report, with due regard to the considerations set out therein with a view to assist in achieving situations conducive to the maintenance of peaceful conditions in the area;

4. *Requests* the Secretary-General, in consultation with the parties concerned, to take steps to carry out these measures and to report, as appropriate, to the General Assembly.

DOCUMENT XI (b). *Aide-mémoire* FROM THE UNITED STATES TO ISRAEL, 11 FEBRUARY 1957.

The United Nations General Assembly has sought specifically, vigorously, and almost unanimously, the prompt withdrawal from Egypt of the armed forces of Britain, France and Israel. Britain and France have complied unconditionally. The forces of Israel have been withdrawn to a considerable extent but still hold Egyptian territory at Sharm el–Sheikh at the entrance to the Gulf of Aqaba. They also occupy the Gaza Strip which is territory specified by the Armistice arrangements to be occupied by Egypt.

We understand that it is the position of Israel that (1) it will evacuate its military forces from the Gaza Strip provided Israel retains the civil administration and police in some relationship to the United Nations, and (2) it will withdraw from Sharm el–Sheikh if continued freedom of passage through the Straits is assured.

With respect to (1) the Gaza Strip—it is the view of the United States that the United Nations General Assembly has no authority to require of either Egypt or Israel a substantial modification of the Armistice Agreement, which, as noted, now gives Egypt the right and responsibility of occupation. Accordingly, we believe that Israeli withdrawal from Gaza should be prompt and unconditional, leaving the future of the Gaza Strip to be worked out through the efforts and good offices of the United Nations.

We recognize that the area has been a source of armed infiltration and reprisals back and forth contrary to the Armistice Agreement and is a source of great potential danger because of the presence there of so large a number of Arab refugees—about 200,000. Accordingly, we believe that the United Nations General Assembly and the Secretary-General should seek that the United Nations Emergency Force, in the exercise of its mission, move into this area and be on the boundary between Israel and the Gaza Strip.

The United States will use its best efforts to help to assure this result, which we believe is contemplated by the Second Resolution of 2 February 1957.

With respect to (2) the Gulf of Aqaba and access thereto— the United States believes that the Gulf comprehends international waters and that no nation has the right to prevent free and innocent passage in the Gulf and through the Straits giving access thereto. We have in mind not only commercial usage, but the passage of pilgrims on religions missions, which should be fully respected.

The United States recalls that on 28 January 1950 the Egyptian Ministry of Foreign Affairs informed the United States that the Egyptian occupation of the two islands of Tiran and Senafir at the entrance of the Gulf of Aqaba was only to protect the islands themselves against possible damage or violation and that 'this occupation being in no way conceived in a spirit of obstructing in any way innocent passage through the stretch of water separating these two islands from the Egyptian coast of Sinai, it follows that this passage, the only practicable one, will remain free as in the past, in conformity with international practice and recognized principles of the law of nations'.

In the absence of some overriding decision to the contrary, as by the International Court of Justice, the United States, on behalf of vessels of United States registry, is prepared to exercise the right of free and innocent passage and to join with others to secure general recognition of this right.

It is of course clear that the enjoyment of a right of free and innocent passage by Israel would depend upon its prior withdrawal in accordance with the United Nations Resolutions. The United States has no reason to assume that any littoral state would under these circumstances obstruct the right of free and innocent passage.

The United States believes that the United Nations General Assembly and the Secretary General should, as a precautionary measure, seek that the United Nations Emergency Force move into the Straits area as the Israeli forces are withdrawn. This again we believe to be within the contemplation of the Second Resolution of 2 February 1957.

(3) The United States observes that the recent resolutions of the United Nations General Assembly call not only for the prompt and unconditional withdrawal of Israel behind the Armistice lines but call for other measures.

We believe, however, that the United Nations has properly established an order of events and an order of urgency and that the first requirement is that forces of invasion and occupation should withdraw.

The United States is prepared publicly to declare that it will use its influence, in concert with other United Nations members, to the end that, following Israel's withdrawal, these other measures will be implemented.

We believe that our views and purposes in this respect are shared by many other nations and that a tranquil future for Israel is best assured by reliance upon that fact, rather than by an occupation in defiance of the overwhelming judgment of the world community.

DOCUMENT XI (c). EXCERPT FROM BROADCAST BY PRESIDENT
EISENHOWER, 20 FEBRUARY 1957.

The Government of Israel has not yet accepted, as adequate insurance of its own safety after withdrawal, the far-reaching United Nations Resolution of 2 February, plus the important declaration of United States policy made by our Secretary of State on 11 February.

Israel seeks something more. It insists on firm gurantees as a condition to withdrawing its forces of invasion.

This raises a basic question of principle. Should a nation which attacks and occupies foreign territory in the face of United Nations disapproval be allowed to impose conditions on its own withdrawal?

If we agree that armed attack can properly achieve the purposes of the assailant, then I fear we will have turned back the clock of international order. We will, in effect, have countenanced the use of force as a means of settling international differences and through this gaining national advantages.

I do not, myself, see how this could be reconciled with the charter of the United Nations. The basic pledge of all the members of the United Nations is that they will settle their international disputes by peaceful means and will not use force against the territorial integrity of another state.

If the United Nations once admits that international disputes can be settled by using force, then we will have destroyed the very foundation of the organization and our best hope of establishing a world order. That would be a disaster for us all.

I would, I feel, be untrue to the standards of the high office to which you have chosen me if I were to lend the influence of the United States to the proposition that a nation which invades another should be permitted to exact conditions for withdrawal.

Of course, we and all the members of the United Nations ought to support justice and conformity with international law. The first article of the charter states the purpose of the United Nations to be 'the suppression of acts of aggression or other breaches of the peace, and to bring about by peaceful means, and in conformity with . . . justice and international laws, adjustment or settlement of international disputes'. But it is to be observed that conformity with justice and international law are to be brought about 'by peaceful means'.

We cannot consider that the armed invasion and occupation of another country are 'peaceful means' or proper means to achieve justice and conformity with international law.

We do, however, believe that upon the suppression of the present act of aggression and breach of the peace there should be a greater effort by the United Nations and its members to secure justice and conformity with international law. Peace and justice are two sides of the same coin.

Perhaps the world community has been at fault in not having paid enough attention to this basic truth. The United States, for its part, will vigorously seek solutions of the problems of the area in accordance with justice and international law. And we shall in this great effort seek the association of other like-minded nations which realize, as we do, that peace and justice are in the long run inseparable.

But the United Nations faces immediately the problem of what to do next. If it does nothing, if it accepts the ignoring of its repeated resolutions calling for the withdrawal of invading forces, then it will have admitted failure. That failure would be a blow to the authority and influence of the United Nations in the world and to the hopes which humanity placed in the United Nations as the means of achieving peace with justice.

I do not believe that Israel's default should be ignored because the United Nations has not been able effectively to carry out its resolutions condemning the Soviet Union for its armed suppression of the people of Hungary. Perhaps this is a case where the proverb applies that two wrongs do not make a right.

No one deplores more than I the fact that the Soviet Union ignores the resolutions of the United Nations. Also no nation is more vigorous than is the United States in seeking to exert moral pressure against the Soviet Union, which by reason of its size and power, and by reason of its veto in the Security Council, is relatively impervious to other types of sanction.

The United States and other free nations are making clear by every means at their command the evil of Soviet conduct in Hungary. It would indeed be a sad day if the United States ever felt that it had to subject Israel to the same type of moral pressure as is being applied to the Soviet Union.

DOCUMENT XI (d). STATEMENT ON ISRAEL'S DECISION TO WITH-
DRAW FROM SHARM EL–SHEIKH AND THE GAZA STRIP BY ISRAELI
FOREIGN MINISTER, MRS. GOLDA MEIR, 1 MARCH 1957.

The Government of Israel is now in a position to announce its plans for full and prompt withdrawal from the Sharm el–Sheikh area and the Gaza Strip, in compliance with General Assembly resolution 1124 (XI) of 2 February 1957.

2. We have repeatedly stated that Israel has no interest in the strip of land overlooking the western coast of the Gulf of Aqaba. Our sole purpose has been to ensure that, on the withdrawal of Israel forces, continued freedom of navigation will exist for Israel and international shipping in the Gulf of Aqaba and the Straits of Tiran. Such freedom of navigation is a vital national interest for Israel, but it is also of importance and legitimate concern to the maritime Powers and to many states whose economies depend upon trade and navigation between the Red Sea and the Mediterranean Sea.

3. There has recently been an increasingly wide recognition that the Gulf of Aqaba comprehends international waters, in which the right of free and innocent passage exists.

4. On 11 February 1957, the Secretary of State of the United States of America handed to the Ambassador of Israel in Washington a memorandum dealing, among other things, with the subject of the Gulf of Aqaba and the Straits of Tiran. This statement discusses the rights of nations in the Gulf of Aqaba and declares the readiness of the United States to exercise those rights on its own behalf and to join with others in securing general recognition of those rights.

5. My Government has subsequently learned with gratification that other leading maritime Powers are prepared to subscribe to the doctrine set out in the United States memorandum of 11 February and have a similar intention to exercise their rights of free and innocent passage in the Gulf and the Straits.

6. General Assembly resolution 1125 (XI) of 2 February 1957 contemplates that units of the United Nations Emergency Force will move into the area of the Straits of Tiran on Israel's withdrawal. It is generally recognized that the function of the United Nations Emergency Force in that area includes the prevention of belligerent acts.

7. In this connection, my Government recalls the statements by the representative of the United States in the General Assembly on 28 January 1957 and 2 February, with reference to the function of the United Nations Emergency Force units which are to move into the area of the Straits of Tiran on Israel's withdrawal. The statement of 28 January, repeated on 2 February, said:

> . . . It is essential that units of the United Nations Emergency Force be stationed at the Straits of Tiran in order to achieve there the separation of Egyptian and Israel land and sea forces. This separation is essential until it is clear that the non-existence of any claim to belligerent rights has established in practice the peaceful conditions which must govern navigation in waters having such an international interest.

8. My Government has been concerned with the situation which would arise if the United Nations Emergency Force, having taken up its position in the area of the Straits of Tiran for the purpose of assuring non-belligerency, were to be withdrawn in conditions which might give rise to interference with free and innocent navigation and, therefore, to the renewal of hostilities. Such a premature cessation of the precautionary measures taken by the United Nations for the prevention of belligerent acts would prejudice important international interests and threaten peace and security. My Government has noted the assurance embodied in the Secretary-General's note of 26 February 1957, that any proposal for the withdrawal of the United Nations Emergency Force from the Gulf of Aqaba area would first come to the Advisory Committee on the United Nations Emergency Force, which represents the General Assembly in the implementation of its resolution 997 (ES-I) of 2 November 1956. This procedure will give the General Assembly an opportunity to ensure that no precipitate changes are made which would have the effect of increasing the possibility of belligerent acts. We have reason to believe that in such a discussion many Members of the United Nations would be guided by the view expressed by Mr Lodge, representative of the United States, on 2 February in favour of maintaining the United Nations Emergency Force in the Straits of Tiran until peaceful conditions were in practice assured.

9. In the light of these doctrines, policies and arrangements by the United Nations and the maritime Powers, my Government is confident that free and innocent passage for international and Israel shipping will continue to be fully maintained after Israel's withdrawal.

10. It remains for me now to formulate the policy of Israel both as a littoral state and as a country which intends to exercise its full rights of free passage in the Gulf of Aqaba and through the Straits of Tiran.

11. The Government of Israel believes that the Gulf of Aqaba comprehends international waters and that no nation has the right to prevent free and innocent passage in the Gulf and through the Straits giving access thereto, in accordance with the generally accepted definition of those terms in the law of the sea.

12. In its capacity as a littoral state, Israel will gladly offer port facilities to the ships of all nations and all flags exercising free passage in the Gulf of Aqaba. We have received with gratification the assurances of leading maritime Powers that they foresee a normal and regular flow of traffic of all cargoes in the Gulf of Aqaba. Israel will do nothing to impede free and innocent passage by ships of Arab countries bound to Arab ports or to any other destination. Israel is resolved on behalf of vessels of Israel registry to exercise the right of free and innocent passage and is prepared to join with others to secure universal respect of this right. Israel will protect ships of its own flag exercising the right of free and innocent passage on the high seas and in international waters.

13. Interference, by armed force, with ships of Israel flag exercising free and innocent passage in the Gulf of Aqaba and through the Straits of Tiran, will be regarded by Israel as an attack entitling it to exercise its inherent right of self-defence under Article 51 of the United Nations Charter and to take all such measures as are necessary to ensure the free and innocent passage of its ships in the Gulf and in the Straits.

14. We make this announcement in accordance with the accepted principles of international law under which all states have an inherent right to use their forces to protect their ships and their rights against interference by armed force. My Government naturally hopes that this contingency will not occur.

PART XII

Arab Unity and Israel
1964-65

THE RIVER JORDAN

As we have seen in the Introduction, the Arab world fell into disunity once more during the early 1960s. A powerful impetus to unity was, however, provided by Israel in 1963. With the near completion of a pumping station on Lake Tiberias, Israel showed that she intended to pump water from the Jordan river system for the purpose of irrigating the Negev. This did not really take the Arabs by surprise for as long before as 1959 Israel had declared her intention to take what she considered her share of the water in the absence of Arab agreement to an overall distribution plan. Such a plan was constructed in 1955 by the late Ambassador, Eric Johnston, a special representative of President Eisenhower. He managed to reconcile conflicting Arab and Israeli claims to the point where agreement at a *technical* level became possible. For purely *political* reasons, however, no agreement was actually ever reached between the Arab States and Israel. For the Arab States to sign an agreement with Israel would be tantamount to recognizing her right to exist. In Document XII (a) we have a brief summary of the Johnston Plan by one of the foremost students of this complex subject.

DOCUMENT XII (a). EXCERPT FROM GEORGIANA S. STEVENS, *Jordan River Partition*, PP. 14–17.

The Israeli argument for her present water programme rests on a *quantitative* water allocation proposed first in the United Nations, and later in a plan evolved in the course of negotiations sponsored by the United States government between 1953 and

1955. This was the Jordan Valley Unified Plan of 1955, often popularly named after its ambassador, Mr Eric Johnston.

In its final form, this plan apportioned some 60 per cent of the water of the Jordan River system to the Arab riparian states and about 40 per cent to Israel. This division was, at one point, accepted by technicians on both sides. While there was no formal document to this effect, Mr Johnston did receive the acquiescence of both sides in the formula allotting the following shares of the system's waters:

Jordan   480 mcm/year
Syria   132 mcm/year
Lebanon   35 mcm/year
Israel   The residue after these amounts claimed as necessary by the Arab riparians. This residual amount would vary with rains evaporation, and droughts, but was estimated at some 466 mcm. This was a reduction from Israel's last-ditch claims to some 550 mcm from the system, but it represented a compromise over the Arab technicians' original proposal of a 20 per cent share for Israel.

The Johnston Plan was concerned with the over-all development to the fullest possible extent of the meagre waters of the Jordan Basin, within the basin, for the benefit of all involved. These included the Syrians and Lebanese as riparians, but more particularly the Jordanians and the great number of unsettled Palestinian refugees in Jordan, as well as the Israelis. The plan did not include provisions for moving water out of the Jordan watershed—an Israeli idea strongly resisted by all the Arab countries. However, at one stage late in the negotiations, when Ambassador Johnston demonstrated that Israel *could* use her share of the waters inside the basin, the Arab technicians showed understanding and conceded, at that time, that Israel might do whatever she liked with her share, provided in-basin needs were fully satisfied.

The negotiations conducted by Ambassador Johnston between 1953 and 1955 have more than historic interest: (1) They marked the beginning of an important stage in American involvement in Middle Eastern Affairs, (2) they set a general pattern for peaceful division of a vital natural resource through patient negotiation, (3) they demonstrated the great sensitivity of the water question in the Middle East. As Mr Johnston undertook his first mission to the area, this political sensitivity over water became immediately apparent. This fact, in turn, had a sobering effect in Washington, where it had been hoped in the early years after the partition of Palestine that the two peoples involved could be brought to some economic accommodation with American financial help.

*

From the above document we can see what has been the crux of the problem. It is neither a matter of shortage of water, nor of failure to agree on its division. Although 77 per cent of the Jordan waters originate in Arab lands, the Arabs showed by their technical agreement in 1955 that they were prepared to give weight to other factors in determining the division to be made. In 1963 Israel simply flouted the Arab world by declaring, despite the Arabs, that she would withdraw from the Jordan up to the limits of the Johnston Plan and, worse, by announcing that the water would be used to irrigate the Negev, an acquisition by Israel in 1948 that has ever stuck in the Arab gullet. As matters have turned out, however, it has not all been plain sailing for Israel. Technical problems have been encountered which throw into question the whole policy of tapping the Jordan. These are explained in Document XII (b).

DOCUMENT XII (b). FURTHER EXCERPT FROM GEORGIANA S. STEVENS, *Jordan River Partition*, PP. 4–12.

Israel's national water conduit

Nineteen sixty-four was to have been the year in which the Negev desert would begin to receive Jordan water, piped from Jisr Banat Ya'qub (Bridge of the Daughters of Jacob) in northern Israel through the 100-mile conduit completed the previous winter. But, although the long-heralded water flow has, in fact, started, it does not come from the Jisr Banat Ya'qub, and very little of it will reach as far as the desert. Instead, the first stage of the flow, during which some 160–180 million cubic metres of water per year is being moved, is drawn from Lake Tiberias and will have to be used mainly to replenish the water tables along the coast. Because their calculated depletion was compounded by droughts, the tables are now so low that agriculture, particularly in Israel's vital citrus orchards, is threatened. Water rationing and strict government control of pumping in this heavily populated region have been in force for several years. Thus the immediate need to relieve the coastal water shortage has, at least temporarily, altered the emphasis on new settlement in the desert.

In addition to this overdraft on her underground water supplies, Israel has encountered two other natural obstacles to her water planning: (1) the salinity of Lake Tiberias and (2) leakage at the site of the first proposed reservoir at Bait Natufa in western Galilee.

Moreover, political obstacles forced Israel in 1953 to desist, at least temporarily, from using the fresher waters at Jisr Banat Ya'qub south of Lake Hulah as her takeoff site. This was due to the fact this site lies within the demilitarized zone between Israel and Syria, an area whose final sovereignty has not yet been determined by the United Nations. It was a Syrian complaint at the United Nations in 1953 that led to the suspension order by the UN Security Council. Subsequently, Israel moved her pumping site to man-hewn caves in a hill at Eshed Kinrot, on the northwest side of Lake Tiberias. This change has been costly, and its drawbacks are becoming increasingly apparent. Thus Syria's objections in 1953 succeeded in both reducing Israel's sweet-water potential and adding greatly to the cost of her National Conduit.

Another difficulty arose after Israel drained the marshes in the Hulah region: the flow of the river there became so rapid that diversion of its waters into the proposed conduit was technically impracticable.

Israel's dependence on diversion of waters from Lake Tiberias has markedly altered the prospects for extensive development of the Negev. Vertical economic expansion, which demands that every new water supply be applied to light industry, now has strong support from official proponents who engage in public debate with those officials who are dedicated to the horizontal extension of strategically placed farm settlements in the Negev. The supporters of vertical development argue that, for every water unit received, light industry contributes to national production thirty times as much as agriculture. . . .

The problem of salinity

The high salinity of Lake Tiberias (increased in drought years) makes the water currently being lifted at Eshed Kinrot and pumped south too salty for general agricultural use. This serious situation has become a political issue in Israel. The question was ventilated publicly in October 1963 at a symposium on the Water Project sponsored by the newspaper *Haaretz* in Tel Aviv. The tone of the meetings was reflected in the comment of one writer: ' . . . the salty waters of the aqueduct . . . have cast a pall on the joy of accomplishment'.

At the symposium, the Project authorities listened to bitter comments on the salinity of the waters being moved at a cost of $110 million. Mr Aharon Wiener[1] explained that the salinity in Lake Tiberias depends on rains but ranges between 270 and 380 parts of chloride to 1 million parts of water. Some of the salt springs in the lake had been detected only during the preceding two years. Whereas about half the chloride comes from visible springs near the edge of the lake, the other half comes from invisible seepage.

To solve the problem of salinity, several devices are being used: (1) mixing of fresh well water with that in the Conduit as it travels southward; (2) attempting to cap or divert the visible salt springs at the southern end of Lake Tiberias; and (3) boring under the lake and pumping the salt out. Such diversions will affect the fishing in the lake, but the need for water is so great that this disadvantage will not deter the water engineers.

Speaking at the 1963 symposium, Mr Dayan assumed that Israel was using 90 per cent of her total water potential of 1,800 mcm. He stated that Israel's territorial settlement was already 90 per cent of the country's potential. Thus he could not envision the establishment of many villages between Beersheba and Bait Shean Valley to the north. He suggested the state was small with a small potential.

Whether this view is extreme remains an unresolved question

[1] Director of Tahal (Water Planning for Israel, Ltd).

in Israel. Meanwhile, some farmers and citrus growers have made a case for delaying use of the conduit water rather than risking further salination of the soil. They accept 170 parts of chloride to 1 million parts of water as usable, except for orange growing, but object that even 170 particles per million (ppm) will eventually salinate the soil. Other have proposed waiting until Tiberias water can be mixed with converted sea water. Some agronomists even suggest that desalted sea water, despite the prevailing cost of conversion, is worth using to save profitable crops. Thus Mr Ra'anon Weitz, head of the Jewish Agency's Settlement Department, has compared the prevailing distilled water cost of I£1.30 per cubic metre with the cost of Conduit water at I£1.00 and found distilled water worth the price. The estimated cost of diverting the salt springs in Tiberias is some $6 million. If this figure is added to the $110 million spent so far on the National Conduit, the figure for delivered Tiberias water will be even higher.

In spite of the cost and technical difficulties involved, many Israeli planners, rejecting Mr Dayan's pessimistic views, continue to call officially for extensive Negev settlement. The Negev now has a population of 150,000. The aim is to add some 10,000 farm families by 1970. Even so, the figure of 10,000 is much lower than that set before the National Conduit's actual potential became apparent. Thus, extensive development of the desert seemed much further off in 1964 than ten years previously, at the height of Israel's optimism about her absorptive capacity. In 1964 the official estimate of her total population increase for the next decade was 750,000. This figure is considered high by outside experts, who calculate that fewer than 250,000 immigrants will have gone to Israel by 1975, and that her total population will grow more slowly than is officially estimated in Jerusalem.

What these calculations indicate is that, in the next decade, there is not likely to be overwhelming pressure on the land in Israel. If this is so, Israel need not feel driven to any of the expansionist moves that her Arab neighbours fear. In the light of this, the Egyptians' fear that dozens of strategically placed settlements might confront them in Sinai seems disproportionate for the time being. Neither the water nor the people will be available for such an internal expansion for 'millions' of settlers envisaged by the Arabs. At most, 60,000 new settlers can be absorbed in the Negev, provided 320 mcm of water per year can be delivered there by 1970.

Nevertheless, discounting a large population increase, Israel's water needs inevitably will grow as she strives for industrialization. It is a question, however, whether Israel any longer expects to rely on Jordan waters for her future industrial needs. The emphasis today is on scientific means of desalting sea water.

*

Notwithstanding the Israeli difficulties, the Arab view is that Israel has no right to divert water from the Jordan river, even within the amounts allowed for in the Johnston Plan. They also maintain that the lands in the Jordan basin need all the water available.

Yet what could the Arab States do? To decide this was the chief object of the January 1964 Arab Summit Conference. At its conclusion a rather general communiqué was issued which showed that the Arab States did not intend to go to war with Israel over the Jordan diversion. However, the Conference, it was announced, had 'adopted practical resolutions necessary to ward off the existing Zionist danger in the technical and defence fields'. What this meant in practice was no more than that plans to reduce the flow of the Jordan were being actively considered and that the Egyptian Lt-General Ali Amer was appointed to command a joint Arab force that it was intended to set up.

The communiqué of the September 1964 Summit Conference boldly proclaimed that work would begin immediately on the plans to develop the Jordan—which meant the diversion of the Jordan's upper tributaries. So to divert the upper Jordan tributaries would indeed make a serious, though not drastic, impact on the water supply to Israel. The threat to begin work was serious enough for the Israeli Prime Minister to respond:

(1) Israel will draw water from Lake Kinneret [Tiberias] within the limits of the quantities laid down in the unified Johnston plan.

(2) Israel will oppose unilateral and illegal measures by the Arab States and will act to protect her rights.

So the Arab States were faced with clear Israeli determination not to permit any diversion of the upper Jordan. As any diversion would have to be made very close to the Israeli frontier, the threat was all too real. Moreover, the Arab States found it difficult to agree on the very necessary measure of stationing troops on one another's territories. They feared their Arab neighbours as well as Israel. Then at the September 1965 (Casablanca) Summit Conference, Lt-General Amer is reported to have said that he would need four years to build up a ground and air force to match that of Israel; and what was more, any diversion scheme would be extremely expensive, technically difficult and unlikely to deprive Israel of all flow from the two tributaries concerned.

The diversion scheme has so far fallen through. At the September 1965 Summit it seems that all Arab States, save the UAR, Syria and Iraq, were either indifferent or opposed to it.

THE EMERGENCE OF THE PALESTINE LIBERATION ORGANIZATION

Arab frustration—the realization that war with Israel was impossible at the present—generated energy in support of a movement to involve the Palestinian refugees themselves in their own destiny. Behind this political initiative lay the promise of military effort by the Palestinians in the only sort of warfare that seemed to lend any hope for success against Israel —that of guerrilla bands. Vietnam, Algeria and Cuba were the ill-understood models in the minds of those who hoped for military success in the more rigorous application of this mode of warfare. As we have seen, guerrilla warfare was not new in the history of the Arab-Israeli conflict. Arab guerrilla attacks seriously disturbed Israel before the 1956 war.

The January 1964 Summit Conference communiqué announced that practical resolutions had been adopted in order to enable the Palestinian people to play their part in liberating their homeland and in determining their destiny. In effect, the Conference endorsed the establishment in September 1963 by the Arab League Council of a Palestine National Assembly, to be formed from among the refugees, and a Palestine Entity. Finance was forthcoming, though not with marked enthusiasm, from the richer and more traditionalist Arab States. On 28 May 1964 a Palestine National Congress convened in Arab Jerusalem, composed of 424 members. The Congress decided principally to set up a Palestine Liberation Organization, to open camps for training of all Palestinians for the liberation battle, and to place all under a unified Arab command. On 2 June 1964 the National Congress proclaimed the Palestine National Charter, of which excerpts are given below. A purely Palestinian movement was struggling into existence and seeking to equip itself with the symbols of legitimacy.

DOCUMENT XII (C). PRINCIPAL ARTICLES OF THE PALESTINE NATIONAL CHARTER, 2 JUNE 1964.

ARTICLE 2. Palestine, within the boundaries it had during the period of the British Mandate, is an indivisible territorial unit.

ARTICLE 6. Palestinians are those Arab citizens who, until 1947, had normally resided in Palestine, regardless of whether they have been evicted from it or have stayed in it. Anyone born after that date of a Palestinian father, whether inside Palestine or outside it, is also a Palestinian.

ARTICLE 17. The partition of Palestine in 1947 and the establishment of Israel are entirely illegal, regardless of the passage of time, because they were contrary to the will of the Palestinian people and its natural right in its homeland, and inconsistent with the general principles embodied in the Charter of the United Nations, particularly the right of self-determination.

ARTICLE 23. For the realization of the goals of this Charter and its principles, the Palestine Liberation Organization shall perform its complete role in the liberation of Palestine in accordance with the Constitution of this Organization.

ARTICLE 24. This Organization shall not exercise any territorial sovereignty over the West Bank region of the Hashemite Kingdom of Jordan, the Gaza Strip, or the Hemma area. Its activities in the liberational organizational, political and financial fields shall be on the national-popular level.

ARTICLE 25. This Organization shall be responsible for the direction of the Palestinian people in its struggle for the liberation of its homeland, in all liberational, organizational, political and financial fields, and also for whatever measures may be required by the Palestine case on the inter-Arab and international levels.

ARTICLE 26. The Liberation Organization shall co-operate with all Arab States, each according to its potentialities; and shall not interfere in the internal affairs of any Arab state.

*

ARAB SOLIDARITY AND ISRAEL

The success of Arab summitry in 1964 and 1965 in creating Arab unity was more apparent than real. The new Saudi Arabian ruler, Feisal, infuriated Nasser by his own attempts, shortly after the September 1965 Summit, to establish his own hegemony over the Arab world on the basis of an essentially Islamic appeal. There were basic differences in attitude between the 'Traditionalist' and 'revolutionary' regimes. The Arab Solidarity Pact signed at the third summit meeting was an attempt to paper over the cracks with its undertaking 'to respect the sovereignty of the Arab States and their regimes in accordance with their constitutions and laws and to refrain from interfering in their internal affairs.' Yet what had really been most instrumental in undermining the success of Arab summitry had been nothing less than an appeal by a noted Arab 'revolutionary' leader for some agreement with Israel. President Bourguiba of Tunisia said what Nasser would perhaps have liked to say, but could not thereafter say without losing the leadership of the 'revolutionary' sector of the Arab world. In this world Bourguiba was much abused for his initiative—and not least by the moderates for thus cutting the ground from under their feet. Surprisingly, but significantly, efforts to expel Tunisia from the Arab League were unsuccessful. Bourguiba claims his views on Palestine will prove correct in the long run. It will be noticed from the excerpts of his speech given below that he actually suggests no concessions to Israel. He recommends negotiation on the basis of the UN Partition Plan of 1947—a plan described by Abba Eban as 'a broken egg'. Israel rejected the substance of the Bourguiba proposals whilst welcoming negotiation. Bourguiba's sin among the Arabs was to dare to suggest negotiation—and therefore, recognition.

DOCUMENT XII (d). EXCERPTS FROM PRESIDENT BOURGUIBA'S
SPEECH TO STUDENTS, 21 APRIL 1965.

I should also like you to know just what I think about the Palestinian problem.

The future will confirm my opinions on this problem. I have expressed them elsewhere. I said we could meet in four or five years' time, when events would have proved me right. I do not just put forward arguments, however well-founded, but I act, for only action is of value. Without action to back them up, arguments remain inoperative. I do not try to impose my point of view. I do not consider myself infallible. I am a man of good will. I am in favour of frank and direct discussion. I should like to have this method adopted, not only by Destourian Youth but by Tunisian as a whole. . . .

On my tour of the Middle East, I visited the Palestinian refugees, whose fate moved me. Being by temperament an upright, serious man, I could not do other than observe that they are being soothed with illusions and that if this goes on, they will be in the same situation twenty years ahead. I have already had the opportunity of telling the Arabs that when one sees one has made a mistake, something else must be found. . . .

Rather than admit this, they try to find excuses. I therefore spoke directly to the refugees to tell them that passion, the desire to return, was entirely natural, that the strength of feelings should in some way act as a driving force, an engine, but an engine by itself may well race if there is no brain capable of controlling the power produced and directing it on the path leading to the objective. However, those concerned fail to see this. It is unimaginable that this notion of the tactics of efficacy should be beyond them. When I tell them that there is possibly a way of inconveniencing Israel, they do no more than insult that country. I remind them that for the last seventeen years the Arabs have been doing nothing but that, without any result. When I talk of tactical methods, they talk of principles, justice, colonialism. But who denies that injustice has been done? . . ·

It seems that certain leaders do not seriously believe in the liberation of Palestine and would gladly forego my advice. This is the real issue. The state of mind prevalent in that part of the world is the same as we came across in Tunisia in Old Destourian circles, thirty years ago. They have found nobody to work out and propose an alternative solution, to open up a new path. For the last seventeen years the course taken has proved a dead end. We, however, applied our method for ten years only and the results are to be seen. At the time, Palestine was in a much better situation than Tunisia. It seemed to be on the eve of independence, as the troops of seven Arab States had made a move to liberate it. You know the outcome. . . .

I have no responsibilities in the Palestinian affair. Years ago I said: in view of Tunisia's geographical situation, it was unthinkable that I should assume responsibility for the struggle in the Palestinian affair, although the Palestinians are our brothers. I only think of helping them by offering advice, which they are free to reject. Any negotiations must be with the Palestinians, not with me. And the Israelis must also clearly say whether they agree to negotiate on the bases I have suggested. My proposal is that all the United Nations resolutions be applied, that is to say the resolution on partition which would make it possible to restore to the Arab Palestinian State a large part of the territories occupied by Israel today and the resolution on the return of the refugees—both decisions being closely linked for reasons of equilibrium. If the Israelis are in good faith, if they sincerely wish to accept such a compromise, they must say so or must at least agree to negotiate on this basis. So far they have not said that they accept this basis for discussion. They merely say they are ready to negotiate with Bourguiba. On what basis would Bourguiba be invited to go to Israel or to receive Israeli representatives? Bourguiba has made precise suggestions. If Israel accepts them a dialogue should be opened with Palestinians and with the Arabs.

The Arabs indeed bear a heavy responsibility in the drama of Palestine, which explains their confusion. War cries and propaganda duels over the radio show that, in their hearts, they feel they have a large responsibility in this drama, since they encouraged thousands of persons to abandon their homes with the promise that they would bring them back by force of arms.

I shall state the problem clearly at the next Arab summit meeting, which is to be held at Rabat. It will be difficult to vacillate or to shirk responsibilities once Israel has agreed to negotiate on the bases I have outlined. If such negotiations were to succeed, they would make it possible not only to recover a large part of the territory of Palestine and restore their homes to the refugees but also at the same time to diminish the climate of war and diminish tension and hatred. Everybody would then be able to breathe once again and their situation would be a distinct improvement on the present one. Matters might well go further and Arabs and Jews might perhaps come to modify their outlook and a climate of co-operation be established between them for the mutual benefit of both sides. It is certain that the situation thus created would be greatly preferable to the present situation in which the two sides face each other and deliberately ignore each other, while Israeli influence steadily gains ground in Africa and Asia.

So this is my position. It is not in the least based on some desire to make me the spokesman of the Palestinian people. I have wanted to give my view on the solution of the Palestinian problem because I am an Arab and the situation of the refugees makes me suffer. Had I been guided by selfish motives I might have used the slogans they are so fond of and assured them that we were ready to die for Palestine. But I feel incapable of such cynicism. I consider it a tragic mistake to try to make our suffering brothers believe that we undertake to see that they return, although no Arab country has an offensive strategy for the liberation of Palestine. This is what emerges from the declarations of Arab staff officers who all talk of amassing arms in order to repulse aggression from Israel. But in actual fact, is any such aggression likely?

Need we recall that in 1956 the entire world stood up to Israel and forced it to withdraw? The same powers which halted Zionist aggression against the Arab countries will intervene to stop the Arabs attacking Israel.

Consequently, all this ironware, assembled at great expense by the army will make no difference to the *status quo*. Likewise, the present arms race is quite useless. Its immediate result is a waste of resources which, with upheavals and *coups d'état*, is jeopardizing the development of the Arab countries. To prepare for an offensive war which cannot be won or for a defensive war which will not take place is a false problem.

The United Nations resolutions

On the other hand, to demand respect for United Nations resolutions cannot but serve our cause, even if Israel refuses to agree. For we would then be on the side of legality, which would put us in a more favourable position in the event of armed conflict. It is quite certain that political positions contribute to the success of armed struggle in so far as they justify it or legitimize it in international opinion. It is important to make sure that everybody is not against us.

My point of view has been expressed clearly. It is now Israel's turn to talk. If the Israelis accept the bases I have proposed, they will, of course, have to negotiate with the Palestinians, who are the principal people involved. In this case the situation would be perfectly clear. But if they reject them, on what bases could the dialogue proceed? What would be the use of going to Tel Aviv or of receiving representatives here, and thus exposing myself to accusations of treachery. Of course I cannot lend myself to this type of misunderstanding.

I do not say that if I had been the Palestinian spokesman I would not have agreed to discussions with the Israelis, as I agreed to discussions with the French whenever I found them ready.

In short, if we have proof that Israel takes matters seriously, we are prepared to contact the other Arab countries and ask them what position should be adopted. But as long as Israel has not agreed to negotiations on the basis I have mentioned I have nothing to put to the Arab leaders. Besides, I know that it is difficult for them to resist certain demagogic tendencies and to appear in the eyes of their own public to be insufficiently patriotic and ardent in the defence of Palestine. This is why I have not too many illusions about the chances of success in this type of venture. Moreover, it should be carried out on firm bases and not on vague rumours about the possibility of contacts with Bourguiba, in Tel Aviv or Tunis. Such rumours are quite unfounded, because Bourguiba has not the slightest intention of putting himself forward as a negotiator in this matter.

L

If the Israelis agree with our suggestions, they should contact our Arab brothers to see what they think. This contact between representatives of the different parties involved can take place in Rome or in any other foreign town. We could facilitate it and, in agreement with President Nasser, try to achieve a result which will change the entire face of the Near East.

But all this does not seem likely to come about just yet. The Israelis do not for the time being want to yield one inch of territory at Jaffa, St John of Acre, Nazareth or elsewhere. On their side, the Arabs mistrust each other so much that it is at present difficult for them to abandon the positions illustrated by Dr Kamhaoui's behaviour at the Congress of Arab Doctors recently held in Tunis.

The Congress of Arab Doctors was not the ideal occasion for discussion of the Palestinian question. But that was beside the point. What mattered to this doctor was to make an impassioned speech. After this, feeling he had salved his conscience, he left it to others to look after the future of the Palestinians. More important for him than the liberation of Palestine was the prospect of cutting an intransigent, heroic figure in the Palestinian cause. He refused to recognize Israel and repeated tirelessly that the land of Palestine could not shelter both Jews and Arabs. He merely forgot that the Jews had been there for the last seventeen years and intended to stay there without bothering too much about what we thought and without taking our attitudes seriously.

PART XIII

The Outbreak of War, 1967

STEPS TO WAR

By 1967 guerrilla warfare waged from Syria had reached new dimensions. Severe Israeli warnings were followed by severe retaliatory action. Nasser claimed that in May 1967 these Israeli warnings to Syria went so far as to threaten to overthrow the Damascus government. If true this was, of course, a very grave development. Nasser referred to the alleged threat in his speech of 25 May 1967, of which we give an excerpt in Document XIII (a).

DOCUMENT XIII (a). EXCERPT FROM SPEECH BY PRESIDENT NASSER, 25 MAY 1967.

Israel has been clamouring since 1956. They spoke of Israel's competence and high standard of training. It was backed in this by the West and the Western press. They capitalized on the Sinai campaign, where no fighting actually took place because we withdrew to confront Britain and France.

Today we have a chance to prove the fact. We have, indeed, a chance to make the world see matters in their true perspective. We are now face to face with Israel. On 12 May a very impertinent statement was made. Anyone reading this statement must believe that these people are so boastful and deceitful and one cannot simply remain silent. The statement said that Israeli commanders announced they would carry out military operations against Syria in order to occupy Damascus and overthrow the Syrian Government. On the same day the Israeli Premier, Eshkol, made a very threatening statement against Syria. At the same time the commentaries said that Israel believed that Egypt could not make a move because it was bogged down in the Yemen. . . .

147

On 13 May we received accurate information that Israel was concentrating on the Syrian border huge armed forces of about 11 to 13 brigades. These forces were divided into two fronts, one south of Lake Tiberias and the other north of the lake. The decision made by Israel at this time was to carry out an attack against Syria starting on 17 May. On 14 May we took action, discussed the matter and contacted our Syrian brethren. The Syrians also had this information. Based on this information Lt-General Mahmud Fawzi left for Syria to co-ordinate matters. We told them that we had decided that if Syria was attacked, Egypt would enter the battle right from the start. This was the situation on 14 May. Forces began to move in the direction of Sinai to take up their normal positions.

News agencies reported yesterday that these military movements must have been the result of a previously well-laid plan. I say that the sequence of events determined the plan. We had no plan before 13 May because we believed that Israel would not have dared to make such an impertinent statement.

*

That a statement including a threat to overthrow the Syrian regime was made by the Israeli Chief of Staff, General Rabin is asserted by E. Rouleau (E. Rouleau, J. F. Held and J. S. Lacouture, *Israël et Les Arabes: Le Troisième Combat* (Paris, 1967), p. 74). But this point has been investigated by W. Laqueur, who, in his authoritative account of the war, writes, 'No one made a statement about overthrowing the Syrian government'. (Walter Laqueur, *The Road to War 1967. The Origins of the Arab-Israel Conflict* (London, 1968), p. 73). He sees the origins of the alleged threats in a United Press dispatch from Jerusalem on 12 May. The dispatch claimed to be inspired by a 'highly placed Israeli source', which spoke of military action to overthrow the regime if Syria-based guerrilla action continued. On the allegation in Nasser's speech about Israeli troop movements we should note that UN observers on the Syrian frontier in fact reported no significant troop movements.

If it is not the case that Nasser was simply looking for a pretext for war—there is a hint of this in a speech of the 26 May—then we must see the war as the last link in a chain of events that stretches far back. Indeed we need to go back to the instabilities of Syrian politics, to the reasons for Syrian support of *El Fatah*. But then if we ask why *El Fatah* existed, we find the answer, as we have seen, still further back in the thicket of Arab-Israeli relations.

Could the chain of events that led to war have been broken at some point? Could Nasser have stopped himself from stumbling into war? Given that he could not avoid putting on a show of strength for the sake of Syria, could he not have stopped there? It was hardly necessary for Egypt to close the Straits of Tiran to Israel as a warning not to attack Syria. This move was in fact justified by Nasser as a return to the *status quo ante* 1956. One interesting suggestion put forward to explain the closure of the Straits is that Nasser did not thereby seek to provoke war (Rouleau, Held and Lacouture, op. cit., p. 110), but rather was intent on creating a position of advantage for himself from which he could negotiate a settlement with Israel. On this thesis he envisaged retaining sovereignty over the Straits—and an Egyptian military presence there—in exchange for certain concessions he would then be in a position to make to Israel. This is probably too fanciful. It seems more probable that Nasser overestimated the strength of the moderates in Israeli politics and the influence of the United States over Israel. He was right to think that the United States would keep out for fear of Russia, but wrong if he thought that Israeli resolve would thereby be seriously undermined, or that Israel could not win a war without western help. To some degree Nasser was perhaps carried away by the general Arab enthusiasm for war. Nasser's spokesman, Haykal, in the newspaper *Al Ahram*, had certainly declared after the closure of the Straits that war was inevitable.

In the statement by President Nasser which we give below (Document XIII (b)) Nasser justifies the closure of the Straits as righting a historical wrong. There is certainly little reason for thinking that Nasser did not really expect U Thant to comply with his request for the withdrawal of the UN Emergency Force—that it was a gesture. Egyptian troops had rendered the Force's Sharm el–Sheikh positions ineffective before the request could be answered; and once Sharm el-Sheikh was occupied Nasser could hardly leave the Straits open. To have done so eould have forfeited respect for his leadership of the Arab world. Eban's view that future historians would see the withdrawal of the UN Emergency Force as the crucial step in the crisis may well turn out to be true. To re-assert control over Sharm el–Sheikh is shown in the document below to be a particular point of pride for the Arabs. The opportune moment seemed to present itself in 1967.

DOCUMENT XIII (b). STATEMENT BY PRESIDENT NASSER TO A PRESS CONFERENCE, 28 MAY 1967.

I am pleased to meet today the representatives of the world and Arab press who are making great efforts to cover the important events which are preoccupying us all. As you all know, the press does not only cover events: it also participates in creating them. I am referring here to a valuable aspect of the press. If the authenticity of reports on any event is important, the form in which we present those reports to the people is no less important. In other words, there is the topic and there is the form in which we present it to others. I feel it is our duty to present to you a picture of reality as we see it. This is part of our responsibility with regard to a situation which may mean peace or war to the entire Arab world and whose effects and repercussions may be felt even beyond the Arab world.

On the other hand, I feel that you who are here on a sacred mission, namely, the freedom of the press, which also has its serious side, namely, influencing world sentiment on certain problems—have the right to ask me to meet you and to answer your questions in person.

I tell you frankly that we are not asking you for anything or trying to keep anything from you. We want to tell you the truth on anything that interests you and to give you details on events as we see them. I have already told you that this is our duty especially in regard to a question concerning peace or war. We are not concerned about the rest. It depends on your professional conscience and your responsibility to the multitudes you serve in all the countries of the world.

I want to add to this preamble before answering your questions. I wish to draw your attention to an important point. The problem all of us are experiencing now and are concerned about

—all of us, statesmen, journalists and the multitudes of peoples —is neither the problem of the Straits of Tiran nor the withdrawal of the UNEF. All these are side issues of a bigger and more serious problem—the problem of the aggression which has taken place and continues to take place on the Arab homeland of Palestine and the continuous threat posed by that aggression against all Arab countries. This is the original problem.

Those who think that the crucial issues of nations and peoples can die and succumb to the symptoms of old age with the passage of time are grossly mistaken. Individuals may succumb to the symptoms of old age, including forgetfulness, but peoples are immortal, rejuvenescent and eternally young. This is specially true in this case, as aggression is not over. It continues to take place and in fact tries to affect and dominate a wider area.

We completely refuse to confine our concern to the subject of the Straits of Tiran or the withdrawal of the UNEF. In our opinion neither topic is open to question. The Straits of Tiran are Egyptian territorial waters, and Egypt has the right of sovereignty over them. No power, no matter how strong—and I am saying this quite clearly so that every side will know its position—can affect or circumvent the rights of Egyptian sovereignty. Any attempt of this kind will be an aggression against the Egyptian people and the entire Arab nation and will result in unimaginable damage to the aggressors.

The subject of the withdrawal of the UNEF is also not open to question. The UNEF came to our territory in the circumstances of the tripartite aggression, the disgraceful collusion which destroyed the moral and material reputation of all the perpetrators. All the secrets of the collusion have been unearthed. They condemn the plotters and brand them with contempt. As I have already said, the UNEF came to our territory with our approval, and its continued existence here depended on this approval. We have now withdrawn our approval and the UN Secretary-General responded faithfully, honestly and honourably to our request. The question of the UNEF is now completely over and is no longer open to discussion.

The circumstances in which we requested the withdrawal of the UNEF are also known to all of you. Syria was threatened.

There was a plan to invade Syria. Measures had been taken and a date set for the implementation of this plan. In the meantime, the voices of Israeli officials were heard openly calling for an advance on Damascus. Naturally, we could not stand idly by when Syria was being threatened with invasion. We could not allow this to be done to Syria or to any Arab country. The UAR armed forces, however, had to move to positions from which they could effectively deter aggression. Many natural developments followed our action. These developments were a surprise to everyone except those who had spread biased propaganda against the Arab nation. They were now caught in the trap they had laid for others. They lied and lied until they believed themselves. Reality therefore took them by surprise.

We do not believe that any sincere man can describe any measure we have taken in the past two weeks as an aggression or even find in it any trace of aggression. Our forces went to Sinai to deter aggression. In the Straits of Tiran we have exercised the rights of Egyptian sovereignty. Any interference with these rights will itself be an aggression. Why? This takes us back to the source, origin, reality and core of the problem. Israel was created by imperialism and by the forces seeking to dominate the Arab nation. We are not the only ones to say this. It is said by others who are today defending the Israeli aggression. They say it on every occasion. Nearly word for word, they say: They have created Israel and are responsible for its security. They have given Israel the biggest part of Arab Palestine. After this first and biggest aggression, they continued to support its aggressive line.

We must now ask ourselves many questions. What has Israel done with the UN resolutions of 1947, 1948 and 1949? The answer: Israel threw them away. What has Israel done with the Security Council's armistice resolutions? The answer: Israel occupied more Palestinian territory after these resolutions. The best example is the port of Eilat, which Israel built on Arab soil at Umm ar-Rashrash. Israel occupied this area after the armistice resolutions. The armistice agreements were signed in February 1949. In March of that year Israel occupied this area, thus trampling on all the Security Council resolutions and the armistice agreements when the ink with which they were signed had hardly dried.

What has Israel done with the rights of Arab refugees and the UN resolutions concerning them? The answer: The refugees are still displaced from their usurped homeland. What has Israel done with the armistice commissions themselves and their members who, in their mission, represented the UN? The answer: When it decided to occupy the demilitarized zone of Al-Auja in 1955 Israel did not hesitate to arrest the truce observers to keep them away from the zone. In any case this was not strange. Israeli aggression went so far as to assassinate the chief truce observer Count Bernadotte, whose report was not favourable to Israeli designs.

What did Israel do in 1956? What does all that Israel did in 1956 mean? The answer: Israel played its role as an imperialist tool. Its role was disgraceful as is now clear from all that has been published about the Suez secrets. Yet Israel claimed victory. In addition to that it tried—and this was obvious—to annex a part of Egyptian territory, namely, Sinai. Ben Gurion announced it. After Suez, Israel's aggressive record continued until the recent threat to Syria, which set off the present crisis. This is the source of the problem. Any attempt to ignore or condone this problem is unacceptable. This is the matter on which the entire Arab nation stands. It is ready to take it up to the last with Israeli aggression and with the United States, which is continuing to back this aggression politically, economically and militarily.

*

IMPORTANCE OF THE STRAITS OF TIRAN TO ISRAEL

How important is unhindered passage through the Straits to Israel? There was some hesitation in Israel after the Straits were closed, but real hesitation was on whether to rely on the United States and other powers to keep the Straits open, or whether Israel should go to war herself to achieve this end. On the economic importance of the port of Eilat there can be little doubt. The document below provides a general view of the factors involved.

DOCUMENT XIII (c). HAROLD JACKSON, 'EGYPTIAN BLOCKADE WOULD CLOSE ISRAEL'S OIL PORT', *The Guardian*, 23 MAY 1967.

The most alarming aspect for Israel of a blockade of the port of Eilat would be the threat to the country's oil supplies. Although no precise figures are officially published for security reasons, a certain amount of delving among different statistics clearly brings out that about 90 per cent of the oil requirements come through Eilat.

According to a magazine published by the Department of Information in Jerusalem, three million tons of oil pass through Eilat annually. The official handbook produced by the Ministry of Foreign Affairs Information Division says that domestic oil production in 1966 was 200,000 tons and that this covers 8 per cent of the country's fuel needs. This in fact gives an aggregate of 2.5 million tons, but some discrepancy is inevitable since the figures have obviously been rounded off.

Thriving port

The oil is piped straight from Eilat to the storage terminal and refinery at Haifa, on the Mediterranean coast. If the situation in the Gulf of Aqaba becomes critical, supplies, which are believed to come largely from Persia, could obviously be diverted there. But this would involve a costly and slow voyage around Africa and through the Mediterranean. It might also involve an uncomfortable hiatus in shipments at a time when the strategic reserves could be depleted rapidly.

Eilat has been the major growth point in the south of Israel since the end of the Egyptian blockade of the Straits of Tiran in 1956. Since the end of the Suez campaign it has grown from a garrison settlement of a thousand or so to a thriving port and holiday resort of about 13,000. Special tax concessions to settlers who stay for two years or more have helped in its growth. Two years ago the harbour facilities were considerably extended on land acquired by the simple means of pushing one of the abundant surrounding mountains into the sea.

Its main purpose in exports is to serve the growing chemical industry in the area around the south of the Dead Sea. The enormous harvest of common salt, magnesium chloride, potassium chloride, magnesium bromide, and calcium chloride, that is reaped from its inhospitable depths goes in increasing amounts to East Africa, India and Japan. Much of it forms the basis for badly needed fertilizers in the developing countries.

These markets are among the fastest-growing sectors of Israel's foreign trade and anything that interrupts its orderly progress will cause anxiety. Altogether about 20 per cent of the country's exports passes through Eilat. Here again, cargo could be diverted to Haifa or to the new modern port of Ashdod which is being developed.

New roads

Domestically, the continued development of Eilat, which depends on its growth as a port, is also the key to the development of the Southern Negev. As communications southwards are built up to meet the port's growing needs, and as the increase in its population leads to increased generating capacity and water supplies, so the civilization of the surrounding biblical wilderness laps out in spreading waves.

Two brand-new roads already cut through the forbidding crags of the Negev and the railway is gradually extending from Beersheba. This is social, as well as economic, investment, but its continuation depends on the functioning of the country's southern outlet. Israel will not collapse if Eilat is paralysed, but it would need to take in its belt a hole or two.

*

Was it really the Egyptian closure of the Straits that made Israel go to war? There is clear evidence that what most worried Israeli leaders, particularly the generals, was the Egyptian build-up of troops in the desert. For reasons of morale and for the sake of the national economy Israel can hardly afford to keep its army, predominantly a *citizen* army, under arms for a long period. But also important was the lack of any real prospect that the United States and other powers would guarantee a passage through the Straits for their own and Israeli ships, using force if necessary. It has been aptly said, 'If neither Egypt nor Israel had struck the first blow, there would have been no war. But neither would there have any re-opening of the Gulf of Aqaba' (Theodore Draper, *Israel and World Politics* (London, 1967), p. 101). There was extreme reluctance on the part of the maritime powers to use force to keep open the

Straits; many baulked at signing a proposed Maritime Declaration which asserted the right of passage on behalf of all shipping sailing under their own flags. The Israelis had little faith in the powers. The crucial meeting between President Johnson and the Israeli Foreign Minister, Abba Eban, on 26 May, conveys nicely the strength of the United States' 'commitment' to maintain the freedom of the Gulf of Aqaba. An authoritative account of the meeting is given below (Document XIII (d)).

DOCUMENT XIII (d). ACCOUNT OF PRESIDENT JOHNSON'S MEETING WITH ABBA EBAN, 26 MAY 1967, BY THEODORE DRAPER, *Israel and World Politics*, PP. 90–1.

The key meeting between President Johnson and Foreign Minister Eban, together with their main advisers and leading officials, took place on 26 May. Eban made an eloquent statement of the Israeli position, which he defined as one of 'surrender or fight'. The President made clear his determination to live up to the commitments made by previous administrations, especially the assurance given by the Eisenhower administration in 1957 to uphold the right of Israel's 'free and innocent' passage in the Gulf of Aqaba. But he also drew attention to the constitutional and congressional difficulties to be faced before the United States could take any action. In the end, Eban put the following question to the President: Would the United States make every possible effort to assure that the Straits of Tiran and the Gulf of Aqaba would be open to free and innocent passage? The President answered: Yes. In return Eban was asked for two weeks to enable the United States to attempt to settle the dispute peacefully.

The Israelis left the meeting with President Johnson feeling that he sincerely intended to take whatever action might be necessary to open the Straits of Tiran and the Gulf of Aqaba to Israeli shipping. But they had also been made acutely aware of the fact that he did not feel that he could act on his own and that much would depend on the international and domestic support he might be able to muster. Meanwhile, Mr Johnson had taken the precaution of obtaining the backing of former President Eisenhower. The latter was called to give his opinion of what the United States had committed itself to in 1957, and he forthrightly answered that he considered it a 'commitment of honour' for the United States to live up to his implicit assurance to former Israeli Prime Minister Ben Gurion that the Straits would be kept open. Eban returned home recommending that President Johnson should be given the chance to see what he could do to reopen the Straits of Tiran one way or another.

*

THE WITHDRAWAL OF THE UN EMERGENCY FORCE

The decision by the UN Secretary-General, U Thant, to withdraw the UN Emergency Force stationed in Sinai gave rise to much criticism. This was reinforced by the publication of a private document prepared by the former UN Secretary-General, the late Dag Hammarskjöld. Of this document U Thant had no knowledge when making his decision. The two documents given below throw light on what, as we have seen, is regarded by some as the most important decision made in the events preceding the June war. Although this is disputable, at least Nasser did not have to face the opprobrium that would have followed any attempt to disarm the Emergency Force. It is arguable that a stronger line by the Secretary-General would have made Nasser hesitate before occupying Sharm el–Sheikh.

We give first an excerpt from the former Secretary-General's private memorandum, which suggests some limitation on the withdrawal of the UN Emergency Force without reference to the General Assembly. In his statement U Thant denies the relevance of the Hammarskjöld memorandum.

DOCUMENT XIII (e). EXCERPT FROM PRIVATE MEMORANDUM ON UN EMERGENCY FORCE BY FORMER UN SECRETARY-GENERAL, DAG HAMMARSKJÖLD, 5 AUGUST 1957.

In my effort to follow up the situation, which prevailed after the exchange in which different stands had been maintained by Egypt and by me, I was guided by the consideration that Egypt constitutionally had an undisputed right to request the withdrawal of the troops, even if initial consent had been given, but that, on the other hand, it should be possible on the basis of my own stand as finally tacitly accepted, to force them into an agreement in which they limited their freedom of action as to withdrawal by making a request for withdrawal dependent upon the completion of the task—a question which, in the UN obviously would have to be submitted to interpretation by the General Assembly.

The most desirable thing, of course, would have been to tie Egypt by an agreement in which they declared that withdrawal should take place only if so decided by the General Assembly. But in this naked form, however, the problem could never have been settled. I felt that the same was true of an agreement to the effect that withdrawal should take place upon 'agreement on withdrawal' between the UN and the Egyptian Government. However, I found it worthwhile to try a line, very close to the second one, according to which Egypt would declare to the United Nations that it would exert all its sovereign rights with regard to the troops on the basis of a good-faith interpretation of the tasks of the force. The United Nations should make a reciprocal commitment to maintain the force as long as the task was not completed. If such a dual statement was introduced in an agreement between the parties, it would be obvious that the procedure in case of a request from Egypt for the withdrawal of UNEF would be as follows. The matter would at once be brought before the General Assembly. If the General Assembly found that the task was completed, everything would be all right. If they found that the task was not completed and Egypt, all the same, maintained its stand and enforced the withdrawal, Egypt would break the agreement with the United Nations. Of course Egypt's freedom of action could under no circumstances be limited but by some kind of agreement. The device I used meant only that instead of limiting their rights by a basic understanding requesting an agreement *directly concerning withdrawal*, we created an obligation to reach agreement on the fact that the tasks were completed, and, thus, *the conditions for a withdrawal established*.

I elaborated a draft text for an agreement along the lines I had in mind during the night between 15 and 16 November in Capodichino [Italy]. I showed the text to Fawzi at our first talk on 16 November and I discussed practically only this issue with Nasser for seven hours in the evening and night of 17 November.

Nasser, in this final discussion, where the text I had proposed was approved with some amendments, showed that he very fully understood that, by limiting their freedom of action in the way I proposed, they would take a very serious step, as it would mean that the question of the extent of the task would become decisive for the relations between Egypt and the United Nations and would determine Egypt's political freedom of action. He felt, not without justification, that the definition given of the task in the UN texts was very loose and that, tying the freedom of action of Egypt to the concept of the task—which had to be interpreted also by the General Assembly—and doing so in a written agreement, meant that he accepted a far-reaching and unpredictable restriction. To shoot the text through in spite of Nasser's strong wish to avoid this, and his strong suspicion of the legal construction—especially of the possible consequences of differences of views regarding the task—I felt obliged, in the course of the discussion, to threaten three times, that unless an agreement of this type was made, I would have to propose the immediate withdrawal of the troops. If any proof would be necessary for how the text of the agreement was judged by President Nasser, this last mentioned fact tells the story.

It is obvious that, with a text of the content mentioned approved by Egypt, the whole previous exchange of views was superseded by a formal and explicit recognition by Egypt of the stand I had taken all through, in particular on 9 and 12 November. The previous exchange of cables cannot any longer have any interpretative value as only the text of the agreement was put before the General Assembly and approved by it with the concurrence of Egypt and as its text was self-contained and conclusive. All further discussion, therefore, has to start from the text of the agreement, which is to be found in document A/3375. The interpretation of the text must be the one set out above.

DOCUMENT XIII (f). EXCERPTS FROM REPORT BY UN SECRETARY-GENERAL, U THANT, ON THE WITHDRAWAL OF THE UN EMERGENCY FORCE, 18 MAY 1967.

The causes of the present crisis

32. It has been said rather often in one way or another that

the withdrawal of UNEF is a primary cause of the present crisis in the Near East. This is, of course, a superficial and over-simplified approach. As the Secretary-General pointed out in his report of 26 May 1967 to the Security Council (S/7906), this view 'ignores the fact that the underlying basis for this and other crisis situations in the Near East is the continuing Arab-Israel conflict which has been present all along and of which the crisis situation created by the unexpected withdrawal of UNEF is the latest expression'. The Secretary-General's report to the Security Council of 19 May 1967 (S/7896) described the various elements of the increasingly dangerous situation in the Near East prior to the decision of the Government of the United Arab Republic to terminate its consent for the presence of UNEF on its territory.

33. The United Nations Emergency Force served for more than ten years as a highly valuable instrument in helping to maintain quiet along the line between Israel and the United Arab Republic. Its withdrawal revealed in all its depth and danger the undiminishing conflict between Israel and her Arab neighbours. The withdrawal also made immediately acute, the problem of access for Israel to the Gulf of Aqaba through the Strait of Tiran—a problem which had been dormant for over ten years only because of the presence of UNEF. But the presence of UNEF did not touch the basic problem of the Arab-Israel conflict—it merely isolated, immobilized and covered up certain aspects of that conflict. At any time in the last ten years either of the parties could have reactivated the conflict and if they had been determined to do so UNEF's effectiveness would automatically have disappeared. When, in the context of the whole relationship of Israel with her Arab neighbours, the direct confrontation between Israel and the United Arab Republic was revived after a decade by the decision of the United Arab Republic to move its forces up to the line, UNEF at once lost all usefulness. In fact, its effectiveness as a buffer and as a presence had already vanished, as can be seen from the chronology given above, even before the request for its with-drawal had been received by the Secretary-General from the Government of the United Arab Republic. In recognizing the extreme seriousness of the situation thus created, its true cause, the continuing Arab-Israeli conflict, must also be recognized. It

is entirely unrealistic to maintain that that conflict could have been solved, or its consequences prevented, if a greater effort had been made to maintain UNEF's presence in the area against the will of the Government of the United Arab Republic.

The decision on UNEF's withdrawal

34. The decision to withdraw UNEF has been frequently characterized in various quarters as 'hasty', 'precipitous', and the like, even, indeed, to the extent of suggesting that it took President Nasser by surprise. The question of the withdrawal of UNEF is by no means a new one. In fact, it was the negotiations on this very question with the Government of Egypt which, after the establishment of UNEF by the General Assembly, delayed its arrival while it waited in a staging area at Capodichino airbase, Naples, Italy, for several days in November 1956. The Government of Egypt, understandably, did not wish to give permission for the arrival on its soil of an international force, unless it was assured that its sovereignty would be respected and a request for withdrawal of the Force would be honoured. Over the years, in discussions with representatives of the United Arab Republic, the subject of the continued presence of UNEF has occasionally come up, and it was invariably taken for granted by United Arab Republic representatives that if their Government officially requested the withdrawal of UNEF the request would be honoured by the Secretary-General. There is no record to indicate that this assumption was ever questioned. Thus, although the request for the withdrawal of UNEF came as a surprise, there was nothing new about the question of principle nor about the procedure to be followed by the Secretary-General. It follows that the decision taken by him on 18 May 1967 to comply with the request for the withdrawal of the Force was seen by him as the only reasonable and sound action that could be taken. The actual withdrawal itself, it should be recalled, was to be carried out in an orderly, dignified, deliberate and not precipitate manner over a period of several weeks. The first troops in fact left the area only on 29 May.

The possibility of delay

35. Opinions have also been frequently expressed that the decision to withdraw UNEF should have been delayed pending consultations of various kinds, or that efforts should have been made to resist the United Arab Republic's request for UNEF's withdrawal, or to bring pressure to bear on the Government of the United Arab Republic to reconsider its decision in this matter. In fact, as the chronology given above makes clear, the effectiveness of UNEF, in the light of the movement of United Arab Republic troops up to the line and into Sharm el–Sheikh, had already vanished before the request for withdrawal was received. Furthermore, the Government of the United Arab Republic had made it entirely clear to the Secretary-General that an appeal for reconsideration of the withdrawal decision would encounter a firm rebuff and would be considered as an attempt to impose UNEF as an 'army of occupation'. Such a reaction, combined with the fact that UNEF positions on the line had already been effectively taken over by United Arab Republic troops in pursuit of their full right to move up to the line in their own territory, and a deep anxiety for the security of UNEF personnel should an effort be made to keep UNEF in position after its withdrawal had been requested, were powerful arguments in favour of complying with the United Arab Republic request, even supposing there had not been other overriding reasons for accepting it.

36. It has been said that the decision to withdraw UNEF precipitated other consequences such as the reinstitution of the blockade against Israel in the Strait of Tiran. As can be seen from the chronology, the UNEF positions at Sharm el–Sheikh on the Strait of Tiran (manned by thirty-two men in all) were in fact rendered ineffective by United Arab Republic troops before the request for withdrawal was received. It is also pertinent to note that in response to a query from the Secretary-General as to why the United Arab Republic had announced its reinstitution of the blockade in the Strait of Tiran while the Secretary-General was actually en route to Cairo on 22 May, President Nasser explained that his Government's decision to resume the blockade had been taken some time before U Thant's departure and it was considered preferable to make

the announcement before rather than after the Secretary-General's visit to Cairo.

The question of consultations

37. It has been said also that there was not adequate consultation with the organs of the United Nations concerned or with the Members before the decision was taken to withdraw the Force. The Secretary-General was, and is, firmly of the opinion that the decision for withdrawal of the Force, on the request of the host Government, rested with the Secretary-General after consultation with the Advisory Committee on UNEF, which is the organ established by the General Assembly for consultation regarding such matters. This was made clear by Secretary-General Hammarskjöld, who took the following position on 26 February 1957 in reply to a question about the withdrawal of the Force from Sharm el–Sheikh:

> An indicated procedure would be for the Secretary-General to inform the Advisory Committee on the United Nations Emergency Force, which would determine whether the matter should be brought to the attention of the Assembly.

The Secretary-General consulted the Advisory Committee befor replying to the letter of 18 May 1967 from the United Arab Republic requesting withdrawal. This consultation took place within a few hours after receipt of the United Arab Republic request, and the Advisory Committee was thus quickly informed of the decision which the Secretary-General had in mind to convey in his reply to the Foreign Minister of the United Arab Republic. As indicated in the report to the Security Council of 26 May 1967:

> The Committee did not move, as it was its right to do under the terms of paragraph 9 of General Assembly resolution 1001 (ES–1) to request the convening of the General Assembly on the situation which had arisen (S/7906, para. 4).

38. Before consulting the Advisory Committee on UNEF, the Secretary-General had also consulted the Permanent Representatives of the seven countries providing the contingents of

UNEF and informed them of his intentions. This, in fact, was more than was formally required of the Secretary-General in the way of consultation.

39. Obviously, many Governments were concerned about the presence and functioning of UNEF and about the general situation in the area, but it would have been physically impossible to consult all of the interested representatives within any reasonable time. This was an emergency situation requiring urgent action. Moreover, it was perfectly clear that such consultations were sure to produce sharply divided counsel, even if they were limited to the permanent members of the Security Council. Such sharply divided advice would have complicated and exacerbated the situation, and, far from relieving the Secretary-General of the responsibility for the decision to be taken, would have made the decision much more difficult to take.

40. It has been said that the final decision on the withdrawal of UNEF should have been taken only after consideration by the General Assembly. This position is not only incorrect but also unrealistic. In resolution 1000 (ES–I) the General Assembly established a United Nations command for an emergency international force. On the basis of that resolution the Force was quickly recruited and its forward elements flown to the staging area at Naples. Thus, though established, it had to await the permission of the Government of Egypt to enter Egyptian territory. That permission was subsequently given by the Government of Egypt as a result of direct discussions between Secretary-General Hammarskjöld and President Nasser of Egypt. There is no official United Nations document on the basis of which any case could be made that there was any limitation on the authority of the Government of Egypt to rescind that consent at its pleasure, or which would indicate that the United Arab Republic had in any way surrendered its right to ask for and obtain at any time the removal of UNEF from its territory. This point is elaborated later in this report (see paras. 71–80 below).

41. As a practical matter, there would be little point in any case in taking such an issue to the General Assembly unless there would be reasonable certainty that that body could be expected expeditiously to reach a substantive decision. In the prevailing circumstances, the question could have been validly

raised as to what decision other than the withdrawal of UNEF could have been reached by the Assembly once United Arab Republic consent for the continued presence of UNEF was withdrawn.

42. As regards the practical possibility of the Assembly considering the request for UNEF's withdrawal, it is relevant to observe that the next regular session of the General Assembly was some four months off at the time the withdrawal request was made. The special session of the General Assembly which was meeting at the time could have considered the question, according to rule 19 of the Assembly's rules of procedure, only if two-thirds or eighty-two members voted for the inclusion of the item in the agenda. It is questionable, to say the least, whether the necessary support could have been mustered for such a controversial item. There could have been no emergency special session since the issue was not then before the Security Council, and therefore the condition of lack of unanimity did not exist.

43. As far as consultation with or action by the Security Council was concerned, the Secretary-General reported to the Council on the situation leading up to and created by the withdrawal of UNEF on 19 May 1967 (S/7896). In that report he characterized the situation in the Near East as 'extremely menacing'. The Council met for the first time after this report on 24 May 1967, but took no action.

4. As has already been stated, the Advisory Committee did not make any move to bring the matter before the General Assembly, and no representative of any Member Government requested a meeting of either the Security Council or the General Assembly immediately following the Secretary-General's reports (A/6730 and S/7896). In this situation, the Secretary-General himself did not believe that any useful purpose would be served by his seeking a meeting of either organ, nor did he consider that there was basis for him to do so at that time. Furthermore, the information available to the Secretary-General did not lead him to believe that either the General Assembly or the Security Council would have decided that UNEF should remain on United Arab Republic territory, by force if necessary, despite the request of the Government of the United Arab Republic that it should leave.

Practical factors influencing the decision

45. Since it is still contended in some quarters that the UNEF operation should somehow have continued after the consent of the Government of the United Arab Republic to its presence was withdrawn, it is necessary to consider the factors, quite apart from constitutional and legal considerations, which would have made such a course of action entirely impracticable.

46. The consent and active co-operation of the host country is essential to the effective operation and, indeed, to the very existence, of any United Nations peace-keeping operation of the nature of UNEF. The fact is that UNEF had been deployed on Egyptian and Egyptian-controlled territory for over ten-and-a-half years with the consent and co-operation of the Government of the United Arab Republic. Although it was envisaged in pursuance of General Assembly resolution 1125 (XI) of 2 February 1957 that the Force would be stationed on both sides of the line, Israel exercised its sovereign right to refuse the stationing of UNEF on its side, and the Force throughout its existence was stationed on the United Arab Republic side of the line only.

47. In these circumstances, the true basis for UNEF's effectiveness as a buffer and deterrent to infiltration was, throughout its existence, a voluntary undertaking by local United Arab Republic authorities with UNEF, that United Arab Republic troops would respect a defined buffer zone along the entire length of the line in which only UNEF would operate and from which United Arab Republic troops would be excluded. This undertaking was honoured for more than a decade, and this Egyptian co-operation extended also to Sharm el–Sheikh, Ras Nasrani and the Strait of Tiran. This undertaking was honoured although UNEF had no authority to challenge the right of United Arab Republic troops to be present anywhere on their own territory.

48. It may be pointed out in passing that over the years UNEF dealt with numerous infiltrators coming from the Israel as well as from the United Arab Republic side of the line. It would hardly be logical to take the position that because UNEF has successfully maintained quiet along the line for more than ten years, owing in large measure to the co-operation of the

United Arab Republic authorities, that Government should then be told that it could not unilaterally seek the removal of the Force and thus in effect be penalized for the long co-operation with the international community it had extended in the interest of peace.

49. There are other practical factors relating to the above-mentioned arrangement which are highly relevant to the withdrawal of UNEF. First, once the United Arab Republic troops moved up to the line to place themselves in direct confrontation with the military forces of Israel, UNEF had, in fact, no further useful function. Second, if the Force was no longer welcome, it could not as a practical matter remain in the United Arab Republic, since the friction which would almost inevitably have arisen with that Government, its armed forces and with the local population would have made the situation of the Force both humilating and untenable. It would even have been impossible to supply it. UNEF clearly had no mandate to try to stop United Arab Republic troops from moving freely about on their own territory. This was a peace-keeping force, not an enforcement action. Its effectiveness was based entirely on voluntary co-operation.

50. Quite apart from its position in the United Arab Republic, the request of that Government for UNEF's withdrawal automatically set off a disintegration of the Force, since two of the Governments providing contingents quickly let the Secretary-General know that their contingents would be withdrawn, and there can be little doubt that other such notifications would not have been slow in coming if friction had been generated through an unwillingness to comply with the request for withdrawal.

51. For all the foregoing reasons, the operation, and even the continued existence of UNEF on United Arab Republic territory, after the withdrawal of United Arab Republic consent, would have been impossible, and any attempt to maintain the Force there would without question have had disastrous consequences. . . .

The 'Good Faith' aide-mémoire of 20 November 1956

71. There remains to be examined whether any commitments were made by Egypt which would limit its pre-existing right

to withdraw its consent at any time that it chose to do so. The only basis for asserting such limitation could be the so-called 'good faith' *aide-mémoire* which was set out as an annex to a report of the Secretary-General submitted to the General Assembly on 20 November 1956.

72. The Secretary-General himself did not offer any interpretation of the 'good faith' *aid-mémoire* to the General Assembly or make any statement questioning the remarks made by the Foreign Minister of Egypt in the General Assembly the following week (see paragraph 74 below). It would appear, however, that in an exchange of cables he had sought to obtain the express acknowledgement from Egypt that its consent to the presence of the Force would not be withdrawn before the Force had completed its task. Egypt did not accept this interpretation but held to the view that if its consent was no longer maintained the Force should be withdrawn. Subsequent discussions between Mr Hammarskjöld and President Nasser resulted in the 'good faith' *aide-mémoire*.

73. An interpretative account of these negotiations made by Mr Hammarskjöld in a personal and private paper entitled '*aide-mémoire*', dated 5 August 1957, some eight and a half months after the discussions, has recently been made public by a private person who has a copy. It is understood that Mr Hammarskjöld often prepared private notes concerning significant events under the heading '*aide-mémoire*'. This memorandum is not in any official record of the United Nations nor is it in any of the official files. The General Assembly, the Advisory Committee on UNEF and the Government of Egypt were not informed of its contents or existence. It is not an official paper and has no standing beyond being a purely private memorandum of unknown purpose or value, in which Secretary-General Hammarskjöld seems to record his own impressions and interpretations of his discussions with President Nasser. This paper, therefore, cannot affect in any way the basis for the presence of UNEF on the soil of the United Arab Republic as set out in the official documents, much less supersede those documents.

Position of Egypt

74. It seems clear that Egypt did not understand the 'good

faith' *aide-mémoire* to involve any limitation on its right to withdraw its consent to the continued stationing and operation of UNEF on its territory. The Foreign Minister of Egypt, speaking in the General Assembly on 27 November 1956, one week after the publication of the 'good faith' *aide-mémoire* and three days following its approval by the General Assembly, said:

> We still believe that the General Assembly resolution of 7 November 1956 still stands, together with its endorsement of the principle that the General Assembly could not request the United Nations Emergency Force to be stationed or to operate on the territory of a given country without the consent of the Government of the country. This is the proper basis on which we believe, together with the overwhelming majority of this Assembly, that the United Nations Emergency Force could be stationed or could operate in Egypt. It is the only basis on which Egypt has given its consent in this respect.

He then added:

> . . . as must be abundantly clear, this Force has gone to Egypt to help Egypt, with Egypt's consent; and no one here or elsewhere can reasonably or fairly say that a fire brigade, after putting out a fire, would be entitled or expected to claim the right of deciding not to leave the house.

Analysis of the 'task' of the Force

75. In the 'good faith' *aide-mémoire* the Government of Egypt declared that, 'when exercising its sovereign rights on any matters concerning the presence and functioning of UNEF, it will be guided, in good faith, by its acceptance of General Assembly resolution 1000 (ES-I) of 5 November 1956'.

76. The United Nations in turn declared 'that the activities of UNEF will be guided, in good faith, by the task established for the Force in the aforementioned resolutions [1000 (ES-I) and 997 (ES-I)]; in particular, the United Nations, understanding this to correspond to the wishes of the Government of

Egypt, reaffirms its willingness to maintain UNEF until its task is completed'.

77. It must be noted that, while Egypt undertook to be guided in *good faith* by its acceptance of General Assembly resolution 1000 (ES-I), the United Nations also undertook to be guided in *good faith* by the task established for the Force in resolutions 1000 (ES-I) and 997 (ES-I). Resolution 1000 (ES-I), to which the declaration of Egypt referred, established a United Nations Command for the Force 'to secure and supervise the cessation of hostilities in accordance with all the terms' of resolution 997 (ES-I). It must be recalled that at this time Israel forces had penetrated deeply into Egyptian territory and that forces of France and the United Kingdom were conducting military operations on Egyptian territory. Resolution 997 (ES-I) urged as a matter of priority that all parties agree to an immediate cease-fire, and halt the movement of military forces and arms into the area. It also urged the parties to the armistice agreements promptly to withdraw all forces behind the armistice lines, to desist from raids across the armistice lines, and to observe scrupulously the provisions of the armistice agreements. It further urged that, upon the cease-fire being effective, steps be taken to reopen the Suez Canal and restore secure freedom of navigation.

78. While the terms of resolution 997 (ES-I) cover a considerable area, the emphasis in resolution 1000 (ES-I) is on *securing and supervising the cessation of hostilities*. Moreover, on 6 November 1956 the Secretary-General, in his second and final report on the plan for an emergency international United Nations Force, noted that 'the Assembly intends that the Force should be of a temporary nature, the length of its assignment being determined by the needs arising out of the present conflict'. Noting further the terms of resolution 997 (ES-I) he added that 'the functions of the United Nations Force would be, when a cease-fire is being established, to enter Egyptian territory with the consent of the Egyptian Government, in order to help maintain quiet during and after the withdrawal of non-Egyptian troops, and to secure compliance with the other terms established in the resolution of 2 November 1956' (997 (ES-I)).

79. In a cable delivered to Foreign Minister Fawzi on 9 or 10 November 1956, in reply to a request for clarification as to

how long it was contemplated that the Force should stay in the demarcation line area, the Secretary-General stated: 'A definite reply is at present impossible but the emergency character of the Force links it to the immediate crises envisaged in resolution 2 November (997 (ES-I)] and its liquidation'. This point was confirmed in a further exchange of cables between the Secretary-General and Dr Fawzi on 14 November 1956.

80. The Foreign Minister of Egypt (Dr Fawzi) gave his understanding of the task of the Force in a statement to the General Assembly on 27 November 1956:

> Our clear understanding—and I am sure it is the clear understanding of the Assembly—is that this Force is in Egypt only in relation to the present attack against Egypt by the United Kingdom, France and Israel, and for the purposes directly connected with the incursion of the invading forces into Egyptian territory. The United Nations Emergency Force is in Egypt, not as an occupation force, not as a replacement for the invaders, not to clear the Canal of obstructions, not to resolve any question or settle any problem, be it in relation to the Suez Canal, to Palestine or to any other matter; it is not there to infringe upon Egyptian sovereignty in any fashion or to any extent, but, on the contrary, to give expression to the determination of the United Nations to put an end to the aggression committed against Egypt and to the presence of the invading forces in Egyptian territory.

81. In letters dated 3 November 1956 addressed to the Secretary-General, the representatives of both France and the United Kingdom had proposed very broad functions for UNEF, stating on behalf of their Governments that military action could be stopped if the following conditions were met:

> (a) Both the Egyptian and Israel Governments agree to accept a United Nations Force to keep the peace.
> (b) The United Nations decides to constitute and maintain such a Force until an Arab-Israel peace settlement is reached and until satisfactory arrangements have been agreed in regard to the Suez Canal, both agreements to be guaranteed by the United Nations.

(c) In the meantime, until the United Nations Force is constituted, both combatants agree to accept forthwith limited detachments of Anglo-French troops to be stationed between the combatants.

These broad functions for the Force were not acceptable to the General Assembly, however, as was pointed out in telegrams dated 4 November 1956 from Secretary-General Dag Hammarskjöld to the Minister for Foreign Affairs of France and the Secretary of State for Foreign Affairs of the United Kingdom.

82. Finally, it is obvious that the task referred to in the 'good faith' *aide-mémoire* could only be the task of the Force as it had been defined in November 1956 when the understanding was concluded. The 'good faith' undertaking by the United Nations would preclude it from claiming that the Egyptian agreement was relevant or applicable to functions which the Force was given at a much later date. The stationing of the Force on the armistice demarcation line and at Sharm el–Shiekh was only determined in pursuance of General Assembly resolution 1125 (XI) of 2 February 1957. The Secretary-General, in his reports relating to this decision, made it clear that the further consent of Egypt was essential with respect to these new functions. Consequently, the understanding recorded in the 'good faith' *aide-mémoire* of 20 November 1956 could not have been, itself, a commitment with respect to functions only determined in February and March 1957. It is only these later tasks that the Force had been performing during the last ten years—tasks of serving as a buffer and deterring infiltrators which went considerably beyond those of securing and supervising the cessation of hostilities provided in the General Assembly resolutions and referred to in the 'good faith' *aide-mémoire*.

PART XIV

The Arabs in Defeat

What was the reaction of the Arabs to defeat in a war with Israel alone? How has the Arab defeat affected the Arab world?

In the short term the Arab States were not demoralized by their defeat. They have not ceased to hurl defiance at Israel. They have frequently likened their defeat to that of the British in France in 1940 and the withdrawal across Suez to the British decision to evacuate from Dunkirk. The parallels are not close, but the right Churchillian slogan has been chosen—in defeat, defiance.

The problem is really with what weapons the battle is to be renewed. To some of the Arabs the only road to victory is through guerrilla warfare, but this view was not supported by the Arab Heads of State Conference held in Khartoum on 30 August 1967.

The Syrian President did not attend this conference, nor did the Syrian Prime Minister, even although he was in fact present in Khartoum. Another notable absence was that of Boumedienne, the Algerian leader; nor was Bourguiba there.

Those Arab States who were represented at the conference by their leaders were the United Arab Republic (Nasser), Jordan, Saudi Arabia, Iraq, the Yemen, Lebanon, Kuwait and the Sudan. The conference did not include, therefore, the elements most hostile to Israel. Even so, the decisions reached revealed anything but a conciliatory, let alone any defeatist, attitude towards Israel. We are here face to face with long-term Arab hostility as well as more immediate and transient defiance.

We give below the resolutions of the Arab Summit Conference (Document XIV (a)), and in Document XIV (b) an excerpt from an editorial in a Syrian newspaper, which demonstrates the Syrian attitude. In the decisions of the Khartoum conference we can note the role of paymaster now being played by the oil-producing states. It may in part be 'ransom' money, but may it not also lead to a measure of control over the Arab world by the more traditionalist Arab regimes? In Document XIV (c) we give a view of the longer-term effect of the defeat on Arab governmental policies and cadres.

DOCUMENT XIV (a). RESOLUTIONS OF THE ARAB SUMMIT CON-FERENCE IN KHARTOUM, 29 AUGUST–1 SEPTEMBER 1967

1. The conference has affirmed the unity of the Arab ranks, the unity of joint action and the need for co-ordination and for the elimination of all differences. The Kings, Presidents and repre-sentatives of the other Arab Heads of State at the conference have affirmed their countries' stand by, and implementation of the new Arab Solidarity Charter which was signed at the third Arab Summit Conference in Casablanca.

2. The conference has agreed on the need to consolidate all efforts to eliminate the effects of the aggression on the basis that the occupied lands are Arab lands and that the burden of regaining these lands falls on all the Arab states.

3. The Arab Heads of State have agreed to unite their political efforts at the international and diplomatic level to eliminate the effects of the aggression and to ensure the with-drawal of the aggressive Israeli forces from the Arab lands which have been occupied since the aggression of 5 June. This will be done within the framework of the main principles by which the Arab States abide, namely, no peace with Israel, no recognition of Israel, no negotiations with it, and insistence on the rights of the Palestinian people in their own country.

4. The conference of Arab Ministers of Finance, Economy and Oil recommended that suspension of oil pumping be used as a weapon in the battle. However, after thoroughly studying the matter, the Summit Conference has come to the conclusion that the pumping of oil can itself be used as a positive weapon, since oil is an Arab resource which can be used to strengthen the economy of the Arab States directly affected by the aggres-sion, so that these states will be able to stand firm in the battle.

The conference has, therefore, decided to resume the pumping of oil, since oil is a positive Arab resource that can be used in the service of Arab goals. It can contribute to the efforts to enable those Arab states which were exposed to the aggression and thereby lost economic resources to stand firm and eliminate the effects of the aggression.

The oil-producing states have, in fact, participated in the efforts to enable the states affected by the aggression to stand firm in the face of any economic pressure.

5. The participants in the conference have approved the plan proposed by Kuwait to set up an Arab Economic and Social Development Fund on the basis of the recommendation of the Baghdad conference of Arab Ministers of Finance, Economy and Oil.

6. The participants have agreed on the need to adopt the necessary measures to strengthen military preparation to face all eventualities.

7. The conference has decided to expedite the elimination of foreign bases in the Arab states.

[additional resolution]

The Kingdom of Saudi Arabia, the State of Kuwait and the Kingdom of Libya have each agreed to pay the following annual amounts, which are to be paid in advance every three months beginning from mid-October until the effects of the aggression are eliminated: Saudi Arabia, £50,000,000; Kuwait, £55,000,000; Libya, £30,000,000. In this way, the Arab nation ensures that it will be able to carry on this battle, without any weakening, until the effects of the aggression are eliminated.

DOCUMENT XIV (b). EXCERPT FROM EDITORIAL IN SYRIAN NEWS-PAPER, *Al-Ba'th*, 31 AUGUST 1967.

Which is better; to carry on the armed struggle or to be content with the chaos of political action? The toiling Arab masses will choose the course of struggle, resistance and sacrifice. The reason is simple. The masses cannot possibly accept a *fait accompli*. . . . The occupied Arab territories will be evacuated by the enemy only through our struggle. The Israeli enemy will be liquidated only by means of force. Anglo-American domination will be shaken only through continued struggle at every economic and military level. . . .

Any other course would be tantamount to deception or perhaps even submision and collusion. In the battle for dignity and survival the masses will achieve a new miracle. They have chosen to fight with all their resources on two fronts; a foreign front to repel the Zionist imperial aggression, and a home front to combat internal defeatism so that every obstacle in the way of their progressive and revolutionary struggle can be removed.

DOCUMENT XIV (c). EXCERPT FROM M. RODINSON, ISRAEL: THE ARAB OPTIONS', *The Year Book of World Affairs, 1968*, PP. 88–92.

Cadres and Policies

In the final analysis either option—the acceptance of the State of Israel, or the pursuit of the contest (implying the presence of numerous gradations and shades as regards modalities)—depends on tactical choices, and may be adopted within a framework of widely varying strategic prospects. Acceptance may be chosen only with careful reference to Arab public opinion and the manner in which this issue is presented to the masses will be of the utmost relevance.

The political cadres which will have to fit a policy of acceptance into an overall programme do exist but are limited in number. Each future prospect must be viewed in the light, not only of the options available in isolation, and in the abstract, but also with due regard to the constitution of the political cadres which will have to execute policy. At present all policies have of necessity to be applied within an ideological framework compatible with the interests and aspirations of certain social groups from which they issued and whose support is needed.

In both Egypt and Syria a certain bourgeois Right wing is ready to relieve the present cadres and to accept the State of Israel within the overall framework of a pro-Western policy abroad and a return to economic liberalism at home, provided only that certain modalities are observed to placate public opinion at home. The political regimes resulting from such a change-over of cadres would be authoritarian in nature under cover of some ostensibly parliamentarian political institutions. If such is to be the course of events, it need not necessarily result in the severance of all political and economic relations with the Socialist bloc. On the whole, regimes of this sort are likely to be similar to those now existing in Saudi Arabia and Morocco. Their main problem will be the extent to which their social support at home enables them to withstand opposition of a possibility virulent nature. Nostalgia for the experiments of the past—greatly idealized, no doubt—could serve to multiply the strength of Left-wing opposition, a condition which is not present in those Arab countries which have known no other political regime. Moreover, a strong Right-wing opposition also could develop and exploit effectively the theme of surrender before the West and Israel.

In some countries—Egypt above all—there exist cadres aiming to establish what—notwithstanding the inadequacy of terminology borrowed from quite a different historical milieu— might be termed 'clerical fascism'. The Muslim Brotherhood, for instance, by its ability to mobilize the masses through the use of Muslim fundamentalist slogans, by calling for the restoration of the pristine purity of Islam, whose abandonment was responsible for all evils, might possess distinct tactical advantages over the cadres just referred to. The adoption of uncompromising positions towards Israel, with political motives reinforced by religious ones, forms an integral part of the Brotherhood's present programme which, however, still has to be tested in practice. Not suspect as regards the attachment of its members to both national and religious values, the Muslim Brotherhood would find it easier to make concessions, especially if these could be presented as tactically unavoidable. Foreign policy, to be sure, will be pro-United States, while at home the repression of all Leftist and democratic trends would be merciless. Liberalism, dressed up in 'Old Islamic' garb, would be the rule in the economic sphere, with the toleration of a small group of powerful capitalists tied to the Western economy and sharing the benefits of power with the new political elite.

It is highly unlikely that the economic policies of regimes of this type would be successful, least of all in Egypt, where the basic conditions of economic activity are unfavourable and where drastic planning would seem to be required if economic breakdown is to be avoided.

Regimes of this type might seek to extricate themselves from their internal difficulties by engaging in adventures abroad. Vocal anti-Israel demagogy could help. United States aid can be taken for granted, notwithstanding subjective preferences entertained among some political leaders in the United States for a purely parliamentary bourgeois type of government. Such a regime would be à la Salazar, at best, or à la Batista, at worst.

Experience has shown that regimes of this kind may survive for a long time, in spite of the general opposition which they tend to arouse at home. Though it might perhaps suit Israel to have countries with regimes of this nature as its neighbours, in the long run the internal fermentation, if it can be contained within safe limits, would prove a liability, and not an asset to the Zionist State.

But the advent of the kind of regime just described is far from inevitable. Strong, anti-imperialist governments may still succeed; but to a large extent their success will depend on the attitude taken by Israel. Clearly, the present military balance will sooner or later impose on those Arab States unwilling to go to extreme lengths the solution of the recognition of the State of Israel in one form or another. But such acts of recognition are certain to weaken the governments advocating them as the internal opposition is liable to charge them with concealed surrender in one way or another.

Israel may encourage tendencies towards recognition in a variety of ways: she can make concessions; accept imperceptible transactions implicitly; resist the temptation of putting forward draconian conditions; and refuse to take too seriously some Arab verbal excesses indulged in merely the better to conceal a policy of moderation in practice. Some of Israel's political leaders, including many regarded as 'hawks' in the past, appreciate the need for an approach along these lines rather well. But, intoxicated with success, the Israeli masses may well be driven into the adoption of unyielding attitudes. Some among Israel's politicians, statesmen and military men are trying to make the most of the opportunites offered by the present state of affairs; while others are content with being carried away by the chauvinistic wave sweeping the country.

Arab anti-imperialist regimes still able to act constructively in the manner indicated above—the Nasser regime in Egypt, for instance (one finds it difficult to identify any single group of politicians in Syria which would fall into that category)—would have to direct their endeavours towards economic and political modernization and independence. This will undoubtedly require difficult internal reconstruction affecting the interests of broad sections of the population, and imply a change of cadres. The old set of politicians is largely discredited. If these drastic measures are not taken and the regime is weakened by the need to come to terms with Israel, then surely one or other of the two above-mentioned cadres is likely to take over.

The alternative to the solutions outlined so far will be the creation of ultra-revolutionary regimes unwilling to accept the recognition of Israel in any way and resolved to continue the war. Such a regime may even consider the continuation of resistance on the Vietnamese model in the event of a military reaction on the part of Israel. A mood of this kind appears to be prevailing among the Left-wing Baathists now in power in Damascus, as well as among the Palestine Liberation Army and among other Palestinian resistance movements, above all *El Fatah*. Some elements within the Left-wing opposition in Egypt would also seem to espouse this point of view.

The chances of success for such an ultra-revolutionary course appear to be few. The Near East is not Vietnam. No doubt the occupation of both Syria and the Nile valley by Israeli forces could raise enormous difficulties for the occupant, as much as regards the submission of the populations in those areas, as in the field of international relations. But the organization of popular resistance in those circumstances would encounter great difficulties, as resistance forces would have at their command few military means and hardly any industrial bases. The Soviet Union might try to help, but she is some distance away. China is even farther away. Internal revulsion in face of attempts to organize a resistance struggle of this kind would be strong. The most likely effect such type of action could have would be to help the anti-revolutionary forces within those areas, greatly assisted by United States and Israeli pressures, to put into power a bourgeois Right-wing or even a clerico-fascist government.

The long-range prospects

We have tried to sketch the prospects at short and medium range. The long-term prospects may be rather different. The June War of 1967 may be no more than the starting point of a new era in the history of the Near East. The blow delivered to the Arab States was so severe that it will almost certainly set off a process of long gestation and preparation on the part of new cadres willing to learn the lessons of the disaster, with the object to eliminate not so much Israel herself as the conditions which have made the Israeli victory possible. There might be radical departures from the pattern of the past. The process is likely to take a long time and to run against many an obstacle. Strong opposition is to be expected from cadres still in office, perhaps particularly where these are pursuing identical objectives. Merciless repression must be expected. These developments will not remain unaffected by the international balance of power, though it would be rash to forecast the precise way in which they will be so affected. It is not altogether impossible that in the end the new cadres will prevail, though it is impossible to say exactly when. It is, however, only after these new cadres have triumphed that the true problems can be stated in all clarity. One of these will be the acceptance of the State of Israel by its Arab neighbours. The solution of this problem will in turn depend to a large extent on the policy that Israel herself is prepared to follow during that period of respite.

PART XV

The United Nations Attempt at a Peace
and the Israeli Nine-Point Peace Plan

The first draft resolution to be submitted to the Security Council in November 1967 was that of India, Mali and Nigeria. It asserted that 'a just and lasting peace in the Middle East must be achieved within the framework of the Charter of the United Nations and more particularly of the following principles', of which the first and most important was that 'occupation or acquisition of territory by military conquest is inadmissible under the Charter of the United Nations and consequently Israel's armed forces should withdraw from all the territories occupied as a result of the recent conflict'. The important point that occupation or acquisition of territory by military conquest was inadmissible significantly did not occur in the American draft resolution, which the Council also considered. Moreover, the American resolution went no further than to say that 'the fulfilment of the above Charter principles requires the achievement of a state of just and lasting peace *embracing* [italics ours] withdrawal of armed forces from occupied territories'. By contrast the Soviet draft resolution required the Security Council to urge that 'the parties to the conflict should immediately withdraw their forces to the positions they held before 5 June 1967 in accordance with the principle that the seizure of territories as a result of war is inadmissible'. Here lay the crux of the matter. Israel wanted to determine the position that would succeed the cease-fire through negotiation with the Arab states. The latter simply demanded Israeli withdrawal. The British resolution seemed to offer the best compromise. It included the inadmissibility of acquisition (but not occupation) of territory by war, though it still viewed Israeli withdrawal as part of a peace settlement, not as a prior condition.

With regard to an Israeli withdrawal, an important point to be noted in the British resolution is its omission of the definite article before 'territories' (Document XV (a), Para. 1 (i)). This is ambiguous. It can mean all, or just some, territories. However, there is no ambiguity in the French text of the Security Council Resolution, which is equally authentic. The definite article is included. It reads: 'Retrait des forces armées israéliennes *des* (italics ours) territoires occupés'. The Indian interpretation, accepted by the Soviet Union, was that 'the United Kingdom draft resolution committed the Council to the application of the principle of total withdrawal of Israel forces from all the territories occupied by Israel as a result of the June conflict. That being so Israel could not use the words 'secure and recognized boundaries' to retain any occupied territory'. The Israeli Foreign Minister retorted that 'for Israel the resolution said what it said. It did not say what it had specifically and consciously avoided saying'. The British representative's view was that 'it was only the resolution that would bind all and he regarded its wording as clear'.

Other points to note are the following. No draft enjoined direct negotiation between the combatants, though the American came nearest to it. The Soviet resolution dropped the condemnation of Israel as an aggressor, which the Soviet Union had insisted upon in the UN General Assembly in the previous June. The Soviet resolution alone excluded any reference to the recognition of the sovereignty of Israel, but the others asserted it only in the context of a peace or settlement. The Soviet and Afro-Asian resolutions hedged about freedom of navigation through international waterways with references to international agreements or international law—a qualification which would leave the matter wide open to interpretation.

We give in Document XV (a) the text of the Security Council Resolution, which is identical with the British draft resolution, and in Document XV (b), President Nasser's comment on it.

DOCUMENT XV (a). SECURITY COUNCIL RESOLUTION, 22 NOVEMBER 1967.

The Security Council,

Expressing its continuing concern with the grave situation in the Middle East,

Emphasizing the inadmissibility of the acquisition of territory by war and the need to work for a just and lasting peace in which every State in the area can live in security,

Emphasizing further that all Member States in their acceptance of the Charter of the United Nations have undertaken a commitment to act in accordance with Article 2 of the Charter,

1. *Affirms* that the fulfilment of Charter principles requires the establishment of a just and lasting peace in the Middle East which should include the application of both the following principles:

(i) Withdrawal of Israel armed forces from territories occupied in the recent conflict;

(ii) Termination of all claims or states of belligerency and respect for and acknowledgement of the sovereignty, territorial integrity and political independence of every State in the area and their right to live in peace within secure and recognized boundaries free from threats or acts of force;

2. *Affirms further* the necessity

(*a*) For guaranteeing freedom of navigation through international waterways in the area;

(*b*) For achieving a just settlement of the refugee problem;

(*c*) For guaranteeing the territorial inviolability and political independence of every State in the area, through measures including the establishment of demilitarized zones;

3. *Requests* the Secretary-General to designate a Special Representative to proceed to the Middle East to establish and maintain contacts with the States concerned in order to promote agreement and assist efforts to achieve a peaceful and accepted settlement in accordance with the provisions and principles in this resolution;

4. *Requests* the Secretary-General to report to the Security Council on the progress of the efforts of the Special Representative as soon as possible.

DOCUMENT XV (b). EXCERPTS FROM SPEECH BY PRESIDENT NASSER, 23 NOVEMBER 1967.

The General Assembly debate ended and we asked for the Middle East crisis to be debated in the Security Council in order to draw the attention of the world to the aggression and the continuation of the aggression. During the contacts it was proposed that the non-permanent members of the Security Council should table a draft resolution, and India presented an Afro-Asian draft resolution supported in clear fraternity by both Nigeria and Mali. The draft resolution, in our view, aimed to achieve some basic guarantees and I would repeat before you, and I want the masses of our Arab nation to know, that there is no full guarantee other than our readiness to take up arms at any time in defence of the principle, the land and the right.

Then Denmark put forward a draft resolution which we rejected at once. The U.S.A. put forward a draft resolution which we also rejected immediately and then Britain came with another draft resolution which tried to compromise between the basic points in the Afro-Asian draft scheme and in the Western draft schemes. From our point of view this British draft resolution is not enough to find a sound solution to the crisis. Then the Soviet draft resolution came, which was reasonable and balanced, and it was clear that the Soviet Union had done well in submitting it, because it was a means of pressure which succeeded at least in reinterpreting the British draft resolution eventually approved by the Security Council. And despite these interpretations put forward at the session of the Security Council—they were formulated by India before the Security Council had approved the British scheme, and were put forward also by the Soviet Union and France, and it was on their basis that the resolution was moved and carried by the Council—despite these interpretations which have contributed some clarifications necessary for the scheme, the British scheme remains inadequate in our view. So whatever happens I say once again, as I am never tired of pointing out: We were not able to obtain guarantees beyond those given by our strength and our readiness to take up arms.

It has been established that the form of phrasing has no value; and it has been established that all phrases are liable to melt in the heat of fire. Are we capable of possessing the possibility of effective armed action or are we not? That is the question. Anything else is of no value.

What is to be done regarding the resolution of the Security

Council? As far as we are concerned, we are studying it and we are consulting our friends about it. There are two indisputable, well defined points as far as we are concerned. Regarding them we accept no give and take. The first is full withdrawal from all Arab territory, from every inch of Arab land occupied in the June battles whether in the UAR or the Hashemite Kingdom of Jordan or the Syrian Arab Republic. This point to us is not subject to any bargaining and the second point is that we shall never allow Israel, whatever the cost, to pass through the Suez Canal. No recognition of Israel. No reconciliation with it. No negotiation. No liquidation of the Palestinian question because it belongs to the Palestinian people. . . .

What should we do with regard to the Security Council Resolution? In our opinion this opens the subject to a general discussion although it is not important in itself. For any resolution that emerges from the Security Council does not mean anything in itself, even if the Afro-Asian or the Soviet draft resolution had been carried, for there is a great difference between a resolution and a solution. In our opinion the involved and vague phrases in which the UN resolutions are couched are not the important thing. The important thing is what takes place in the field. Will Israel actually withdraw from all the territories occupied during the June battles or not? Here lies the decisive barrier between words and action.

*

The Security Council resolution was not a success because the Arabs and the Israelis interpreted it in different ways; and there was little or no chance of resolving differences, if they could be resolved, while the Israeli government insisted on direct negotiations and Nasser said no negotiation, no recognition.

The conflict dragged on in this depressing way until Israel, in October 1968, rather suddenly declared she was going to advance peace proposals. There was a stir of hope, but any hope was dashed when the peace proposals emerged. There was no real change in Israeli policy; there were no suggestions in detail; above all there was hardly any evidence of any move in the direction of modifying the principle of direct negotiation.

We give in Document XV (c) the Israeli peace proposals, not because they add anything new to the history of the conflict, but because they summarize the most recent official Israeli position.

We should bear in mind that these peace proposals were probably aimed at a larger than Arab audience. They were in part a response to a Soviet peace plan presented to Washington in September 1968 and leaked to the Press. The Soviet proposals apparently required (1) a return by Israel to her pre-5 June borders, (2) a strong UN presence in evacuated areas, (3) a declaration by Arab States ending their state of war with Israel and (4) a Four-Power guarantee of peace by the United States, the Soviet Union, Britain and France. If progress were made on this basis, then other issues could be taken up by Israel and the Arab states through the UN.

Quite apart from the Israeli demand for a negotiated peace as a prerequisite to withdrawal, there were two undesirable features, for the West and for Israel, in the Soviet proposals. First, and more important, the Four-Power guarantee would give Russia a legitimate reason for maintaining a military presence in the Middle East. Second, Israel could hardly be expected to accept a plan that required her to hand over occupied territory to a UN force after her recent experience of the effectiveness of such a force.

As though to leave no doubt of American support for the Israeli position, the day after the promulgation of the Israeli peace plan President Johnson announced he had authorized negotiations for the sale of the highly prized Phantom jets to Israel. The tone of the Arab reaction was affected by their indignation at the projected supply of the strike aircraft to Israel. However, as there was nothing new in the plan, there could hardly be a positive response from the Arab states, Phantom jets or not. The Egyptian counter-proposal was to advocate a stage-by-stage implementation of the Security Council Resolution to be worked out by Dr Jarring under the supervision and the guarantees of the Security Council. According to the Egyptian Foreign Minister, this stage-by-stage implementation would amount to a peace settlement. The Israeli Foreign Minister gave short shrift to this idea.

'The timetable idea has no value whatever in this context.

How can you have a timetable for something to which you have not agreed? It is only when you have negotiated an agreement and when you have signed peace that you can raise the problem of implementing what was signed and of fixing the time and the sequence of carrying out what has been signed. But to talk about a timetable which concerns a peace which has not been signed and which has not been agreed upon, and which has not been negotiated—this is fundamentally fallacious. . . .

There is no such thing as a self-implementing resolution. Those who drafted the resolution and those who supported it have said to him, the Egyptian Foreign Minister, and to me that it is not self-executing. It is a list of principles which can help the parties and guide them in their search for a solution, because it lists the claims, the main claims, which both parties make against each other, but it has no life of its own. . . '
(Interview with Israeli Foreign Minister, Abba Eban, by Y'aqov Reuel, 11 October 1968.)

DOCUMENT XV (c). ISRAELI NINE-POINT PEACE PLAN, 10 OCTOBER 1968: EXCERPT FROM STATEMENT TO UN GENERAL ASSEMBLY BY THE ISRAELI FOREIGN MINISTER.

My government has given intensive consideration to the steps that we should now take. Our conclusion is this. Past disappointment should not lead to present despair. The stakes are too high. While the cease-fire agreements offer important security against large-scale hostilities, they do not represent a final state of peace. They must of course be maintained and respected until there is peace. They must be safe-guarded against erosion by military assault and murderous incursion. But at the same time the exploration of a lasting peace should be constant, unremitting, resilient and, above all, sincere. My government deems the circumstances and atmosphere afforded by our presence here as congenial for a new attempt. We suggest that a new effort be made in the coming weeks to co-operate with Ambassador Jarring in his task of promoting agreement of the establishment of peace.

It is important to break out of the declaratory phase in which the differences of formulation are secondary and in any case legitimate, in order to give tangible effect to the principles whereby peace can be achieved in conformity with the central purposes of the United Nations charter, or the Security Council resolution and with the norms of international law. Instead of a war of words, we need acts of peace.

I come to enumerate the nine principles by which peace can be achieved:

(1) *The establishment of peace*

The situation to follow the cease-fire must be a just and lasting peace, duly negotiated and contractually expressed.

Peace is not a mere absence of fighting. It is a positive and clearly defined relationship with far-reaching political, practical and juridical consequences. We propose that the peace settlement be embodied in treaty form. It should lay down the precise conditions of our coexistence, including a map of the secure and agreed boundary. The essence of peace is that it commits both parties to the proposition that their twenty-year old conflict is at a permanent end.

Peace is much more than what is called 'non-belligerency'. The elimination of belligerency is one of several conditions which compose the establishment of a just and lasting peace. If there had previously been peace between the states of our area and temporary hostilities had erupted, it might have been sufficient to terminate belligerency and to return to the previously existing peace. But the Arab-Israel area has had no peace. There is nothing normal or legitimate or established to which to return. The peace structure must be built from its foundations. The parties must define affirmatively what their relations shall be, not only what they will have ceased to be. The Security Council, too, called for the establishment of peace and not for any intermediate or ambiguous or fragmentary arrangement such as that which had exploded in 1967.

(2) *Secure and recognized boundaries*

Within the framework of peace we are willing to replace the cease-fire lines by permanent, secure and recognized boundaries between Israel and each of the neighbouring Arab states, and to carry out the disposition of forces in full accord with the boundaries agreed under the final peace. By this means the central purposes of the Security Council resolution of 1967 will be fulfilled. We are willing to seek agreement with each Arab state on secure and recognized boundaries within a framework of permanent peace.

It is possible to work out a boundary settlement compatible with the security of Israel and with the honour of the Arab states. After twenty years it is time that Middle Eastern states ceased to live in temporary 'demarcation lines' without the precision and permanence which can only come from the definite agreement of the states concerned. The majority of the United Nations have recognized that the only durable and reasonable solutions are agreed solutions serving the common interest of our peoples. The new peace structure in the Middle East must be built by Arab and Israeli hands.

(3) *Security agreements*

In addition to the establishment of agreed territorial boundaries we should discuss other agreed security arrangements designed to avoid the kind of vulnerable situation which caused a breakdown of the peace in the summer of 1967. The instrument establishing peace should contain a pledge of mutual non-aggression.

(4) *The open frontier*

When agreement is reached on the establishment of peace with permanent boundaries, the freedom of movement now existing in the area, especially in the Israel-Jordan sector, should be maintained and developed. It would be incongruous if our peoples were to intermingle in peaceful contact and commerce only when there is a state of war and cease-fire—and to be separated into ghettos when there is peace. We should emulate communities of states, as in parts of Western Europe. Within this concept we include free port facilities for Jordan on Israel's Mediterranean coast and mutual access to places of religious and historic associations.

(5) *Navigation*

Interference with navigation in the international waterways in the area has been the symbol of the state of war and, more than once, an immediate cause of hostilities. The arrangements for guaranteeing freedom of navigation should be unreserved, precise, concrete and founded on absolute equality of rights and obligations between Israel and other littoral states.

(6) *Refugees*

The problem of displaced populations was caused by war and can be solved by peace. On this problem I propose:

A conference of Middle Eastern states should be convened, together with the governments contributing to refugee relief and the specialized agencies of the United Nations in order to chart a five-year plan for the solution of the refugee problem in the framework of a lasting peace and the integration of refugees into productive life. This conference can be called in advance of peace negotiations.

Under the peace settlement joint refugee integration and rehabilitation commissions should be established by the signatories in order to approve agreed projects for refugee integration in the Middle East, with regional and international aid.

As an interim measure my government has decided, in view of the forthcoming winter, to intensify and accelerate action to widen the uniting of families scheme, and to process 'hardship cases' among refugees who had crossed to the East Bank during the June 1967 fighting. Moreover, permits for return which had been granted and not used can be transferred to other refugees who meet the same requirements and criteria as the original recipients.

(7) *Jerusalem*

Israel does not seek to exercise unilateral jurisdiction in the Holy Places of Christianity and Islam. We are willing in each case to work out a status to give effect to their universal character. We would like to discuss appropriate agreement with those traditionally concerned. Our policy is that the Christian and Moslem Holy Places should come under the responsibility of those who hold them in reverence.

(8) *Acknowledgement and recognition of sovereignty, integrity and right of national life*

This principle, inherent in the Charter and expressed in the Security Council resolution of November 1967 is of basic importance. It should be fulfilled through specific contractual engagements to be made by the Governments of Israel and of each Arab State to each other—by name. It follows logically that Arab Governments will withdraw all the reservations which they have expressed on adhering to international conventions, about the non-applicability of their signatures to their relations with Israel.

(9) *Regional co-operation*

The peace discussion should examine a common approach to some of the resources and means of communication in the region in an effort to lay foundations of a Middle Eastern community of sovereign states.

PART XVI

Continuing Problems: Guerrilla Warfare, the Military Balance, Jerusalem, Refugees

---

GUERRILLA WARFARE

Now that Israel occupies the Gaza Strip and the West Bank of the Jordan, guerrilla warfare has taken on a new menace. There is now a substantial Arab population under Israeli rule. This new million provides a latent civilian base for Arab guerrilla fighters, a factor which gives them much greater hope than before June 1967.

Improved prospects for guerrilla warfare combine with an increased determination to wage it. The security situation on the West Bank has been a serious problem for Israel, as evidenced by a number of bomb outrages, including one in Jerusalem in November 1968 and by numerous demonstrations against Israeli rule. The Israelis seem quite able to contain the situation at present, but they are clearly worried.

In these new circumstances for guerrilla warfare what are the guerrilla aims? They emerge from the interview, given in Document XVI (a), below, of the *El Fatah* guerrilla leader. Yet whether the circumstances have so changed since 1967 that there is now a good chance for success is clearly doubted by many Arabs, including Haykal, whose views we give in Document XVI (b). Haykal, it will be recalled, is regarded as Nasser's mouthpiece.

One important factor in the success or failure of the guerrillas is whether King Hussein continues to permit them to operate from his territory. A showdown with a relatively small guerrilla band, the Victory Group, in early November 1968, showed that the King was still master. But if he allows the guerrillas too much authority they may well oust him. There is a crucial balance of forces in Jordan, where strong units of the Iraqi armed forces are also stationed. The aim of Israeli policy is to oblige Hussein to take action against the guerrilla bands. Israel has generally sought to achieve this by a policy of severe retaliation for guerrilla attacks; but with Hussein hanging on to power rather precariously such a policy might now cause him to lose hold of power altogether. An assessment of the prospects for guerrilla warfare by a student of military affairs is given in Document XVI (c). It clearly presents a very real threat to Israel if properly pursued.

DOCUMENT XVI (A) EXCERPTS FROM RADIO ALGIERS. INTERVIEW OF LEADER OF *El Fatah*, YASIR ARAFAT (ABU AMMAR), BY HARRASH BIN JADDU, 5 JUNE 1968.

Q. Our first question is when and how did the Palestine national liberation movement come about and how have its activities increased?

A. Our movement, the Palestine national liberation movement, *El Fatah*, was formed in 1956 following the Israeli-French-British aggression and during the occupation of the Gaza sector. Since then we, the Palestine people, have been thinking in terms of action and formed the Palestine national liberation movement. We trained youth and collected arms secretly until we set off our revolution on 1 January 1965 under the name of the General Command of the Asifah Forces.

Q. What are the political objectives of the Palestine national liberation movement, *El Fatah*—and is it possible to define the development of the movement as far as it concerns the future of Palestine and in particular of the Jews in Palestine?

A. Our aim is to liberate our homeland Palestine from the Israeli occupation, to eliminate the Zionist-imperialist presence and to establish an Arab Palestine State in which all religions coexist.

Q. What then are the means to attain these objectives?

A. We believe only in one means—the means of armed

struggle in which we have full faith for the liberation of our country and the regaining of our land.

Q. As for the armed struggle with which the Palestine national liberation movement, *El Fatah*, is concerned, what are its methods and stages?

A. The armed struggle as far as our movement is concerned means the waging of an armed revolutionary people's war. Accordingly, in the initial stage of our action our one aim is to [win over] the masses of our people and make them live in a revolutionary climate in which all the people should be in the right position to take on their full responsibilities under the leadership of a struggling revolutionary vanguard, the General Command of the Asifah Forces. We depend on long-term war strategy.

Q. What is the method of political action and [what are the] contacts with the occupied territories of the Arab countries, and what is required of the Palestinian compatriot in Palestine and outside.

A. The fact is that we depend on the development of the revolutionary spirit in our people both inside and outside our occupied land. We believe that this cannot be divorced from the struggle of our Arab peoples. We believe that revolution cannot be undertaken in isolation from the people, for it is the people who nourish and sustain and are the main support of every popular revolutionary movement.

Q. Where does the political programme of the Palestine national liberation movement, *El Fatah*, fit in technically, strategically, militarily and politically within the framework of total Arab policy?

A. The fact is that our armed revolution of 1965 was a rebellion against the mentality of surrender in the Arab region. This fact was proved by the unleashing of our action after 5 June. In rising up we acted on the assumption that the people's war is the road to liberation. This theory has been confirmed all along since 1 January, for the people's liberation war is the effective and sure means which has succeeded in many places and in the experience of many peoples. The best proof is the Algerian revolution which showed how, after a seven-year struggle, Algeria was able to seize independence. Thanks to the struggle of its sons and the sacrifice of 1,500,000 martyrs, Algeria—that country once described as French—returned to the bosom of the Arab motherland. There are also our brothers in Vietnam who are at present successfully engaged in the same experiment. We have entered upon the threshold of this new experiment.

Q. Talking about Algeria, what are the present relations between the Palestine liberation movement, *El Fatah*, and Algeria; what is the history, as well as the present and future state, of these relations; and what role can Algeria play to step up and strengthen Palestine *fedai* action?

A. In fact our contact with the Algerian revolution before and after independence began when we were only a theoretical movement, before starting our armed struggle. This was in 1959, '60 and '61. When Algeria became independent, we were invited to establish a Palestine office in Algiers. In the further course of events the good relations continued but we cannot say much about them. We can say, however, that when Algeria triumphed, the Algerian revolution ended in the Maghrib so that the Palestine revolution should begin in the Arab East.

Q. Has the movement any relations with the outside world, and if so, what are they and what is expected of them regarding the present situation, and also what is expected from outside help, and the explanation of the issue, etc.?

A. The fact is that our revolutionary movement has many such contacts some of which we keep secret, as dictated by the tactics of the battle, while the rest we make known in conferences which we attend, such as the one we recently attended in Cuba or others in various parts of the world. All these relations aim at strengthening, intensifying and consolidating the revolution.

Q. What steps have you taken or will you take to widen and develop these relations?

A. We have made a start. No doubt every revolutionary movement has its own methods in strengthening such contacts, above all the help from our brothers who believe in our cause, especially those in the Arab States who help us in developing and strengthening these relations.

Q. Regarding the Arab Palestine struggle, there are various organizations which may have different political tendencies but are all working or wanting to work for the liberation of the Palestine homeland. Now what are the methods of co-operation existing at present between these various organizations and the Palestine national liberation movement, *El Fatah*?

A. The fact is that we fully believe in the unity of the Palestine struggle. This unity cannot be established overnight, especially after twenty years of misery endured in many lands following our misfortune in 1948. We have taken many steps to strengthen relations between us and these organizations, and we shall always continue as a revolutionary vanguard to widen these contacts and meetings until the final unification and fusion takes place, whether through direct contact or by means of our brothers in these organizations. We are firmly convinced that true union is the one which takes shape on the battlefield, forged by guns and sealed with the blood of martyrs. I think the battle of Karamah of which you must have heard was the best proof of the unity of these organizations. . . .

Q. During the liberation revolution in Algeria, the *fedayeen* in Algeria carried out armed actions inside the towns and villages. Can you define the word *fedai* as it applies to the Palestine national liberation movement *El Fatah*?

A. Brother, *fedai* action is part of our armed revolution. This is the true meaning of the *fedai* action because it is part of the total revolution, no more and no less. Revolution means using arms, words, positive struggle, passive struggle, strikes, defiance such as that displayed by our people against the enemy occupiers—this is what revolution means. They include *fedai* operations by special units of our men against the enemy.

DOCUMENT XVI (b). EXCERPT FROM H. HAYKAL, 'DEATH AND HOPE', *Al-Ahram*, 16 AUGUST 1968.

I met Abd al-Majid for the first time at my office about a year ago during the distressing and sorrowful days that followed June 1967. He immediately impressed me as a different man, out of the ordinary. . . . He was a Palestinian youth whose consciousness was aroused after the 1948 setback. . . . He became an officer in the Jordanian Army. . . . When the six-day war came in June 1967 he was a battery commander near Jerusalem. . . . When everybody complied with the cease-fire decision, his rebellion against the decision was irresistible. He bade farewell to his comrades-in-arms in the Jordanian battery and infiltrated alone into the occupied territory, where he contacted *El Fatah* and joined its military wing, Asifah. He assumed an important command position. He then spent his days and nights challenging danger, facing an enemy dizzy with a victory that no mind had envisaged. His responsibilities then took him to Cairo to establish co-operation between Fatah and the UAR. He believed that such co-operation would bring about a quantitative and qualitative improvement for the resistance.

I remember that at that time I explained to him my view on the resistance. I told him: The Arab world is full of people who see only black and white without any shades in between. . . . In my estimation, I said, the Palestine resistance has a great role, but I am with those who believe that its role is not decisive in the liquidation of the Israeli aggression. Those who think it will be decisive are, in my opinion, lazy or ill-informed. They are lazy people who want to give the responsibility to others to save themselves the trouble and remain silent, or they do not know the facts about the Arab confrontation with the Israeli enemy in the present circumstances. . . . As for the current situation in the Arab world, the Palestinian resistance is hampered, though not constricted by the following factors that are difficult to ignore:

(1) The human ratio of the resistance forces to their enemy in the occupied territory is not like the present ratio in Vietnam or that which existed in Algeria. For example in North and South Vietnam there are about 40,000,000 Vietnamese, while the enemy confronting them numbers 500,000 US soldiers. In Algeria there were 10,000,000 Arabs and 400,000 enemy French soldiers against them. In Palestine, inside the occupied territory, the Arabs number less than 1,000,000 and the enemy over 2,000,000, with 250,000 men under arms.

(2) The nature of the Palestinian terrain is not like Vietnam's with its thick forests, nor like the Algerian terrain with

its rugged mountains. There, the forests and the mountains served as natural hideouts for the resistance, whereas in Palestine the plains are exposed and the hills are not big. Also, the Palestinian land is limited and narrow and helicopters are used extensively.

(3) Around Vietnam there are shelters in which the resistance can prepare itself out of the enemy's reach—such as China and North Vietnam. The situation was similar in Algeria, with Tunisia and Morocco next door and Libya and Egypt close by. The Palestinian resistance, however, does not have any such secure shelters in which it can prepare itself out of the enemy's reach. The enemy is prepared to strike at any place in the Arab world, which has been defeated and has not yet recovered its strength.

Yet, all these and other factors do not detract from the great role of the Palestinian resistance—rather, they increase its importance and make it a political, military, and human necessity. The role of the Palestinian resistance is, therefore, as follows:

(1) To continue to strike during the period between the two battles—the battle of 5 June, in which the Arab world was defeated, and the inevitable battle to rectify that defeat. . . .

(2) The continuation of resistance has an important moral effect because it eliminates the fear which the Israeli enemy is trying to implant in the heart of the Arab fighter. . . .

(3) Resistance is causing material embarrassment and psychological confusion to the enemy.

(4) By strengthening its positions in the face of all the obstacles, the resistance may be able to play a major role in the battle with the enemy behind his lines when the decisive hour strikes.

(5) Resistance, and this is the human aspect of its role, will symbolize the Palestinian element. Propaganda has tried to eliminate its existence, and even the feeling of its existence.

(6) Finally, the resistance—particularly because of the enemy's overwhelming superiority—will by its courage and sacrifice give the Arab struggle its finest legends and epics. . . .

This then, is the role of the resistance. It is one of the most splendid and noble roles, but not a decisive one. I mean that the resistance cannot achieve the liquidation of the Israeli aggression, which is a broader responsibility. It is the responsibility of the entire Arab nation on a broader and wider front, with complete concentration and mobilization. . . .

DOCUMENT XVI (c) EXCERPT FROM G. KEMP, *Arms and Security: The Egypt-Israel Case*, PP. 13-14.

Guerrilla war

The military advantages of retaining parts of the West Bank may be offset by the disadvantages (both political and military) of incorporating the new Arab population into Israel. It is a question of balancing 'maps' and 'chaps'.

A proper guerrilla war mounted by Arab 'freedom fighters', and supported by the Arab countries and the Arab population in Israel, could prove to be extremely costly in financial, military, and political terms for Israel. It is not that Israel would become the arena for a war of 'national liberation', but rather for terrorism similar to that practised by Jewish groups during the Mandate, by the FLN and OAS in Algerian cities, and the Viet Cong in South Vietnam. The scope for such activities would be limited in the first place to sabotage and terrorism in both urban and rural areas, but neighbouring Syria, Jordan, and Lebanon could provide routes for infiltration and possible sanctuary. Furthermore, the possible effectiveness of well-trained terrorists operating in the new Israeli-occupied territories cannot be ignored. Arab terrorists could harass a great many of the military command, control, and communication installations that are essential for the type of rapid response tactics in which the Israelis have until now excelled.

Israeli leaders have tended to play down the threat from terrorism, arguing that the comparison with the activities of the various extremist groups during the Mandate is not very realistic. The British used a velvet glove against the local population then and had no stomach for the operation; Israel would react very differently. The massive reprisal raids against guerrilla bases in Jordan in late 1967 and 1968 suggest that she is prepared to be tough; whether these methods would be successful is another question.

It may well be that terrorism would be one alternative offensive strategy for the Arabs to seriously consider given their present impotence against Israel's strength, but it is difficult to believe that a fourth Arab-Israeli war would be restricted to this type of campaign. An effective terrorist campaign against Israel would require some co-operation from the local population, as well as sanctuary in a friendly neighbouring country. Though the West Bank could provide the local co-operation and the East Bank the sanctuary, some movement of the Arab population would reduce the danger of co-operation, and mining the banks of the Jordan and the construction of an electric barrier along the 50-mile stretch of that river between Lake Tiberius and the Dead Sea could reduce the danger of infiltration.

If terrorist attacks against Israel continue it would seem that short of a major war, the best military strategy for her to adopt would be to develop more well-trained helicopter-borne troops either to counter-attack against guerrilla sanctuaries, or to engage them in action on Israeli-held territory. Under such circumstances some priority might be given for further purchases of assault helicopters.

*

THE ARAB-ISRAELI MILITARY BALANCE AND ARMS CONTROL

It is tempting to compare the military strength of nations by reference simply to the quantities of modern weapons held. There is some value in making a start with comparison in this way, but the objection is that quantities of weapons held, even when allied with demographic and economic information, can be misleading. We need also to know about the qualities of the different types of weapons held, their suitability for the environment, the skill and determination with which they are handled and other similar factors. As a necessary start to comparison we can see from Document XVI (d) (i) how in sheer holdings of arms the Arab states are greatly superior to

Israel. Can arms holdings be controlled? In Document XVI
(d) (ii) we have a further excerpt from G. Kemp's study that is
devoted to the problem of arms control and its alternatives and
the role of nuclear weapons in the Arab-Israeli conflict. This
study takes into account the more complex, often unquantifiable,
factors that often lie uncounted in the background. Elsewhere
in his study the author makes it clear that the prime Egyptian
problem does not lie in shortage of equipment, but in inadequate training. This is the sort of factor difficult to allow for in
comparing strengths or establishing any arms control policies.

DOCUMENT XVI (d) (i) COMPARATIVE HOLDINGS OF ARMS: ISRAEL
AND THE PRINCIPAL ARAB STATES (EXTRACTED FROM *The Military
Balance, 1968-69*, INSTITUTE OF STRATEGIC STUDIES)

State	Total Armed Forces	Army	Tanks	Combat Aircraft
Israel	275,000	255,000	895	270
UAR	211,000	180,000	700	400
Syria	60,500	50,000	430	150
Jordan	55,000	53,000	230	20
Iraq	82,000	70,000	575	215
Totals for Arab States	408,500	353,000	1,935	785

DOCUMENT XVI (d) (ii) FURTHER EXCERPTS FROM G. KEMP, *Arms
and Security: The Egypt-Israel Case*, PP. 22-5

Arms control?

Even if the United States and Soviet Union were to reach an
understanding on the dangers involved in the transferring of

certain types of conventional weapons to their respective friends, the political differences between Israel and the Arab world are so fundamental to the problem of stability in the Middle East, that it has to be asked whether arms control, which has usually implied greater regulation of the existing force levels, has any relevance at all. Members of that apparently fast-vanishing group, the arms controllers, have hoped that in the long run increased stability would result from arms control agreements which would lead to improvements in the political climate and the reduction of arms levels and defence expenditures. The initial and important objective in any external and local arms-control agreement imposed on a conflict area must be to work towards a more stable *military* situation, which will allow basic political disagreements to be tackled with less risk of war. This may entail a net increase in certain types of arms deliveries. Arms-control proposals that advocate only cut-offs and embargos have more chance of acceptance in areas not so plagued with such irreconcilable inter-state conflicts, e.g. in South America and sub-Saharan Africa. The worst area in which to attempt to impose limits on force levels is one where the adversaries are involved in major conflict, and consider strong military forces to be essential.

The Arab countries have suffered a military defeat comparable to Dunkirk and the fall of France. It is naive to suppose that these countries will accept proposals that weaken their capacity to fight Israel. It may be that economic necessity and reason will force them to modify their more extreme military plans, but an external arms-control agreement would almost certainly be denounced as a *diktat*, a further example of great power self-interest, and another indicator of Chairman Mao's contention that the industrial powers are tacitly part of an 'Unholy Alliance'. And Israel will continue to insist that, without a political settlement, she must remain militarily superior.

Alternatives

Rather than attempt to suggest blueprints for peace in the Middle East, it would seem more helpful to approach the control problem cautiously, and ask what arms structures the local powers feel they really need, and what effect these would have on the local and international power balance, and how, if at all, can the arms supplier adjust their transfers to enhance, rather than erode, the uneasy peace? This approach may conceivably generate helpful suggestions about the inter-relationship between weapons and security in local conflict areas, and, in turn, may offer alternative policies within the context of a political climate that is basically hostile.

The quantitative classifications of weapons to be found in the country sections of *The Military Balance* (published annually by the Institute for Strategic Studies) and other statistical publications provide an extremely useful ready-reckoner for determining the relative force levels. To those who are acquainted with the performance of weapons systems, this presentation, also, tells something of respective force capabilities. But to be as precise as possible about the military balance between two or more adversaries, force levels must be examined in a more functional way. . . .

This approach offers no panacea for the problems that must be faced but the arms control itself has never been regarded as a panacea. Arms-control measures, however rigorous or far-reaching, can only reduce, never remove, the likelihood of armed conflict between sovereign states and, most important, can never be divorced from politics. If arms-control policies are to contribute to long-term stability, there has to be political agreement in more areas than those relating to the use of force.

The main difficulty of proposing any comprehensive agreements on arms levels in the Middle East continues to be the political and military asymmetry between Israel and the Arab countries. If one accepts that in the months before the June war, Israel was not intent on the conquest of Jordan, Sinai, and the Golan Heights, but that the Arab countries were, for various obvious reasons dissatisfied with the *status quo*, one facet of this asymmetry becomes clear: though Israeli political aspirations favoured the broad terms of the *status quo*, her military strategy was best suited for 'offensive' operations—in other words was designed to defend Israel by containing Arab military power on Arab soil. Alternatively, the Arab political ambitions favoured change, but their military posture against Israel was not geared in June 1968 for short-term offensive operations. This asymmetry is greater since the June War. Israel is more satisfied with the territorial *status quo*; the Arabs more dissatisfied. Yet Israel is now probably in a stronger military position from which to conduct both offensive and defensive military operations.

The most significant asymmetry concerns the Egyptian and Israeli perceptions of such concepts as 'victory', 'defeat', 'stability', and 'balance of power'. Most Arab countries openly admit that they were decisively beaten in June 1967, but they argue that they lost a battle, not a war; just as they lost battles in 1948 and 1956. The loss of 15,000 Egyptian soldiers in the 1967 war may have been appalling but it was not disastrous. Egypt has survived as a nation state and would probably continue to survive if 115,000 men were to be killed. For Israel the position is very different. The Israelis argue that they cannot afford to lose one battle, and for that reason their policy must be to avoid a fourth war by deterring what they clearly failed to deter in 1967. If deterrence fails, then they must have the capacity to win again speedily, and with small loss of life. These objectives can only be achieved by reaching a real political settlement or by maintaining a clear military superiority by modernizing weapons inventories, and adjusting territorial boundaries. The Israelis do not believe the long-term Arab objective—the destruction of the Jewish state of Israel—has changed, though it is admitted that for tactical reasons the short-term Arab objective may be more moderate and accommodating.

The Arab countries, and especially Egypt, are as well aware of the basic weaknesses of Israel as they are of Israel's present military superiority. In the absence of a settlement, their strategy is a simple one; to improve their military position to the point when they have the ability to win just one battle. Or they do not even have to 'win' a battle, merely to raise the costs of an Israeli 'victory' to the point where the kill-ratio becomes intolerable for Israel. Arab strategists can argue that Israel would not survive in her present form if casualties, in the tens of thousands, were sustained in a war or battle. It is for this reason that groups like *El Fatah* would almost welcome an Israeli occupation of Amman, Damascus, or Cairo; such an undertaking would strain Israel's manpower, weaken her international status, and set the scene for a real war of national liberation. Equally the clashes in September 1968 between Jewish and Arab Israelis in Tel Aviv, following a terrorist attack in the bus station there, indicates that the Israeli population itself could become more polarized in future.

Since many Israelis understand the logic of this strategy, one cannot expect them to fall into the trap of occupying more territory, but rather to concentrate on building up an even stronger military machine for decisive surprise attacks on Arab military positions.

Nuclear weapons and the arms race

It is widely known that Israel has a fairly advanced nuclear research programme. The most important facility, located at Dimona in the Negev, has been operational since 1964; and if a reprocessing plant were used to extract plutonium from the fuel rods it could provide enough (between 6–12 kilograms) for at least two bombs a year. It is doubtful whether Israel could build a reprocessing plant without the news leaking out although there can be no certainty of this. In addition, Israel has a missile research programme and has been co-operating with the French company, *Dassault*, in development of the MD 620 surface-to-surface missile mentioned on p. 10 [of Kemp's book]. It is, therefore, quite possible that within 2–3 years Israel could build up a small nuclear capacity, and probably explode a test bomb within 18 months. Initially the atomic bomb could be carried in a specially adapted combat aircraft, or even one of *El Al*'s Boeing 707s. Given the short distances involved, Israel would be able to threaten the two most important Egyptian targets, Cairo and the Aswan Dam.

The present conventional weapons equation between Israel and the Arab countries suggest that it is the latter, not Israel, who can make the best military case for nuclear weapons as their alternative strategic options, conventional war or guerrilla war, at present seem so unattractive. But where could they get the necessary technical and financial backing to develop, build, maintain, and operate a nuclear capability? The Soviet Union will presumably not supply Egypt with nuclear know-how whatever she may do in the way of nuclear guarantees. Chinese nuclear assistance seems equally improbable, at least for the next few years.

If nuclear weapons entered the Middle East as a result of indigenous effort, the prospect for long-term stability would remain uncertain. Perhaps an Israeli nuclear weapons programme would have such an important lead-time over any possible indigenous Egyptian programme, that an era of military stability might ensue, based on Israel's ability to deter Egyptian or combined Arab aggression. This would seem to be a dubious argument. What would Israel consider constituted Arab 'aggression'? Would she threaten to use nuclear weapons if terrorist activity continues; and if so, against whom? It is doubtful whether a nuclear weapon developed in the near future would buy Israel any more security than she at present enjoys, and it would certainly increase her already high defence budget and weaken her case internationally.

Since the chances of a multilateral agreement to restrict arms supplies to the Middle East seem low, the external powers, especially the United States and Soviet Union, may have to supply more conventional weapons to their clients, to avoid becoming embroiled in conflict, to live up to their respective pledges to both sides, and to prevent the eventual spread of nuclear weapons. The offer made by Mr Kosygin on 1 July 1968, to consider some agreement with the United States to control arms supplies to the area had an unrealistic ring about it, given the preconditions laid down (an Israeli withdrawal to the pre-June 1967 boundaries). The Soviet Union probably realizes that any attempt to invoke a joint embargo on certain supplies without an Israeli withdrawal would almost certainly be unacceptable to the Arab countries, who would then have to turn elsewhere for arms. Given a Soviet desire to exercise some restraint over Arab military ambitions, a continuation of arms supplies would seem, from the Russian point of view, the best way to retain influence.

France and Britain probably have more to gain politically and economically by increasing, rather than limiting, arms sales to the countries of the Middle East. The deal announced between Britain and Libya in May 1968 for air-defence missiles is one of the several lucrative arms orders that are to be won in the Middle East. French policy has already shown its opportunistic nature. Short of a miracle, the 'mad momentum' of the conventional arms race will continue at increased costs to all participants, and with the increased probability of the introduction of very advanced weapons systems into local inventories.

What options are there, then, for the external powers, who at present do not want another war and yet cannot get themselves out of the quagmire? Doubtless, the four major external suppliers have professional committees who are well aware of the subtle military and political nuances of arms transfers to Middle East countries. Armed with the relevant graphs, curves, and costs, they are in a much better position than any outsider to describe in detail what effect the transfer of System X will have on a local balance. However, since the United States, the Soviet Union, and France do not co-operate in determining what systems shall be transferred (there is some co-operation between the United States and Britain), it is difficult for professional military analysts to make much sense of the pattern of transfers, unless they can predict the significant political factors that in the last resort affect all major weapons inputs.

*

JERUSALEM

Another continuing problem is Jerusalem. Of the territories occupied by Israel since June 1967, this is one whose return the Israeli government has frequently declared to be non-negotiable, though reports in late 1968 suggested a somewhat moderating attitude.

To surrender Jerusalem permanently to Israel would be a great blow to Arab pride. It is also a matter that raises animosity towards Israel in the Muslim world generally.

In Document XVI (e), below, we give excerpts from early UN resolutions on the subject of Jerusalem—resolutions much quoted by Arab writers. Document XVI (f) contains excerpts from official American 'White House' statements issued just before and just after the merger of East and West Jerusalem was carried out. The American statements stress the interests of the three great religions with claims on Jerusalem, but also refer to the 'international status' of the city. As we can see, this is not however the wording of the original UN resolutions, which require an 'international regime'. Document XVI (g) gives the text of the Pakistani-sponsored UN General Assembly Resolution of 4 July 1967—a resolution on which the United States abstained. In Document XVI (h) we have excerpts from a statement of the Israeli position by the Israeli Foreign Minister. We may note in this statement the Israeli contention that any international interest in Jerusalem can relate only to the Holy Places.

DOCUMENT XVI (e). UN RESOLUTIONS ON JERUSALEM, 1947 AND 1948

Excerpt from the 1947 UN Partition Plan

The City of Jerusalem shall be established as a *corpum seperatum* under a special international regime and shall be administered by the UN.

General Assembly Resolution, 11 December 1948

In view of its association with three world religions, the Jerusalem area, including the present municipality of Jerusalem, plus the surrounding villages and towns . . . should be accorded special and separate treatment from the rest of Palestine and shall be placed under effective United Nations control.

DOCUMENT XVI (f). WHITE HOUSE STATEMENTS ON JERUSALEM, 28 JUNE 1968

The President said on 19 June that in our view 'there must be adequate recognition of the special recognition of three great religions in the Holy Places in Jerusalem'. On this principle he assumes that before any unilateral action is taken on the status of Jerusalem there will be appropriate consultation with religious leaders and others who are deeply concerned. Jerusalem is holy to Christians, to Jews and to Moslems. It is one of the great continuing tragedies of history that a city which is so much the centre of man's highest values has also been, over and over again, a centre of conflict. Repeatedly, the passionate beliefs of one element have led to exclusion or unfairness for others. Men of all religions will agree that we now must do better. The world must find an answer that is fair and is recognized to be fair. That could not be achieved by hasty unilateral action, and the President is confident that the wisdom and good judgment of those now in control of Jerusalem will prevent any such action. . . .

The hasty administrative action taken today cannot be regarded as determining the future of the Holy Places or the status of Jerusalem in relation to them. The United States has never recognized such unilateral action by any State in the area governing the international status of Jerusalem. . . .

DOCUMENT XVI (g). UN GENERAL ASSEMBLY RESOLUTION ON JERUSALEM, 4 JULY 1967

The GENERAL ASSEMBLY

DEEPLY CONCERNED at the situation prevailing in Jerusalem as the result of the measures taken by Israel to change the status of the city,
(1) CONSIDERS that these measures are invalid.
(2) CALLS UPON Israel to rescind all measures already taken and to desist forthwith from taking any action which would alter the status of Jerusalem.
(3) REQUESTS the Secretary General to report to the General Assembly and the Security Council on the situation and the implementation of the present resolution not later than one week from its adoption.

DOCUMENT XVI (h). EXCERPTS FROM STATEMENT BY ISRAELI FOREIGN MINISTER, MR ABBA EBAN, ON JERUSALEM, 12 JULY 1967

The resolution presented on 4 July by Pakistan and adopted on the same date evidently refers to measures taken by the Government of Israel on 27 June, 1967. The term 'annexation' used by supporters of the resolution is out of place. The measures adopted relate to the integration of Jerusalem in the administrative and municipal spheres and furnish a legal basis for the protection of the Holy Places in Jerusalem.

I now specify the character and effect of the measures adopted on 27 June:

The Holy Places

The Protection of Holy Places Law provides that 'the Holy Places shall be protected from desecration and any other violation and from anything likely to violate the freedom of access of the members of the different religions to the places sacred to them or their feelings with regard to those places. Whoever desecrates or otherwise violates a Holy Place shall be liable to imprisonment for a term of seven years. . . .' During the previous nineteen years there had been no such legislation to protect the Holy Places in Jerusalem. Since 27 June sacred buildings desecrated since 1948 have been restored, and houses of worship destroyed during the Jordanian occupation are being rebuilt.

Civic co-operation

One of the most significant results of the measures taken on 27 June is the new mingling of Arabs and Jews in free and constant association. The Arab residents within the walls had been cut off for 19 years from all contact with the residents of the newer parts of the city. Today they are free to renew or initiate contacts with their Jewish neighbours in Jerusalem and elsewhere in Israel. The residents of the city outside the walls now visit the Old City.

There is a profound human and spiritual significance in the replacement of embattled hostility by normal and good-neighbourly relations. It is especially appropriate that ecumenical habits of thought and action should take root in the city from which the enduring message of human brotherhood was proclaimed with undying power in generations past.

Municipal services

In the hills of Judea, where Jerusalem is situated, there is an acute shortage of water. The Old City is now connected with the general water supply system, and all houses are receiving a continuous supply of water double the quantity available to them in the past.

All hospitals and clinics are already functioning. In the past no health services existed for the young within the framework of the school system, nor were there any health stations for mother- and child-care. These services are now being established.

There was no social welfare system in the Old City. Today all the inhabitants of Jerusalem enjoy the same welfare rights. The municipality has already begun extending its welfare services to those for whom none have been available in the past. . . .

Compulsory education regulations have been extended to all parts of the city. None of those arrangements affect the existing private education network.

*

The universal interest

The measures taken by my Government to secure the protection of the Holy Places are only a part of Israel's effort to ensure respect for universal interests in Jerusalem. It is evident from UN discussions and documents that the international interest in Jerusalem has always been understood to derive from the presence of the Holy Places.

Israel does not doubt her own will and capacity to secure the respect of universal spiritual interests. It has forthwith ensured that the Holy Places of Judaism, Christianity and Islam be administered under the responsibility of the religions which hold them sacred. In addition, in a spirit of concern for historic and spiritual tradition, my Government has taken steps with a view to reaching arrangements to ensure the universal character of the Holy Places. In pursuance of this objective, the Government of Israel has embarked on a constructive and detailed dialogue with representatives of universal religious interests. If these explorations are as fruitful as we hope and expect, the universal character of the Holy Places will for the first time in recent decades find effective expression.

*

REFUGEES

The problem of the refugees has been made more complex by the June 1967 war. In the first place, there are now more refugees if we include in the definition those persons newly displaced by the war, though these are not for the most part registered refugees on the books of UNWRA. Second, many of the registered refugees from the 1947/48 war fled to the East Bank of the Jordan, and some to Syria in June 1967.

It is not possible to say exactly how many refugees there are now because the figures are in doubt—as they must be after the upheavals that have taken place. We can only produce some rough approximation.

From an examination of the documents from which extracts are given below we arrive at the following broad conclusions as to numbers of refugees.

There are probably 250,000 to 350,000 newly displaced persons in the Arab countries surrounding Israel. Of these between 115,000 and 175,000 are former refugees who have moved from the West Bank and Gaza, principally to the East Bank, but some to Syria and elsewhere. Altogether there were, in June 1968, over 900,000 UNWRA registered refugees actually receiving rations—the minimal provision—but many others receive medical, educational and other services. In fact, the total number of registered refugees as at June 1968, is 1,364,294, but this figure does not necessarily reflect the actual refugee population owing to factors such as unreported deaths and undetected false registration. In short, the war has not only increased the numbers of refugees, it has also resulted in there being large numbers of displaced persons, who may or may not become refugees, registered with UNWRA. Thanks to the efforts of UNWRA the refugees will not starve or lack elementary shelter, but their plight in every other respect is unenviable.

Clearly a first step is to enable those displaced by the war to return to where they were. To this end the Security Council, in June 1967, 'called upon Israel to ensure the safety, welfare and security of the inhabitants of the areas where military operations had taken place and to facilitate the return of those inhabitants who had fled the area since the outbreak of hostilities'. (Security Council Resolution 237 (1967)).

We give below excerpts from the 1967 and 1968 UNWRA Reports and an excerpt from an article which examines the problems set for Israel by her occupation of the West Bank.

DOCUMENT XVI (i). EXCERPT FROM REPORT OF COMMISSONER-GENERAL OF UNWRA FOR PALESTINE, I JULY 1966–30 JUNE 1967, PP. 11–14.

34. On 2 July the Commissioner-General had learnt of the announcement by the Government of Israel that they were prepared to allow the return to the West Bank of the Jordan of those persons who had fled across the River Jordan as a result of the hostilities. He immediately appealed to all those who might still be contemplating leaving their homes to stay where they were, and urged all concerned, on grounds of common humanity, to encourage those persons who had already left to return to their former place of residence, and to do everything to allay the fears which deterred them from going back. In making this appeal, he stressed the fact that UNWRA's capacity to assist these persons was far greater on the West Bank, where the Agency had the necessary camps, installations and other facilities.

35. On 10 July, the Government of Israel issued rules concerning the return of these persons. The arrangements for the return were the subject of prolonged negotiations between the International Committee of the Red Cross and the Governments of Israel and of Jordan. The date of 10 August 1967 had originally been set by the Israel Government as the final day of submission of applications for return; at a later stage, however, the date of 31 August was set for the completion of the actual return. The rules provided that applications were to be submitted on special forms, through the Red Cross, by heads of families and other adults whose permanent place of residence as on 5 June was on the West Bank, and who had crossed over to the East Bank in the period between 5 June and 4 July. The application forms were to be accompanied by passports, identity cards, UNWRA registration cards or specially designed UNWRA certificates which would afford evidence of residence

P*

on the West Bank. No application would be approved if the return of the applicant was considered by the Israel Government to involve a risk to security or legal order. The cases of residents of the West Bank who went abroad prior to 5 June and who wished to return would be treated separately, within the framework of arrangements for the reunion of families, by means of application to the diplomatic missions of Israel abroad.

36. The application forms were issued on 12 August and in the following days UNWRA staff members worked with Jordan government and Red Cross officials to help the many thousands of persons anxious to submit applications for return to the West Bank. In the event permits were issued only during the remainder of August and the return arrangements came to an end on 31 August. However, with the expiry of the 31 August deadline, the Government of Israel informed the Secretary-General (A/6795) that those whose applications had been approved but who had not managed to return would be permitted to do so within a fixed period of time. In addition, it announced that West Bank residents could apply for the return of members of their families, and that individual applications based on special hardship could be made. In the time available before putting the text of this report into final form, it has not been possible to reconcile entirely the figures relating to the return arrangements. From Amman it is reported that some 40,000 application forms were completed and submitted in respect of approximately 150,000 persons (out of the 200,000 who are reported to have crossed over to the East Bank). Israel has stated that the number of applications actually received by them amounted to only some 32,000 and related to only about 100,000 persons. The number of applications approved and permits issued is stated on the Jordan side to be 5,122 (relating to 18,236 persons) and on the Israel side to be 5,787 (relating to 20,658 persons). The number of persons who had actually crossed by 31 August was reported from Amman to be 14,150 and from Jerusalem to be 14,056. It is evident that only a small fraction of the total number of persons applying to return have so far been permitted to do so. Among those permitted to return, it appears that there were very few former inhabitants of the Old City of Jerusalem, very few from among the refugees formerly living in UNWRA camps on the West Bank and from

among the displaced persons who were accommodated in the tented camps set up in East Jordan since the hostilities. The number of refugees registered with UNWRA who have been permitted to return is reported to be only about 3,000 out of the 93,000 who crossed to the East Bank before 4 July and who were therefore *prima facie* eligible to return in accordance with the conditions stipulated by the Government of Israel. The Jordanian authorities have also reported that, in some cases, permits have been issued for some members of the family but not for others; the procedure for the submission of applications required that adult sons and daughters should apply separately from the rest of the family and this has resulted in cases where families were faced with the choice of either leaving a son or daughter behind or of losing their opportunity of return. It is clear from the figures given above that the hopes which were generated at the beginning of July that at least the bulk of the displaced persons would be able to return to the West Bank in pursuance of the terms of the Security Council's resolution 237 (1967) have not been realized. The reasons for the frustration of these hopes are disputed and are not a matter on which the Commissioner-General believes he can helpfully comment in present circumstances. However, from personal observation, he and his staff in Amman are able to record that the Jordanian authorities did all that was humanly possible to ensure that those whose applications to return were approved were promptly informed and were given every assistance in re-crossing the river. Nevertheless the bulk of the displaced persons remain on the East Bank and, whatever the reason may be and wherever the responsibility may lie, have not been able to return to their former homes.

37. Faced with this massive human problem, the Commissioner-General feels that he can only reiterate that UNWRA's capacity to help will be much greater if the refugees return to their previous camps and homes on the West Bank where UNWRA'S installations and facilities already exist.

DOCUMENT XVI (j) EXCERPTS FROM REPORT OF COMMISSIONER-GENERAL OF UNWRA FOR PALESTINE, I JULY, 1967–30 JUNE, 1968, PP. 2 AND 4–8.

5. In Lebanon the Agency's services continued to function

normally throughout the past year. The number of refugees registered with UNWRA was 166,264 at the end of June 1968 and the number receiving rations was 103,727. . . .

6. In Syria also the Agency's established services have functioned more or less normally. The number of refugees registered with UNWRA was 149,537 at the end of June 1968 and the number receiving rations was 100,503, including 4,583 added as a result of the emergency. . . .

8. The most urgent task confronting the Agency in Syria during the past year has been the provision of temporary shelter and other essential services for the registered refugees uprooted from the Quneitra area, now occupied by Israel. The total number of these newly displaced refugees is 17,500. Most found shelter in the homes of relatives and friends or in rented accommodation in Damascus and elsewhere, but, by the end of 1967, some 4,500 were accommodated in three tented camps, two on the outskirts of Damascus and one at Dera'a. The number of displaced refugees seeking accommodation in the tented camps, however, continued to increase and, at the request of the Syrian authorities, UNWRA established a further tented camp in the Damascus area and expanded one of the camps established last autumn. At 30 June 1968, there were 7,746 refugees living in the tented camps. During the bitterly cold and stormy winter of 1967/1968, the refugees living in the tented camps in Syria had to face much hardship and discomfort. UNWRA sought to alleviate the misery of life in these camps by providing stoves for heating, bedding, concrete floors under the tents, surfaced pathways and roads, and ditches for surface drainage through the camps. The Agency has supplemented the food ration with additional protein and enlarged the hot meal programme for the newly displaced refugees in these camps, as well as for those living outside who are in special need. Syrian displaced persons from the southern area, estimated at 100,000, have been provided with food, shelter and other services by the Government of Syria, and UNWRA'S help has not been required.

9. In Jordan, there were some 724,000 refugees registered with UNWRA before the hostilities, including persons who

were temporarily residing outside of the Agency's area of operations. After the exodus to east Jordan, the number of registered refugees still residing on the West Bank is estimated by the Agency at about 245,000 and the number in east Jordan at about 455,500, plus some 38,500 registered refugees from Gaza who have entered east Jordan since the hostilities. However, the total figure of 494,000 refugees will include some unreported deaths and absences.

10. At the time of writing this report, the situation in east Jordan is still confused as a result of the movements of population that have continued throughout the year and the difficulty of obtaining accurate figures. In addition to the 494,000 registered refugees shown in UNWRA records as now located in east Jordan, the Government of Jordan has registered some 237,500 displaced persons from the West Bank plus about 8,500 displaced persons from Gaza, a total of 246,000 displaced persons—which, when added to the 494,000 UNWRA registered refugees, would bring the total number of refugees and displaced persons living in east Jordan to 740,000. However, there is, doubtless, some duplication between the UNWRA registrations and those of the Government, as well as within each group, and efforts are now under way to identify and eliminate these extra registrations. The actual number of rations issued to all recipients in east Jordan during June 1968 was 590,000. Of these, 350,000 were issued to UNWRA-registered refugees and the remaining 240,000 to Government-registered displaced persons. Those receiving rations represent about 40 per cent of the total population of east Jordan. . . .

11. Paragraphs 34 to 38 of last year's report (A/6713) described the result of the arrangements made in July and August 1967, under which slightly more than 14,000 persons returned to the West Bank. Since then, some others have been able to return on grounds of special hardship or family reunion. For the period September 1967 to 30 June 1968, the total figure is given as 2,000 by Jordan and as 3,000 by Israel. However, these numbers are exceeded by the numbers of persons who have moved from the West Bank and the Gaza Strip to east Jordan over the same period. Some easing of the difficulties faced by the refugees and other displaced persons in east Jordan has

resulted from the greater freedom of movement across the river Jordan in both directions, which has been permitted in recent months. Nevertheless, the Commissioner-General feels that he should reiterate once again that UNWRA's capacity to help will be much greater if, in accordance with Security Council resolution 237 (1967), which was endorsed by the General Assembly, the inhabitants who had fled are allowed to return to the places where they were living before the hostilities and where UNWRA's installations and facilities already exist. The General Assembly's attention is also called to the references to this matter in the resolutions adopted by the International Conference on Human Rights on 7 May 1968 (A/7098); by the Economic and Social Council in resolution 1336 (XLIV) adopted on 31 May 1968, which endorsed resolution 6 (XXIV) adopted by the Commission on Human Rights on 27 February 1968; and by the World Health Assembly on 23 May 1968, which is reproduced as annex IV of this report. The Commissioner-General also hopes that the return to the territories now occupied as a result of the June 1967 hostilities ought to be considered, and the return permitted at the earliest possible date and without waiting for the achievement of the 'just settlement of the refugee problem' to which Security Council resolution 242 (1967) refers. This, in the belief of the Commissioner-General, would conform to the wishes of the vast majority of the refugees concerned.

12. Meanwhile, during the past year, UNWRA has done its best, in close co-operation with the Jordanian authorities and with a number of voluntary agencies, to cope with the apalling problem of the great mass of refugees and other displaced persons who now eke out a miserable existence in east Jordan. One of the first difficulties faced by the Agency was that, since its administrative headquarters within Jordan were previously in Jerusalem, a completely new administrative structure had to be established in Amman. At the request of the Government of Jordan, UNWRA has accepted responsibility for running all of the six tented camps (population 78,400) now established on the uplands in east Jordan. As already mentioned, UNWRA has also undertaken, at the Government's request, the whole responsibility for ration distribution. Schools have been improvised for the children in the tented camps and for displaced

refugee children living elsewhere. In all, schooling in east Jordan has had to be provided by the Agency for 20,000 more children than before the hostilities. . . .

14. On the West Bank, UNWRA's services recovered quickly from the disruption caused by the hostilities and have functioned in a regular and effective way throughout the year. During the first weeks of the school year, attendance at the UNWRA UNESCO schools was affected by general unrest and was both low and subject to sudden fluctuations. The three UNWRA training centres were similarly affected. But since November attendance has been regular and the schools and training centres have been running smoothly, with only occasional difficulties arising from the political uncertainty prevailing on the West Bank. Some school classes were handicapped by a lack of textbooks [as explained in paragraphs 17-19] but these difficulties were partly overcome by the preparation by UNWRA of teaching notes. The UNWRA health services have also operated regularly and without serious difficulty during the year. In both education and health matters, after initial questions of policy and jurisdiction had been explored with the authorities, the Agency has been left to carry on its work with little restriction or interference and, in general, the co-operation between UNWRA and the Israel authorities continued to be effective. Extensive revision of UNWRA's registration records and ration rolls has been necessary because of the large movement of refugees from the West Bank to east Jordan. In the process of rectifying the records, efforts have also been made, in accordance with General Assembly resolution 2341 (XXII), to ascertain deaths or absences which had not previously been recorded. Technical problems involved in ascertaining and reflecting such information in registration records have been under study. Consultations have also been held with the technical staff of the Government of Israel on the reconciliation of the UNWRA statistics with those produced in the census conducted by that Government in September 1967. More recently, emphasis has shifted to the statistics produced from the issue of identification cards. Against the Agency's current estimate of about 245,000 registered refugees remaining on the West Bank (including

Jerusalem) the number of rations being distributed by the Agency is 140,000 for normal recipients. Assistance was given during 1967 to some 6,000 emergency cases not previously registered with the Agency, but responsibility for this group was assumed by the Government of Israel at the beginning of 1968. The Agency has been assured that the level of assistance for this group will be maintained.

15. In Gaza, the aftermath of the hostilities has been painful and prolonged and the Agency's services felt the effects of the succession of incidents and security measures, such as curfews, interrogations, detentions, and, on some occasions, the demolition of houses which followed. In addition, economic activity, always precariously based in Gaza, has slumped and the demand for the Agency's services, particularly supplementary feeding, has increased. The full range of the Agency's services was quickly re-established after the hostilities, and has been maintained. Between 40,000 and 45,000 registered refugees are believed to have left Gaza since the hostilities. The Agency's current estimate of the total number of registered refugees remaining in Gaza is about 265,000. The number of rations being issued by UNWRA in Gaza is 206,638 for regular recipients and 2,435 for emergency cases. As on the West Bank, the revision of the UNWRA registration records to reflect the movement out of Gaza, as well as deaths not previously reported, has been a major task. . . .

16. In the United Arab Republic, UNWRA has during the past year met the cost of relief support provided by the United Arab Republic authorities for some 3,000 registered refugees from Gaza. (The total number of registered refugees now in the United Arab Republic is believed to be considerably larger and the Government estimates the number of refugees and other displaced persons from Gaza at 13,000.)

DOCUMENT XVI (k). EXCERPT FROM DON PERETZ, 'ISRAEL'S NEW ARAB DILEMMA'', *Middle East Journal*, VOL. 22, NO. 1 (1968), PP. 49–53.

Israeli policies and problems of administration in occupied areas

The situation in the occupied areas differs greatly from that following the 1947-48 and 1956 wars with the Arab states. Far more territory has been occupied, including all the land disputed in the Palestine conflict. Thus the approximately 8,000 square miles controlled by Israel within the 1949 armistice frontiers has been enlarged about four times to include all Sinai, the Gaza Strip, the Jordanian West Bank (with East or Arab Jerusalem), and Jawlan. (The total areas of Israel and the occupied territories is about 35,000 square miles.)

Whereas in 1948 only about 150,000 leaderless Palestinians remained in Israel, there are now about ten times that number of Arabs constituting about a third of the population under Israel jurisdiction. (The estimate of an Arab population equal to one third the Jewish population includes some 300,000 Israeli Arabs.) The present Arab population includes several former Jordanian Cabinet ministers, ambassadors, high ranking government officers, judges, clerics, lawyers, physicians, engineers, journalists, educators and other professionals. The problems faced by Israel in dealing with the occupied territories are not only more numerous but far more complex than those ever before faced in its dealings with Arab residents.

In 1956-57 Israeli forces destroyed roads, military establishments and other Egyptian installations before departing from Sinai and the Gaza Strip. Army policy now is to extend highways, rebuild military posts, and otherwise improve the infrastructure indicating that there will be no hasty evacuation from any of the occupied territories.

Public opinion in Israel as indicated by the press, the pronouncements of political leaders and other leading citizens daily becomes more resistant to departure for both sentimental and practical reasons. Only the Arab wing of the bifurcated Communist party, and Mapam have openly opposed retention by Israel of certain occupied territories. The press and leaders of most other political groups have on several occasions made known their opposition to return of any, or in some instances, return of large parts of the Arab territories. The leaders of Mapai, the kingpin in the present war coalition government, have not made public their position on the occupied regions. Within Mapai, however, there are differences of opinion about the future of the territory and its inhabitants. Some support the Mapam proposal to return much of the West Bank to Jordan;

others favour the concept of a 'Greater Israel' in which all territory will be retained.

Within two months after the war leaders of several political parties took definite stands against return of land to the defeated Arabs. Labour Minister Yigal Allon told a gathering of his Ahdut Ha'avoda Party that 'Israel's eastern border must be the River Jordan and the halfway line through the Dead Sea. This was a viable frontier with Jordan, and a permanent Israeli presence by settlement of this region will ensure the nation's security,' he warned. 'The Golan Heights is no less part of ancient Israel than Hebron and Nablus, for did not Jephtha judge there?' he asked. Allon stated that he preferred a cease fire arrangement along the new borders to armistice agreements that would again lead to renewed war. Israel could not settle its border problems by military and diplomatic means alone, he stated. The liberated areas could be suitably developed by settling them with Jews in co-operation with the Arab populations.

At approximately the same time Israel's Defence Minister, Major General Moshe Dayan, one of the founders and leaders of the new Rafi Party, addressed his followers along similar lines. 'All the areas we have taken, including the Suez and the Rama [Golan Heights], are dear to us.' He too called upon Jewish history and Israel's security as reasons for retaining the 'new territories'.

More recently Israel's Chief Sephardic Rabbi gave religious sanction to retention of the occupied territories. In answer to a question about the *halachic* status of the area he replied that no religious or secular authority, including the Israel government, has the power to yield a single inch. 'The land was promised to us by the Almighty, and all the prophets foretold its return to us. Therefore, it is forbidden for any Jew ever to consider returning any part whatsoever of the land of our forefathers.'

Mapam's six-point peace programme contains the only suggestion by any of Israel's major parties for return of territory. The plan calls for keeping border changes related to security reasons to 'an absolute minimum'. It opposed 'programmes of annexation of the West Bank of Jordan into the State of Israel, as expressed by various members of the Cabinet'. However, Mapam also calls for inclusion of the Gaza Strip, the ridges of the Golan Heights and Jordanian Jerusalem within

Israel's enlarged borders. Mapam also would refuse to evacuate any territory until a peace settlement is achieved.

An alternative to annexation has been suggested by a group of private Israeli citizens representing a wide range of political opinions, including many who formerly supported establishment of a binational state. Their proposals call for a federation of Palestine (Eretz-Israel) to include the State of Israel, the West Bank and Gaza, with 'Greater Jerusalem' as its capital. Neighbouring Arab states would also be encouraged to join. The jurisdiction of the federation would include economic, trade, transportation, communications, education, culture and other activities, and 'will be determined dynamically, by the process of growing mutual trust and co-operation'. This leaves only the Arab faction of the Communist party with a programme calling for immediate and complete evacuation of the occupied territories.

Integration into Israel of Arab Jerusalem has already become 'non-negotiable'. The former Arab municipal structure, educational system, police force, and public services have all been united with those in Israel's capital and the 65,000 to 70,000 Arab occupants of the former Jordanian city are now considered to be Israeli residents.

Although policy towards other occupied areas is not quite so decisive, the general trend is towards a similar, if not identical, form of integration. The major and as yet unanswered problem confronting Israelis is what to do about the large Arab population for which their government would be responsible if complete integration of the occupied areas occurs. Given present rates of population growth, the Jews would become a minority within a decade in a 'Greater Israel' including Gaza and the West Bank. Fear of becoming a minority in an 'Arab Israel' accounts for Mapam's abandonment of its traditional binational programme and for the party's desire to return the West Bank to Jordan.

Many who favour a 'Greater Israel' are among the strongest opponents of binationalism because they fear diluting the country's 'Jewish character'. One answer to this dilemma was recently offered by the Secretary-General of Rafi, Shimon Perez. He foresaw possibilities of encouraging Arab emigration. 'There is the phenomenon in the modern world,' he pointed out 'of roaming from village to city and from agriculture to industry. In the Arab world industrial development was delayed by several generations, but the twentieth century arrived in the Arab world with the assistance of oil wells which made possible employment and enrichment of many. Why prevent the movement of emigrants from underdeveloped agriculture in Judah and Samaria to the oil industries of Kuwait and Bahrein?' he asked. Perez believed that under appropriate conditions tens of thousands of Arabs would flock to the oil rich Arab countries, forgetting the era when they had been refugees.

Since the Six Day War there have been increasing calls by the Israel government and Jewish Agency for a great increase in Jewish immigration to balance the large Arab population in the new territories. By December Jewish settlements were set up in Sinai, the West Bank and Jawlān, although there seemed to be few indications of large-scale Jewish immigration to the new territories.

Meanwhile, Israel has taken full responsibility for administration and government in the occupied areas. Arab Jerusalem is under civil administration but the Jawlān, the West Bank and the Gaza-Sinai areas are governed by high ranking army officers. Each of the three military governates is subdivided into districts under lower ranking officers. Local officials such as mayors, town clerks, judges, teachers, welfare workers, and even a few Jordanian appointed police officers have been asked to continue in their posts. Although many Palestinians refused to serve under, or to receive their salaries from, Israel, there are hundreds who have remained. Some who did not wish to become refugees remained in their posts because they had no alternative income. Others felt duty bound to the Arab communities they were serving. A few envisaged possibilities of co-operation with Israel until the fate of the occupied areas would be determined.

The military governors have been assisted in their administration by civilian specialists seconded from various Israel government departments including the ministries of education, agriculture, social welfare, health, finance and others.

Long-range development policy for the occupied areas is being devised by a complex of civilian committees comprised of some two hundred specialists in a variety of fields. They include agriculturalists, urban planners, hydrologists, petroleum engineers, sociologists and demographers. While many of these committees work independently of each other, they are supposedly co-ordinated in the prime minister's office. Included among their responsibilities are plans for redistributing and relocating Arab populations in the Gaza Strip and West Bank. Their micro-economic planning includes an overall survey of resources and populations with possibilities of integrating the occupied areas into Israel's economy, their return to the Arab states, or continued administration of parts of them. Israeli policy towards both the old and new refugees will be largely determined by overall plans for the occupied areas. Indications are that repatriation of any substantial number of refugees will be discouraged, especially in view of the high Arab birth rate. Except for the 14,000 West Bank residents who were permitted to return last August, there has been no large-scale official return to occupied territory. On the other hand, exodus from Israel-held regions continues at the rate of a few thousand per month. Some unofficial repatriation occurs where the Jordan River is shallow enough to permit crossings on foot or by motor vehicles. One Israeli hydrologist has suggested flooding the River in the Beisan Valley as a deterrent to unauthorized infiltration.

At the micro-economic level there are plans for pilot projects resettling some 2,000 refugee families, two-thirds in agriculture and one-third in non-agricultural occupations on Jordanian government state lands in the Jordan Valley.

The annual report of UNWRA observed that few former inhabitants of the Old City of Jerusalem and very few refugees formerly living in UNWRA camps on the West Bank were permitted to return during the August repatriation. There has been some speculation that refugee camps and installations on the West Bank may be used for resettling refugees from the Gaza Strip.

Israelis who have been developing plans for the occupied areas reason that their efforts will not be wasted even if the areas are returned to the Arab countries. If economic rehabilitation succeeds, not only will the refugees, the indigenous populations and the Arab countries benefit; it will also be to Israel's advantage to be surrounded by fewer displaced Palestinians.

Conclusion: For Further Discussion

It is perhaps tempting to think that quarrels between nations must rest on a clash of material interests. It is natural for us to look at the concrete issues about which nations disagree. Are there then specific points of dispute between Arabs and Israelis whose solution would set Arab-Israeli relations to rights?

Let us consider, first, the problem of Israeli access to the southern seas. It has apparently been a crucial factor in the course of Arab-Israeli relations—a prime cause of war in 1956 and 1967. If the Arab States again denied Israeli access to the Indian Ocean, it would no doubt become a cause of conflict once more. Access is commercially important for Israel. Yet we must surely ask whether Israeli access to the Indian Ocean constitutes a commercial loss, or any other danger to the Arab States. Is there any real problem at all in the sense that any vital interest is involved?

Or again, take the problem of the division of the Jordan waters. It was partly the lack of an agreed solution on this—and Israel's declared intention to draw water up to the limits of the Johnston Plan—that occasioned renewed Arab-Israeli hostility in 1964. Yet, bearing in mind broad Arab-Israeli agreement on the division of waters proposed in the Johnston Plan, can we say there is a real problem here?

As we have seen, another issue is that of Jerusalem, whose recent absorption into Israel has been much resented by the Arabs and by Muslims elsewhere. Professor Arnold Toynbee, who describes himself as a Western spokesman for the Arab cause, has said that annexation of Jerusalem 'would make genuine peace between Israel and the Arabs impossible' (Arnold Toynbee and J. L. Talmon, 'The Argument Between

Arabs and Jews', *Encounter*, September 1967, p. 69). Yet he does not altogether rule out acceptance of Israeli sovereignty in return for some concessions by Israel. Jerusalem is a difficult issue and the wisdom of the Israeli action extremely dubious, but may it not be that the issue is even now just negotiable? The difficulty is perhaps that Israel is so convinced of the essential justice of her case that she will not regard Jerusalem as a matter requiring compensation to the Arabs elsewhere.

We come much closer to the core of the Arab-Israeli conflict when we consider the refugee problem. There are two possible solutions to it—or at least there were before the 1967 Israeli victory. One was that advocated by the United Nations, namely return to their lands in Israel for those who wished and compensation for the remainder. The other, which Israel favours, is the compensation of refugees and their resettlement in other Arab lands. In rejecting this solution the Arabs are concerned with justice; and they accept that the cause of justice may require sacrifice—even by the refugees themselves. They would ask, 'Are not the honour and dignity of the Arab people at stake'. Why should Arabs be displaced from their lands and turned into refugees for the sake of Jewish refugees— and for immigrants who are no longer refugees? On the Israeli side, re-admission of large numbers of refugees would upset the balance between her Jewish and Arab population. For Israel it is partly a matter of security, partly a matter of the equation that has developed between Jewish Home and Israeli State. And do not the Jews, they ask, have a better historic claim to Palestine than the Arabs?

The refugee problem has always been crucial, but has always been seen as linked to the boundaries issue. The UN Conciliation Commission insisted on this link in 1949. The Arabs have always wanted to resettle Arabs on the lands they left; and they insist that those who fled from territories lying between the 1947 UN Partition Plan and the 1949 Armistice Agreements' borders would live under Arab rule. In other words Israel would retire to the Partition Plan borders. This Israel has refused to discuss.

Boundaries' and refugees' problems have in the past been closely tied together, but is this any longer the case? Since June 1967 the territorial changes have been so tremendous that the boundaries problem surely overshadows that of the refugees. Save that of compensation, the old solutions seem irrelevant. The pressing Arab problem is simply how to get Israel to hand back her territorial gains from the June war without having to negotiate and recognize her existence. Even if negotiation took place, would the Arab States agree to, say, a smaller West Bank area for Jordan, no Golan Heights for Syria? And what concessions could Israel offer in return for acceptance of an Israeli Jerusalem?

In the light of recent events the old Arab plans for refugees look more and more unrealistic, but many Arabs think that realism is to be despised in this context and that in the long run it is better to stick to their principles; and for this they may be admired. Some of the Arabs would not even now be prepared to accept the return to the 1947 Partition Plan frontiers as a satisfactory solution. Some would allow a Jewish refuge in an Arab-controlled Palestine. Others believe that, like the crusaders, the Israelis will eventually wither away, a foreign plant in Middle Eastern soil; others strive to hasten this historical process—now by means of guerrilla warfare, the only means open. But as it resolves itself for the more moderate Arabs, the Arab-Israeli problem is essentially now one of frontiers. Yet to say this does not make the problem either manageable or soluble. For the differences between Arab and Jew do not stem from narrow, materialistic considerations, but from a clash of fundamental convictions about the right to sovereignty over Palestine. Consequently, and paradoxically, it is only perhaps by a sympathetic understanding of, and respect for, the *depth* of each other's convictions that the climate for some sort of compromise will ever be produced.

CO-EXISTENCE OR WAR?

If Arabs and Israelis cannot agree can they co-exist? Co-existence would surely count for much. Quite apart from the human suffering that it produces, the great harm of the periodic heating-up of the conflict that we have seen is that it powerfully militates against mutual understanding at the most profound level. For this reason alone it is, therefore, necessary to discover which factors have been important in turning this cold (or tepid) war into a hot one in 1956 and 1967. Such an enquiry must always produce no more than tentative results, but will it not help us to conjecture on the present situation? Is there any likelihood that the present cease-fire arrangements will persist without another war breaking out? From a brief comparative analysis of the major factors that led to the 1956 and 1967 wars we can perhaps suggest for further discussion those factors in the present situation that would seem to make for war.

To put it in the broadest terms, there were two main reasons for the 1956 and 1967 wars. First, the Israelis have always had a morbid appreciation of the sheer vulnerability of their tiny state. Second, the Arabs have always deeply resented the injustice done to Arab refugees and have naturally enough interpreted Israeli attitudes in this regard as evidence of the Israeli expansionism they always stress and often genuinely fear. Consequently, they are perpetually hostile to Israel and provocative.

In order to activate Israeli and Arab emotions to the point where war becomes well-nigh inevitable, certain factors seem crucial. On the Israeli side their sense of vulnerability was in 1956 and 1967 enhanced by (1) massive supplies of arms to the Arabs by Eastern bloc countries, (2) severe Arab guerrilla attacks that deeply affected the ordinary Israeli's sense of personal security, (3) the Arab closure of the sea routes to the Southern seas, and (4) concentrated aggressive measures against Israel taken by the three dangerous border Arab States, Egypt, Syria and Jordan. These factors operated in 1956 and 1967 and led to the Israeli attacks. In 1956 Israel was further moved to an aggressive policy by the guarantee of Western military support, by anxiety at the removal of the British presence from Suez and by the failure of the West to win over to their side Egypt and Syria—though this might have entailed unwelcome concessions by Israel.

On the Arab side, their hostility towards Israel increased very greatly in 1955/56 and in 1966/67, thereby enhancing Israel's sense of vulnerability. One reason for this is the sheer frustration engendered by Israeli success in simply flouting Arab opinion. The Israeli development of the port of Eilat, or, in 1964, the Israeli water-carrier scheme, demonstrated this

Israeli imperviousness to Arab hostility. Another factor in raising the level of Arab hostility is Israeli re-arming, which intensifies Arab suspicions of Israeli 'expansionism'. (Egypt did not obtain arms from the East until after the Israeli-French arms deal of 1952.) Another factor is heavy Israeli retaliation for Arab guerilla attacks, which seems to outrage rather than intimidate the Arabs in the long run. Then again, to judge from the 1967 experience, Arab hostility increases when inter-Arab disputes are at their worst. Disputes about leadership of the Arab world can easily turn into disputes about who is most anti-Israel. In this connection we might note that among the modernists in the Arab world nationalism is now powerfully reinforced by socialism, but this does not entail less hostility towards Israel. As the alleged protégé of the 'imperialist' powers, in Arab eyes Israel is firmly located in the capitalist camp. She is regarded as the agent of capitalist economic imperialism. In the normal course of affairs—if we were concerned with a simple mechanical balance—Israel would now draw closer to the conservative Arab traditionalist states and all might be well. Unfortunately for Israel, however, it is not such a balance. Anti-Israeli feeling is a permanent feature of the make-up of the traditionalist Arab States. Arab hostility towards Israel is founded not only in nationalism and anti-imperialism, but also in religion.

Another factor that raises the temperature is incessant, bellicose anti-Israeli propaganda. In his speeches Nasser often remarks of his enemies that 'they lied and lied till they deceived themselves'. Arab leaders may not in fact come to believe in the extravagancies their radios broadcast, but they have to act as if they do—and this is the road to the self-deception Nasser has perceived in others. Then again there is the baleful influence of the major powers. Their role in inflaming the dispute—Britain and France in 1956 and Russia in 1967—has been considerable, if not always intentional. If the powers become closely involved in using the dispute for their own ends then there is the danger that the tail will wag the dog.

If these temperature-raising agents on both sides lie dormant, then perhaps there is some possibility of co-existence, if not of peace. Are they dormant now, in 1969, or are we witnessing a repetition of history?

We must ask first whether Israel is now as vulnerable as before and therefore prepared to strike first at the sign of an Arab attack. We can straightway see that strategically she is not. Her territory is now extended in Syria and Jordan to make her own defence much less precarious than it was. Moreover, she occupies the Sinai buffer. There is still the problem of guerrilla warfare, but Israel seems able for the present to contain its effects within bounds. As to communications, Israel has access through the Straits of Tiran as a result of the war and Suez is closed to all shipping, not just her own. On this occasion Israel has not been forced back by the United States to the 1949 Armistice lines; and she has the prospect now of American armaments. Her security is therefore much better provided for.

On the Arab side, their fears of Israeli expansionism have been deepened. The fear that occupied territories may be annexed by Israel lends urgency to Arab demands for their restitution. With this Arab territory in Israeli hands the Arabs just cannot now sit back and co-exist. They have to do something, yet their military capacity and above all, their self-confidence is now very much in doubt after their defeat. Extensive Russian re-armament cannot in the short term do much for the underlying qualities of training and morale that are essential for victory. President Nasser has announced (September 1968) that Egypt is no longer in the state of preparation, but of liberation, though he suggests that liberation is not feasible just yet. Egyptian public opinion seems set on war. What sort of liberation war, however, is now feasible? Have we not really seen the end of any Arab hope of a classic military defeat of Israeli armed forces? If this is the case, then are there new factors in the situation that will work against a repetition of history? The only sort of warfare that seems possible in the near future is that waged by the guerrillas. This is important for the Arab-Israeli conflict as it keeps it for ever in motion, for ever on the stage. Even more significant, perhaps, is the fact that the guerrilla war of liberation is led by Palestinians. Since 1964 the Palestinians themselves have begun to take the initiative. The Arab *States* are now rather in the background. Their efforts to liberate Palestine have failed. Now, it is said in the Arab world, it is up to the Palestinian people to recover their lost land. Dependent as they are on the support of the Arab States, often divided among themselves and sometimes at odds with Jordan, Syria or the UAR, and bereft of any territorial base, do the Palestinians really have much hope? Perhaps their only hope is an accommodation with Israel, at the expense of Jordan, that would result in an independent Arab Palestine on the West Bank, but this is an arrangement that could presumably only be made by the moderate Palestinians, not by the guerrilla bands. There have been signs that Jordan might indeed agree to such a solution, but then would the other Arab states really allow it to happen? If they were to throw up moderate, but very strong, governments, they might just do so. At present their governments are too precariously balanced to be able to offer much hope. Nevertheless it is clear that the Palestinian Arabs are now more important than they have ever been. With tempers as they are there is little chance of an independent West Bank state being created. Why should Israel agree to create a hostile neighbour? There seems more chance that the Palestinians in Jordan might unseat King Hussein.

If the Arab *States* are to challenge Israel again, what they need is help. Russia is prepared to supply this, but probably not to the point of encouraging the Arab States to start a war. It might be argued that Russia is prepared to push Egypt to the point of a local war for control of the Suez Canal, whose re-opening would be valuable for Russian communications to the Far East. Such a war would also divert attention from unpopular Russian policies in Eastern Europe. But the signs are that Russia does not want to risk a Third World War for the sake of the Middle East. A local war might break out if the Arabs believe that Russia will in fact come to their aid, or if Israel continues to use attack as the best form of defence.

Russian policy at the moment is probably either (1) to keep the Arab-Israeli pot just on the boil, or (2) to obtain a peace of which Russia would be one of the guarantors with a legitimate physical presence in the Middle East. An Arab-Israeli peace that rendered the Russian role in the Middle East redundant could hardly be to Russian liking. Arab demands for arms have given the Soviet Union an opportunity to implant herself in just that part of the Middle East the British so long and so tenaciously defended. Would not the Arab-Israeli dispute have been forced to a solution in 1949 if Britain, on the way out, and the United States on the way in, had only realized how powerful an agent of policy it could become in Russian hands? In the hiatus between the British withdrawal and the American assumption of power in the Middle East the Arab-Israeli conflict was not properly controlled. Would the Soviet Union have entered the Middle East anyway? Would not the inter-Arab rivalries which we have described have been sufficient opportunity for intervention? The answer must be yes. But the Arab-Israeli dispute produces very ambivalent attitudes in the West, with the result that the Western Powers can easily be caught off balance. Western interests and loyalties are very divided on the Arab-Israeli conflict. Anxious about oil, about the Suez Canal, sometimes about the spread of socialism and the fate of traditionalist rulers and allies, the West has also to face a conscience about the fate of the Jews of Europe during the Second World War, the half-promises to Zionism and the powerful Jewish lobbies. Russia can reap all the benefit of supporting one side; the West must support neither, and is consequently criticized by both.

Yet a policy of inaction, of wait and see, must surely be now more than ever the worst policy. The longer Israel has to hold on to her gains from the June war, the more difficult will any solution become. To examine at every turn what prospects there are for peace is the urgent task to which all students of the subject—and not only governments—should address themselves. It is hoped that a study of the modest collection of documents in this book will have revealed the contours of the Arab-Israeli problem; and that fertile minds will be stimulated further to seeking new ways of approach to what is one of the world's most intractable problems.

Appendix

Although questions are constantly raised in the text, a selection of topics for discussion is set out below for the convenience of the reader.

1. On what grounds do Arabs deny the historic right to live in Palestine claimed by the Jews?
2. Were the promises made by the Allied Powers to Jews and Arabs during the first world war really incompatible?
3. To what extent was Britain successful in fulfilling her obligations under the terms of the Mandate for Palestine?
4. How close to settlement was the Arab–Israeli dispute in 1948–49 and why was agreement not reached?
5. What has been the effect of Russian re-entry into the Middle East on the Arab-Israeli problem?
6. How important a part of the Arab-Israeli problem has been the dispute over the allocation of the waters of the River Jordan?
7. Should the U.N. Secretary-General, U Thant, have agreed to the UAR's request in May 1967 for the withdrawal of the UNEF?
8. Are the conditions for the success of Arab guerrilla warfare against Israel present in the Middle East?
9. Were the causes of the 1956 and 1967 wars basically similar?
10. In what ways has the Arab refugee problem been altered by the 1967 war?
11. What are the differences between the Israeli and Arab interpretations of the Security Council Resolution of 22 November 1967?
12. What are the implications of the Arab defeat in 1967 for the political stability of the Arab states?
13. Is an embargo on supplies of arms to Israel and the Arab Middle Eastern States desirable and feasible?
14. What part has Israel played in the dissensions that have occurred between Arab States in the Middle East?

Guide to Further Reading

THE MIDDLE EAST AND THE WEST

LEWIS, Bernard, *The Middle East and the West*, London: Weidenfeld & Nicolson, 1964.
MUNROE, Elizabeth, *Britain's Moment in the Middle East, 1914–56*, London: Chatto & Windus, 1963.

ARAB NATIONALISM AND ZIONISM

ANTONIUS, G., *The Arab Awakening*, London: Hamish Hamilton, 1938. A useful critique of Antonius may be found in KIRK, G. E., *A Short History of the Middle East* (7th ed., London: Methuen, 1964) Appendix II.
COHEN, I. *The Zionist Movement*, ed. and rev. by B. G. Richards, New York: Zionist Organization Bureau, 1946.

THE DEVELOPMENT OF THE CONFLICT

(*1*) *To 1948*

HOWARD, H. N., *The King–Crane Commission*, Beirut: Khayats, 1963.
HUREWITZ, J. C., *The Struggle for Palestine*, New York: W. W. Morton & Co., 1950.
NATHAN, R. R., GASS, O. and CREAMER, D., *Palestine: Problem and Promise, an Economic Study*, Washington, D.C.: Public Affairs Press, 1946.
SYKES, Christopher, *Cross Roads to Israel*, Nel Mentor Books, London: Collins, 1965. Good on British and Zionist policies.

(*2*) *1948–57*

BERGER, Earl, *The Covenant and the Sword: Arab–Israeli Relations, 1948–56*, London: Routledge & Kegan Paul, 1965.
MONCRIEFF, A. (ed.), *Suez Ten Years After*, London: B.B.C., 1967. Broadcasts from the B.B.C. Third Programme.
STOCK, Ernest, *Israel on the Road to Sinai, 1949–56*, London: O.U.P., 1968. Has sequel on 1967 war.

WINT, G. and CALVOCORESSI, P., *Middle East Crisis*, London: Penguin Books, 1957. A very good introduction to the Suez Crisis.

(3) From 1957

DRAPER, Theodore, *Israel and World Politics: Roots of the Third Arab-Israeli War*, London: Secker & Warburg, 1968.

HOWARD, M. and HUNTER, R., *Israel and the Arab World: The Crisis of 1967*, London: Institute for Strategic Studies, 1967. A succinct introduction.

KERR, Malcolm, *The Arab Cold War, 1958-64*, London: O.U.P., 1964. A Chatham House Essay.

LAQUEUR, Walter, *The Road to War, 1967: The Origins of the Arab-Israel Conflict*, London: Weidenfeld & Nicolson, 1968.

(4) General

RODINSON, Maxime, *Israel and the Arabs*, London: Penguin Books, 1968.

Index

Algeria, 28
  and Middle East Politics, 20
  and 1967 War, 173
  and Palestine Liberation, 195
  example of, 139, 194–5, 197–9
  French withdrawal from, 16
Aqaba, 29, 30, 31
  Gulf of, 15, 19, 22, 117, 125–6, 129–31, 155–6, 160
Arab armaments, *see references under* Armaments
  armies, 13–15, 84, 109, 138–40
  boycott, 12, 15, 21, 101–3, 116–17, 121, 185
  economic development, 144, 174–5, 223–5
  Christians, 2
  guerillas, 18–19, 22, 25, 106, 116–20, 123, 139–40, 147–9, 173, 179, 192–200, 228–32
  Higher Committee, 76–7
  homeland of Palestine, 139–40, 151, 153, 174, 193, 196,
  independence, 6–11, 30, 49, 56–8, 60, 64–5, 73, 77, 85–7, 89
  instability, 22, 24, 144, 149, 232
  League, 11, 28, 84, 86–8, 90, 139, 141
  Legion, 16, 118
  masses, 175–6, 184, 194
  moderates, 141, 228, 232
  nation, 56–7, 151–2, 175, 184, 199
  nationalism, 2, 4, 6–7, 20, 45, 54, 72, 85, 152, 230
  occupied territory ('48), 15, 26, 93, 144, 197, 221
  occupied territory ('67), 24, 26–7, 174–5, 181, 194, 197–8, 203, 207–72, 212–19, 219–25, 226–8, 231, 233
  public opinion, 149, 176–7, 229
  rebellion, 11, 72
  solidarity, 141, 174
  State, 30, 60, 62
  State in Palestine, 26, 32, 73, 80–2, 87, 143, 223, 232
  State of Palestine, 77, 80–2, 86–7, 89–90, 121, 193, 228
  States and Jordan Waters, 132–3, 137–9, 229
  States and Israel ('49–67), 15, 91–3, 97, 103, 121, 123, 131, 137, 141–6, 229
  States and 1948, 13, 14, 84–90
  States and P.L.O., 140–1
  Summit Conferences, 21–2, 24, 138–9, 141, 144, 173–5
  unity, 20–1, 132, 139, 141, 174, 230, 233
  Confederation of — States, 30, 60, 62
  joint — force, 138–9
  Palestinian — people, 1–3, 8–11, 13–14, 49, 51, 77, 84–5, 87–90, 139–40, 143–6, 174, 185, 193–4, 196, 231–2
  unified Arab command, 140
Arabia, 44–5
Arabian Peninsula, 8, 20, 22, 62
Arabism, 107, 109
Arabs, and imperialism, 7, 16, 20–1, 88, 107, 152–3, 175–6, 178–9, 193, 230
  and Palestine (to '47), 8–12, 35, 45, 47–54, 64–5, 72, 76–7

Arabs,
  and Partition, 10–15, 26, 49, 72, 77–8, 87–8, 92–3, 140–1, 143–4, 227–8
  and socialism, 17, 19–22, 141, 176–7, 179, 193–4, 230–3
  and state of war, 101, 116–21, 186
  and traditionalism, 17, 19, 21–2, 140–1, 174, 177, 179–80, 230, 233
  in and after 1967, 147–53, 173–80, 183, 186, 191–207, 212–21, 228–32
  Palestinian — in Israeli territory, 93, 197, 199, 205, 220–5
Armaments, Algerian, 104
  American supply of, 108–10, 113, 186, 201, 206–7, 231
  Arab States', 105, 144–5, 201, 229, 231–2
  British supply of, 108–10, 113, 117, 206–7
  Chinese supply of, 206
  Czech supply of, 17, 104, 106, 110–11, 115, 117, 119
  Eastern bloc supply of, 17, 112, 114, 229–30
  Egyptian, 17–18, 25, 104, 106–17, 201, 230
  French supply of, 16, 104, 108–10, 113, 115, 121, 205–7, 230
  in Sykes–Picot, 62
  Iraqi, 104, 106, 201
  Israeli, 16, 104–5, 109, 113, 115–16, 120–1, 186, 201, 205, 230–1
  Jordanian, 104, 201
  nuclear, 205–6
  Soviet supply of, 25, 110–13, 117, 186, 201, 206–7, 231–2
  Syrian, 201
  Western bloc supply of, 21, 104, 107, 109, 113–14, 116
Armistice, agreements, 14–15, 91, 97, 101–3, 227

boundaries, 33, 152
demarcation lines, 98–100, 104–5, 124, 126, 170, 172, 231
demilitarized zones, 135, 153
regime, 15–16, 18, 97, 101–2, 105, 118, 135, 152, 170
Israel–Egyptian —, 97–101, 124–5
Mixed — commissions, 101, 153
Arms Race, 15, 21, 25, 104–5, 107, 109, 111, 113, 117, 144, 201–7, 229–30
Asifah, 193–4, 197
Aswan Dam, 18, 205

Baath, 20–1
Balfour Declaration, 5–6, 42–5, 47–9, 52, 63, 65, 67, 75, 82, 85, 233
Ben Gurion, David, 18, 117, 120, 153, 157
Britain, after 1967 War, 25, 176, 181–2, 184, 186, 206–7
  and Balfour Declaration, 5–6, 42–5, 47–9, 52, 63, 65, 67, 75, 82, 85, 233
  and Egypt, 107–10, 113
  and Husain–McMahon, 4, 6, 48, 55–9, 65, 85
  and Jewry, 6, 38, 40–2, 63, 67
  and Jordan/Transjordan, 16–17, 19, 20, 73, 118
  and Kuwait, 20
  and Middle East politics, 16–17, 19–20, 108–10, 116, 232–3
  and 1967 War, 24
  and 1923 Peace Settlement, 7–8, 64–5, 67
  and Suez crisis, 18, 115–16, 229
  and Suez war, 19, 124, 147, 151, 170–2, 193, 230
  and Sykes–Picot, 5–7, 30, 55, 59–63
  and Tripartite Declaration, 15–16, 104–5

Britain,
  and Zionism, 5–7, 42–7, 52–3,
    63, 85, 233
  as Palestine Mandatory, 9–14,
    67–73, 75–81, 83, 85–9, 199
  British, supply of armaments,
    108–10, 113, 117, 206–7
  withdrawal from empire, 16–
    18, 229

Communism, 19, 20
Cuba, 195
  example of, 139

Diaspora, *see* Jewish, — Dispersion

Egypt, 28
  after 1967 War, 173, 176–9,
    183–7, 196–9, 204–5, 220,
    232
  and Algeria, 16, 104, 198
  and armaments, 17–18, 25,
    104, 106–17, 201, 230
  and Britain, 8, 16, 107–9,
    115–16
  and development, 179
  and Gaza, 14, 93, 123, 140,
    220
  and guerillas, 18, 106, 116
  and imperialism, 16, 21, 107,
    110, 179
  and Iraq, 20, 114
  and Israeli expansionism, 137,
    230
  and Jordan, 23, 114
  and Jordan Waters Plans, 139
  and massive retaliation, 18,
    106, 116
  and Middle East Politics, 16,
    18, 108, 111–14
  and 1967 War, 23–5, 147–53,
    155, 157–72, 204, 229
  and neutrality, 112
  and Palestinian nationalism,
    22, 116, 196–9, 231–2
  and public opinion, 23, 177,
    179, 231

  and Russia, 25, 110–14, 117,
    232
  and Saudi Arabia, 20, 22, 141
  and state of war, 101, 116–21
  and Suez Crisis, 18–19, 115–
    16, 229
  and Suez War, 123–6, 130,
    147, 157–9, 161, 167–72
  and Syria, 20–2, 147–9, 151–3
  and Tiran and Sanafir, 15,
    22–3, 117, 123, 125–6, 130,
    149, 151–2, 155, 162, 166
  and UN Emergency Force, 19,
    22, 149–51, 157–72
  and USA, 18, 107–9, 110, 113
  and Yemen, 20, 147
  in World War I, 4
  independence of —, 8, 107–8,
    110–13, 179
  Israeli-exclusion from Suez by
    —, 15, 21, 101–3, 116, 185
  left wing opposition in —, 179
  right wing in —, 176–8
  socialist revolutionary regime
    in —, 16, 20–1, 106–10, 112,
    115, 179
Eilat, 32, 33, 152–5, 229
El Fatah, 22, 149, 179, 192–7,
  204

Fedayeen, 18, 117–20, 195–6
  See also references under Arab
  guerillas
France, after 1967 War, 184
  and 1923 Peace Settlement,
    7–8, 31
  and Suez Crisis, 18–19, 115–
    16
  and Suez War, 18, 124, 147,
    151, 170–2, 193, 230
  and Tripartite Declaration,
    15–16, 104–5
  in World War I negotiations,
    5, 7, 30, 58, 60–3
  armaments supply by —, 16,
    104, 108–10, 113, 115
  North African empire of —, 8,
    16, 108–9, 145, 195, 197

Gaza, 18–19, 29–34, 119, 123–5,
129, 192–3, 217, 220–5
Raid, 18, 106, 116
Arab refugees from —, 212,
217, 220
Egyptian administration of
—, 14, 93, 123, 140, 220
Germany, 39, 47
in World War I, 4–6
Jewry in —, 36, 38–9, 52
Golan (Jawlan, Rama), 27, 203,
221–2, 224, 228
Guerilla warfare, *see* Arab gueril-
las

Herzl, Theodore, 5, 42, 47, 82
Holy Places, 58, 73, 77, 84–5, 91,
190–1, 208–12
Husain, Sharif of Mecca, 4, 6,
29, 55–9, 60, 65
Hussein, King of Jordan, 22,
192–3, 232

Imperialism, and capitalism, 21,
230
and Israel, 21, 152–3, 230
and Zionism, 88, 176, 193
in 1923 Peace Settlement, 7
hostile to Arabs, 7, 16, 20–1,
88, 107, 152–3, 175–6, 178–
9, 193, 230
economic —, 230
International Court of Justice,
13, 49, 70, 101, 126
Iraq, 28, 77
after 1967 War, 173, 193
and armaments, 104, 106, 201
and Baath, 20–1
and Egypt, 20, 114
and Israel, 97
and Jordan, 23
and Jordan Waters Plans, 139
and Kuwait, 20
and Middle East politics, 16,
104
mandate, 7, 64
independence of —, 8, 31
1958 revolution in —, 19–20

revolutionary socialist regime
in —, 20–1
Islam, 1–2, 4, 22, 25, 41, 56, 141,
177
Holy Places of —, 190–1, 207,
209, 211, 226
Israel, after 1967 War, 24–5, 33,
181–3, 185–91, 203–4, 220–
5, 231–3
and Afro-Asia, 144, 154–5,
226, 229–31
and Arab guerillas, 18–19, 25,
106, 116–20, 123, 139, 147–
8, 179, 192–3, 197–200,
229–32
and Arab States ('49–67), *see*
Arab States
and Arabs (after 1967), 24–5,
174, 176–80, 181–91, 216,
220–5, 226–8
and armaments, 16, 104–5,
109, 113, 115–16, 120–1,
186, 201–2, 205–7, 230
and capitalist imperialism, 21,
152–3, 230
and Jerusalem, *see* Jerusalem
and Jordan Waters, 132–9, 229
and 1967 War, 22–4, 123,
147–9, 152–7, 203–4
and refugees, *see* Refugees,
Arab Palestinian
and Russia, 18, 23–4, 181–2,
186
and Suez Canal, 15, 21,
101–3, 116, 185, 231
and Suez Crises, 17–18, 115–
16, 229
and Suez War, 19, 123–31,
144, 151, 153, 166, 170–1,
193, 221
and state of war, 101, 116–21,
186, 188
and Syria, 22–3, 147–9, 152–3,
175–6
and Tiran, 15, 19, 22–3, 33,
117, 123, 125–6, 129–31, 149,
151, 153–7, 160, 162, 166,
183, 190, 231

Israel (*contd.*),
and Tunisia, 141–6
and UN, *see* UN
and USA, 15–17, 19, 21, 23,
    93, 104–6, 113, 116, 123–30,
    132–4, 149, 153, 155–7,
    181–2, 186, 201–2, 206–8,
    231
in 1948–49, 14–15, 82–4, 152,
    229
Arab boycott of —, 12, 15, 21,
    101–3, 116–17, 121, 185
Arabs within —, 84, 93, 192,
    197, 199, 200, 205, 220–5
Armistice Agreements with
    —, *see* Armistice
Greater —, 222–3
immigration into —, 14, 83–4,
    137, 224, 227
negotiation with —, 14, 15,
    21, 93, 97, 133, 141, 143–6,
    149, 174, 181–2, 185–8,
    207, 223, 227, 228
population of —, 26, 34, 93,
    137–8, 155, 197, 205, 221,
    223, 227
recognition of —, 146, 174,
    176, 178–80, 182–3, 185–6,
    188, 191, 227–8
State of —, 14, 47, 82–4, 95,
    176, 178, 204, 222–3, 227
withering away of —, 228
Israeli, — agression, 151–3, 174–
    5, 182, 184, 197, 199
economic development, 93,
    95, 120, 132–9, 153–5, 223–
    5
expansionism, 18, 27, 121–2,
    137, 229–31
military stategy, 117–18, 120–
    2, 137, 155, 200, 203–5,
    231–2
moderates, 119, 149
retaliation policy, 17–18, 25,
    106, 116, 147, 153, 193,
    199–200, 230
territory, 14–15, 19, 24–7, 33,
    91–3, 95, 123, 143, 183,
    186, 188–9, 221, 227–8, 231
occupied territory, 24–7,
    123–7, 129, 153, 174–5,
    181–3, 185–6, 192–4, 197,
    199–200, 207–12 213–15,
    217–20, 220–5, 226–8, 231
political parties, 221–3
public opinion, 118–20, 178–
    9, 205, 221

Jarring, Gunnar, 25, 183, 186–7
Jawlan, *see* Golan
Jerusalem, 29–33, 43, 75, 140,
    210
after 1967 War, 25–7, 190–2,
    207–12, 214, 220–8
and border incidents, 119–20
and UN, 80–1, 87, 207–9, 211
and US, 207–9
in 1948–49, 14, 26, 88, 91
in 1967 War, 24, 207
Holy Places in —, 73, 77, 84–
    5, 91, 190–1, 208–12
Jewish, — National Home, 6–9,
    11, 44–5, 49–50, 63–4, 67–8,
    73, 76, 82, 85–6, 227
nationalism, 3–5, *and see
    under* Zionism
people, 37, 39, 44, 63, 67, 75,
    82–4
population in Palestine, 2–3,
    26, 41–3, 46, 68, 72, 75–6,
    84–5
problem, 35–43, 74, 76, 82
refugees, 11–12, 74, 227–8
State, 9–10, 14, 32, 44, 50,
    52, 73, 80–3, 85, 87, 204,
    223
Agency, 68–70, 75–6
Commonwealth, 75–6
Dispersion, 3, 5, 12, 35–42,
    82–3
immigration and settlement in
    Palestine, 3–5, 8–9, 11–14,
    26, 38, 40–2, 45, 49–51, 69,
    72, 74–6, 80, 82–5
immigration into Israel, 14,
    83–4, 137, 224, 227

Jewish,
lobbies, 52–3, 233
nation, 74, 84
Jewry, — and Britain, 6, 38,
40–2, 63, 67
and Europe, 3, 5, 11–12,
35–9, 41–4, 52, 74–6, 82–3,
85, 233
and Palestine, 2–3, 5–6, 40–2,
44, 50–1, 63, 67–8, 82–4
and Russia, 5–6, 18, 35, 42,
44, 47
and USA, 6, 35–6
Johnston, Plan, 132–4, 138, 226
Jordan (kingdom), 28
after 1967 War, 26, 185, 192–3,
212–19, 221–5, 228, 231–2
and armaments, 104, 201
and Britain, 16–17, 19, 73, 118
and Egypt, 23, 114, 118
and guerillas, 25, 199, 229
and Jordan Waters Plans, 133
and massive retaliation, 25,
17, 116, 119, 193
and Middle East Politics,
16–17, 104, 118
and 1956 War, 118–19, 229
and 1967 War, 24, 173, 197,
203, 229
and Palestine Liberation Organization, 140
and USA, 19–20
independence of Trans —, 8
West Bank and Jerusalem
incorporated into Trans—,
14, 33, 104, 140
see also Westbank, Jerusalem
Jordan (river), — after 1967
War, 222
and guerilla warfare, 200
and refugees, 213, 225
Valley, 225
both sides of — part of Palestine, 7
dispute over waters of —, 21,
132–9, 226, 229
Jordanian East Bank, 212–15,
200, 217–19

Kinneret, see Tiberias
Kuwait, 20, 28, 173, 175, 224

Lausanne Protocol, 92–4
League of Nations, — Covenant,
7, 49, 64–7, 77, 85, 87–9
Mandates, see Mandate
Lebanon, 28, 54
after 1967 War, 173, 215
and border incidents, 119
and guerillas, 199
and Jordan Waters Plans, 133
and USA, 19–20
independence of —, 8
mandate of —, 7, 31, 64
Libya, 28, 175, 198, 207

McMahon, Henry, 4, 6, 29,
55–9, 65
Mandate, — instruments, 7, 64
system, 7, 49, 65–7, 85
territories, 31, 32
and see references under each
Mandate territory
Morocco, 8, 28, 36, 177, 198

Nasser, Gamal Abd el, — after
1967 War, 182–5, 192, 231
and Bourguiba, 141, 146
and China, 18
and Czech arms, 106–14
and Jordan, 118
and guerillas, 116
and Middle East politics, 16,
19–20, 22, 112–14, 118–19,
141
and 1956 War, 19, 157–9, 164,
168
and 1967 War, 22–4, 147–53,
161, 173
and propaganda, 230
and USA, 18–19, 107–110,
113
regime, 19, 179
Nazism, 52, 76, 83
Negev, 26, 132, 134–5, 137–8,
152, 155, 205
Neutralism, 112

Oil, 20, 114, 153–4, 174, 195, 224, 233
Ottoman Empire, 28
  and Jewry, 41–2
  administration and policy, 1–3, 29, 55, 59, 84, 87
  in 1923 Peace Settlement, 8, 49, 65–7, 69
  in World War I, 4, 48, 60, 62
  end of —, 4–5, 7

Palestine, — and Jewry, 2–3, 5–6, 40–3, 44, 50–1, 63, 67–8, 75–6, 82–3
  and UN, see UN
  and Zionism, 5–6, 43, 74–6, 82–4, 88, 144, 176, 193, 233
  in 1947–8, 12–14, 26, 49, 78–91, 143
  Liberation Army, 22, 179
  Liberation Organization, 139–41
  Liberation Struggle, 39–40, 116, 143–4, 146, 175, 179, 193–6, 199, 231–2
  National institutions, 22, 139–41
  People's War, 194
  population, 1–3, 26, 34, 41, 44, 85, 197
  resistance, 179, 197–9
  revolution, 193–6
  territory, 1, 7, 10, 31, 68, 140, 144–5, 152, 197–8, 221–5, 227
  under the Mandate, 8–12, 31, 46, 48–9, 53, 64–5, 67–75, 77, 82–3, 85
  Arab Higher Committee of—, 76–7
  Arab homeland of —, 139–40, 151, 174, 193, 196
  Arab State in —, 26, 73, 80–2, 87, 143, 223, 232
  Arab State of —, 77, 80–2, 86–7, 89–90, 121, 193, 228
  Arabs and Mandated —, 8–12, 35, 45, 47–54, 64–5, 72, 76–7

Britain and Mandated —, 8–14, 65, 67–73, 75–6, 79–81, 83, 85–9
  binational state of —, 223
  economic development of —, 9, 45, 75, 82
  federal state of —, 78, 223
  Jewish immigration and settlement in —, 3–5, 8–9, 11–14, 26, 38, 40–2, 45, 49–51, 69, 72, 74–6, 80, 82–5
  Jewish National Home in —, 6–9, 11, 44–5, 49–50, 63–4, 67–8, 73, 76, 82, 85–6, 227
  Jewish State in —, 14, 50, 52, 73, 80–3, 85, 87, 223
  Partition of —, see Partition
  sovereignty over —, 228
  unitary state of —, 9–12, 89–90
  Zionist–Arab agreement on, 46
  Zionists and Mandated Palestine, 9–10, 64–5, 72, 74–6, 199
  Zionist State in —, 52
Palestinian, — Arab people, 1–3, 8–11, 13–14, 49, 51, 77, 84–5, 87–90, 139–40, 143–6, 174 185 193–4, 196, 231–2
  Arabs in Israeli territory, 93, 197, 192, 199, 205, 221, 223–5
  masses, 194
  moderates, 232
  refugees, see Refugees, Arab, Palestinian
  Economic Union of —, States, 79, 84, 134
Partition, abandonment of —, 11
  1956 proposals for —, 12
  1947 plan of —, 12, 14–15, 26, 32, 49, 76, 78–84, 87–8, 92–3, 134, 140–1, 143–5, 227–8
  1937 plan of —, 10, 32, 72–4

Partition (*contd.*),
UNSCOP recommendation of
—, 12, 76
Peace, — after 1948, 91–2, 94, 97–8, 100–104
after 1967, 25, 174, 181, 187–8, 222, 232–3
Conference, 44
Settlement 1923, 7–8, 31
Peel Commission, *see* Royal Commission on Palestine 1936–7
Persia, 29–31, 36, 53, 154
Picot, Georges, 5–7, 30, 59–63
Poland, 5, 35–6, 38, 47
Power blocs, Eastern —, 17, 111–12, 114, 177, 229–30
industrial —, 202
maritime —, 129, 131, 155–6
Great — and Suez Crisis, 118, 120, 122, 230
Great — to 1923, 4, 8, 65, 67
Western — after 1967, 177, 184, 186, 223, 233
Western — and 1949–56, 15–16, 21, 104–6, 108, 111–14, 229
Western — and 1967 War, 23–4, 230
Western — and partition, 74
see also, Britain, France, Russia, USA

Rama, *see* Golan
Refugees, Arab Palestinian —
and Jordan Waters Plans, 133
and Liberation of Palestine, 139, 142
and UN, *see* UN
Israeli attitude to (to 1966)—, 91–5, 153
Israeli attitude to (from 1967) —, 190, 212–25, 227–8
numbers of —, 34, 212, 214, 216–17, 219–20
origin of —, 13–14, 88, 143
problem of —, 25, 88, 91–6, 121, 125, 142–5, 227–9

Royal Commission on Palestine 1936–7 ('Peel'), 9–10, 12, 32, 35 *seq.*, 72–4
Russia, — after 1967 War, 24–5, 179, 181–2, 184–6, 206–7, 231–3
and Balfour Declaration, 5
and Middle East politics, 16–17, 53, 106, 111–14, 233
and 1967 War, 23–4, 149, 230
and Suez War, 19, 128, 144
and Sykes–Picot, 59–60, 62
armaments supply by —, 25, 110–13, 117, 186, 201, 206–7, 231–2
Jewry and —, 5–6, 18, 35, 42, 44, 47

Sanafir, *see* Tiran and Sanifir Islands
Sanjak, 29
Saudi Arabia, 28, 77, 177
after 1967 War, 173, 175
and Egypt, 20–2
and intra Middle East politics, 22, 141
and Yemen, 20–1
establishment of —, 8
Sinai, —after 1967, 137, 221, 224
in 1956–57, 19, 118, 123, 126, 153, 221
in 1967, 23–4, 148, 152, 155, 157, 203
Campaign, *see above* Sinai in 1956–57, *and see* Suez War
Sharm el-Sheikh, 19, 33, 124–5, 129, 149–50, 157, 152–3, 166, 172
Soviet Union, *see* Russia
Sudan, 8, 28, 114, 173
Suez Canal, — after 1967 War, 222, 231, 232
and 1967 War, 173
and the West, 233
and World War I, 4
British withdrawal from, 16–17, 229

Suez Canal (*cntd.*),
exclusion of Israel from —, 15,
21, 101–3, 116, 121, 183,
185, 190, 231
nationalization of —, 18, 115
Suez War 1956, 19, 104, 115,
121, 123–31, 144, 147, 151,
153–4, 170–1, 229, 230
Sykes, Mark, 5–7, 30, 59–63
Syria, 28, 54
after 1967 War, 24, 27, 173–6,
179, 185, 212, 216, 228,
231–2
and Baath, 20, 179
and border incidents, 119
and Demilitarized Zone, 135
and Egypt, 20–2, 147–9, 151–2
and guerillas, 22, 25, 147–9,
199
and Jordan Waters Plans, 133,
135, 139
and 1956 War, 119, 229
and 1967 War, 22–4, 147–9,
151–3, 229
independence of —, 8
instability of —, 22, 24, 149
mandate of —, 7, 31, 64
revolutionary socialist regime
in —, 20–2, 179
right wing in —, 176

Tiberias, city of —, 41, 88
lake of (Kinneret), 119, 132,
134–7, 148, 200
Tiran, — and Sanafir Islands,
15, 19, 125–6
Straits of —, 22–3, 33, 117,
123, 125–6, 129–31, 149,
151–7, 160, 162, 166, 183,
190, 231
Transjordan, *see* Jordan
Tripartite Declaration, 16, 104–
5, 118, 121
Tunisia, 28
and Algerian War, 198
and Arab League, 141
and Arab Unity, 21–2
and the Destour, 142–3

and Israel, 21–2, 141–6
and Liberation of Palestine,
143
French position in, 8, 145
Turkey, 16, 53, 111, 114
and see references under Ottoman
Empire

UN, — after 1967 War, 24–5,
181–91
and Armistice Regime, *see*
Armistice
and Jerusalem, 80–1, 87, 207–
9, 211
and Jordan Waters Plans, 132,
135
and 1967 War, 25, 157, 160–9
and Palestine Question (1947–
48), 12–15, 32, 49, 53, 76–
84, 87–91, 97–101, 118,
143, 152
and retaliation policy, 18
and state of war, 15, 101–3
and Suez Canal, 15, 101–3
and Suez Crisis/War, 124–31,
157–9, 161, 163–4, 166–72
Armistice Resolutions, 97–100,
102, 152
Charter and principles, 48–9,
77, 79, 84, 87, 89, 127–8,
131, 140, 181, 183, 191
Conciliation Commission on
Palestine, 15, 91–7, 101, 227
Emergency Force, 19, 22, 123,
125–6, 129–30, 149–51,
157, 172, 186
mediators, 14, 101, 153
refugee resolutions, 92, 94,
143–5, 152–3, 212–13, 215,
218–19, 227
RWA, 95, 212–20, 225
Secretary General, 100–1,
124–6, 130, 151, 157–72,
183, 209, 214
Special Representative, 25,
183, 186–7
Truce Supervision Organization, 102, 148, 153

UN (*contd.*),
Arab States members of —, 8, 54, 88
establishment of —, 11, 87–8
USA, after 1967 War, 176, 178, 180–2, 184, 186, 201, 206–9, 231
aid, 178
and capitalist imperialism, 21, 53, 176
and Egypt, 18, 107–10, 113
and Eisenhower Doctrine, 19–20
and Israel, 15–17, 19, 21, 23, 93, 104–6, 113, 116, 123–30, 132–4, 149, 153, 155–7, 181–2, 186, 201–2, 206–8, 231
and Jewry, 6, 35–6
and Jordan Waters Plans, 132–3
and Lebanon, 19–20
and Middle East politics, 16–17, 233
and 1967 War, 23–4, 149, 153, 155–7
and Suez Crisis, 18, 116
and Suez War, 19, 123–9, 144, 231
and Tripartite Declaration, 15–16, 104–5
and Zionism, 53, 74–6
armaments supply by —, 108–10, 113, 186, 201, 206–7, 231
partition proposals by —, 12

Vietnam, example of —, 139, 179, 195, 197–9
Vilayet, 29, 55, 58–9

West Bank, — as independent Arab Palestine, 232
in Sykes–Picot Agreement, 7
incorporated into Transjordan, 14, 104, 140
Arab refugees from —, 212–15, 217, 219–20
Israeli occupation of —, 24, 33, 192, 199–200, 212, 221–5, 228
population of —, 34
World War I, 4–7, 35, 37–9, 47, 52, 65, 85
II, 75, 83, 86, 111, 233
III, 232

Yemen, 20, 28, 147, 173

Zion, return to, 42–4, 82–3
Zionism, — and Britain, 5–7, 42–7, 52–3, 63, 85, 233
and imperialism, 88, 176, 193
and Israeli expansionism, 121
and Jordan Waters, 138
and USA, 53, 74–6
as Jewish Nationalism, 5, 11, 35
Zionist, — aggression 88, 144, 176
Arab agreement on Palestine, 46
Movement, 5, 42, 83
State, 32, 52, 178
World — Organization, 5, 42–3, 46–7, 68, 75, 82
Zionists, — and Palestine (to '47), 5–7, 9–12, 42–8, 50–2, 63, 65, 72, 74–6, 85, 87–8, 199, 233
and Palestine (1948), 12–14, 82–4
and Partition, 10, 12, 72–4